LIFELONG RETIREMENT PLANNING

for Local Government Employees

With start-up grants and loans from the Ford Foundation and the International City Management Association, the ICMA Retirement Corporation (RC) was formed by local government officials in 1972 as a nonprofit, tax-exempt organization. RC was the first to offer deferred compensation as a retirement program for mobile public employees.

In 1984, RC expanded its "product line" by introducing administration of the 401(a) money purchase plan for local governments. In 1988, RC attained the milestone of $1 billion in total plan assets.

RC is governed by a Board of Directors familiar with local government concerns. The Board is responsible for carrying out the overall management of the organization, including investment administration and regulatory compliance. As a nonprofit corporation, RC's foremost goal is to provide high quality service to public sector employees.

The International City Management Association is the professional and educational organization for chief appointed management executives in local government. The purposes of ICMA are to enhance the quality of local government and to nurture and assist professional local government administrators in the United States and other countries. In furtherance of its mission, ICMA develops and disseminates new approaches to management through training programs, information services, and publications.

Managers, carrying a wide range of titles, serve cities, towns, counties, councils of governments, and state/provincial associations of local governments in all parts of the United States and Canada. These managers serve at the direction of elected councils and governing boards. ICMA serves these managers and local governments through many programs that aim at improving the manager's professional competence and strengthening the quality of all local governments.

The International City Management Association was founded in 1914; adopted its City Management Code of Ethics in 1924; and established its Institute for Training in Municipal Administration in 1934. The Institute, in turn, provided the basis for the Municipal Management Series, generally termed the "ICMA Green Books."

ICMA's interests and activities include public management education; standards of ethics for members; the *Municipal Year Book* and other data services; urban research; and newsletters, a monthly magazine, *Public Management*, and other publications. ICMA's efforts for the improvement of local government management—as represented by this book—are offered for all local governments and educational institutions.

LIFELONG RETIREMENT PLANNING

for Local Government Employees

EDITED BY

Patricia Walsh

*Published by the International City Management Association
in cooperation with the ICMA Retirement Corporation*

This book is intended to help local government
employees by presenting practical ideas and
information from diverse sources. The views
expressed in this book are those of the contributors
and are not necessarily those of the International City Management Association or the
ICMA Retirement Corporation.

Library of Congress Cataloging-in-Publication Data

Lifelong retirement planning for local government employ-
    ees / edited by Patricia Walsh
        p. cm.
    Bibliography: p.
    ISBN 0-87326-054-6
    1. Retirement—United States—Planning. 2. Retirement
income—United States—Planning. I. Walsh, Patricia.
II. ICMA Retirement Corporation.
HQ1064.U5L545 1988
646.7'9—dc19   88-13347
                                                    CIP

Printed in the United States of America.
939291908988
54321

ABOUT THE EDITOR

Patricia Walsh served as senior editor for Action for Independent Maturity, the preretirement division of the American Association of Retired Persons (AARP), and later for the association's Worker Equity Department.

While with AARP, she oversaw the development of the Association's highly regarded retirement planning programs, publications, and training materials. The Association's preretirement planning program, "Think of Your Future," is offered by hundreds of major corporations and smaller businesses to their employees approaching retirement age. She also developed *Working Age*, a newsletter about employment issues affecting midlife and older workers, and served as editor of *How to Plan Your Successful Retirement*, published by AARP and Scott, Foresman and Company.

Pat Walsh is currently a freelance writer specializing in retirement planning and employment issues. Two of her articles, "Work in the Future" and "Getting Organized," appear in this volume.

ABOUT THE AUTHORS

Following are the affiliations of the contributors to *Lifelong Retirement Planning for Local Government Employees* at the time of writing:

David S. Arnold is an editorial consultant and was for many years the editor of the ICMA Municipal Management Series.

Caroline Bird is the author of seven books exploring social change. Her latest, *The Good Years*, looks at the part today's "ageless" pioneers are playing to make life better in the twenty-first century.

Barbara Blossom is a freelance writer residing in Vestal, New York.

Elwood N. Chapman is the author of over a dozen self-help books, including *Your Attitude Is Showing*.

Walter W. David is a senior vice-president at Morley Properties, an investment firm specializing in real estate in Maitland, Florida.

Jack Egan is an assistant managing editor for *U.S. News and World Report*.

Diane Harris is a staff writer with *MONEY* magazine.

Marie Hodge is a contributing editor of *50 PLUS*. Her column "Money Talks" appears regularly.

Morton Hunt writes frequently on the behavioral and social sciences for the *New York Times Magazine* and other magazines.

Walter Kiechel III is a columnist and editor for *FORTUNE* magazine.

Katie Leishman is a writer living in Brooklyn. Her articles on social issues have appeared in *McCalls*, *The Atlantic Monthly*, and other major magazines.

Jeanne L. Reid is a staff writer for *MONEY* magazine.

Charles Schaeffer is the executive editor of *Changing Times* magazine.

Doralie Denenberg Segal is a cardiovascular physiologist with the U.S. Food and Drug Administration and is a freelance writer on health-promotion and disease-prevention topics.

Gene Swearingen is vice-president, Participant Services Division of the ICMA Retirement Corporation's Washington, DC, office.

Margot L. Tripi is senior service advisor, Participant Services Division of the ICMA Retirement Corporation's Washington, DC, office.

Richard Weatherington is a freelance writer on financial topics who contributes frequently to *Modern Maturity* magazine.

Julie Whitmore writes frequently on financial and health care topics for a variety of publications.

Clint Willis is a staff writer with *MONEY* magazine.

Retirement today is . . . the beginning of a new, lengthy, important stage of life, rich with promise and well worth planning for.

—Hugh Downs

CONTENTS

FOREWORD

Not too long ago, local government employees who participated in well-funded pension plans would look ahead to age 65, lots of leisure time, and maybe buying a recreational vehicle for cross-country travel. Some will still do that, but for most the ground rules have changed. Some are retiring earlier; others are switching jobs and occupations much more frequently; and all are contending with a financial world that is much more complicated.

We no longer talk about retirement as if it were an end point like birth, marriage, and death. It has changed to a process that should be built into life planning from the thirties on. Police officers, firefighters, planners, managers, supervisors, and others employed by cities, counties, and other local governments are—or should be—concerned with the lifelong planning that points toward the later years—not the "golden years" but the continuation of living.

Lifelong Retirement Planning for Local Government Employees has been jointly published by ICMA and the ICMA Retirement Corporation, to provide a convenient starting point for those persons in local government who want to explore their lifestyles, manage their assets, and develop strategies for the future. This book will help you develop your personal retirement program and build a solid foundation, personally as well as financially, for your later years.

The Introduction to this book provides background on your responsibilities for lifelong retirement planning and the benefits to be gained. The three parts of the book cover personal relationships, leisure time, occupational choices, housing choices, and other aspects of lifestyle; insurance, Social Security, tax-deferred retirement programs, and other aspects of financial planning; and record keeping, wills, estates, and other aspects of income and asset management. The Conclusion provides a few personal guidelines to help you get started.

We gratefully acknowledge the work of three persons who made this book possible: Patricia Walsh, the editor, who organized the book, selected the chapters, and wrote the introductory sections and two of the chapters; Robert B. Morris, director of training services, ICMA Retirement Corporation, who participated in book planning and reviewed all of the chapters; and David S. Arnold, who was a liaison between the editor and the staff representatives from ICMA and ICMA-RC, wrote the Conclusion, and prepared the manuscript for the ICMA publications department. Our thanks go also to Alice R. Markham, the ICMA publications editor who copyedited the manuscript and shepherded it through all phases of production, and to the individuals and organizations who granted ICMA permission to reprint their materials.

Finally, we hope this book will help you explore life now and in the years ahead as part of your lifelong retirement planning.

Peter L. DeGroote
President
ICMA Retirement
   Corporation

William H. Hansell, Jr.
Executive Director
International City
Management Association

Introduction:
Why Plan for Retirement?

Patricia Walsh

Retirement today is for most of us a truly individual decision. We have more choices than ever before as to what we'll do in retirement, where we'll live, when we'll retire, and even how we'll retire.

Many people continue to take traditional, full retirement, often as early as possible. Others prefer the growing options for phased retirement—gradual withdrawal from work. They opt for fewer hours, or sometimes a less demanding job, with an employer for several years before retiring completely. Still others find that cyclical retirement—from one job to another, full- or part-time job, even a new career—suits them best.

A personally satisfying, financially secure retirement, however you define it, must be planned for, and the earlier the better. Planning for retirement offers tremendous rewards. If you are well prepared—psychologically, physically, and financially—your retirement years can be the best years of your life. Planning will reward you with financial independence, peace of mind, a sense of control over your life, the freedom to explore new opportunities, and confidence that you are ready to meet almost any challenge that might arise.

The consequences of not planning can be tremendous too. You could wind up with too much time and too little money, leaving you vulnerable, constricting your options, and even making you dependent on family, friends, or public assistance.

How long should you plan for?

No longer is retirement a few work-free years at the end of a career. We are living longer, healthier lives. With increased life expectancy, many retirements are spanning twenty, thirty, or more years. Yet many people underestimate just how long they have to plan for. And 168 hours a week for twenty, thirty, or more years is a lot of time.

What year do you want to retire in? How old will you be then? How many more years can someone that age expect to live? Here are the latest life expectancy estimates from the U.S. Bureau of the Census:

Your age	Life expectancy	
	Men	Women
20	52.7 more years	59.3 more years
30	43.5	49.7
40	34.3	40.1
50	25.6	30.9
60	17.9	22.5
65	14.6	18.6

Bet that you'll beat the averages and live even longer. Couples must also plan for the probability that the wife will survive her husband. Women typically outlive men the same age by about seven years. Because they often marry men older than themselves, many women spend ten, twenty, or more years as widows. Planning for these years requires special attention to finances, housing, and insurance.

What is retirement planning?

Retirement planning involves defining your desired retirement lifestyle (what you want to do and where you want to live) and then figuring out how you will finance that lifestyle in both early and later retirement. Ideally, retirement planning is just an extension of your lifelong planning that focuses on your middle and later years.

The answers to your lifestyle and financial questions come only after a great deal of thought, research, and experimentation as you obtain more insights into yourself and more information about various options.

Not long ago, when retirement was more or less uniform for most people, retirement planning was fairly simple and straightforward. That's no longer the case. Take financial planning. The responsibility and risk for long-term financial security are shifting from government and business onto you. At the same time, the world of finance is becoming increasingly complex. A financial strategy that appears sound today may become obsolete in only two or three years, much less fifteen or twenty years into retirement.

People at every age and income level must be able to continually review and revise their financial situation. Evaluating and applying professional advice from financial planners, lawyers, accountants, and other specialists is part of this process.

When should you start planning?

Whether you're thirty years from retirement or just one year away, now is the time to get started. This book provides suggestions, insights, and information you can use to make your future more satisfying and secure.

For example, if you are in your thirties, retirement planning is probably a low priority. Yet, your generation will have to supply a greater percentage of its retirement income from savings, investments, and work than preceding generations. Fortunately, you can do much now to lay a solid foundation for your retirement years while raising a family and building a career. The decisions you are making today—about saving, changing jobs, buying a house, taking a training course—will largely determine the resources and options open to you later.

Whatever your age or income level, our overriding goal in preparing this book is to help you launch your personal retirement planning program. If *you* don't do it, it simply won't get done.

Part One will help you identify your desired retirement lifestyle. We'll look at adjustments in roles and relationships, health and fitness, meaningful use of time, work options in retirement, and how to select the kind of housing and community that will support and enhance your retirement lifestyle.

In Part Two, you will assess your current financial status, develop a tentative retirement budget based on the lifestyle choices you made in Part One, and then consider strategies you can employ now to achieve your retirement goals.

Part Three discusses additional strategies for protecting your resources and your future. They include having the right kinds and amounts of insurance, setting up an effective record-keeping system, working with a financial planner, and estate planning.

The quizzes, exercises, and checklists throughout the book will help you gauge where you are in your retirement planning and what you need to do next. The sources of information at the end of each part will guide you to organizations and publications that can provide in-depth information on particular topics.

How should you proceed?

As you consider each retirement planning topic, it might be helpful to follow this step-by-step procedure:

- Acquire up-to-date information. Too much is changing too fast to base your decisions on assumptions you've held for years, whether the topic is how much to budget for a long-awaited trip or the current market value of your house.
- Discuss issues with family and friends, especially retired friends. They know you best and can help you evaluate choices. *But the decision is entirely yours.* Of course, if you are married, retirement planning is a joint project calling for discussion, sensitivity, negotiation, and compromise.
- Develop a trusted team of professional advisers and then use them to obtain specific answers to financial, legal, tax, and other technical questions.
- Select definite lifestyle and financial goals; but remember, at this point, that nothing is cast in concrete. You're free to change your mind.
- Write down actions you need to take. Specify due dates for completing them. When will you enroll in a financial planning course at the community college? When will you make out your will? When will you start exercising regularly? When will you spend more time with your kids, doing what?
- Test out potential retirement roles and activities before you retire. Get a part-time job, volunteer at the youth center, join a bowling league. Discard those that don't work and try others. Having new roles and activities in place will ease the transition to retirement by providing the structure, commitment, and companionship previously provided on the job.
- Review and update your plans regularly as you obtain more insights and information.

One more suggestion

Before you launch your retirement planning program by reading this book, take a few minutes to ask yourself honestly what work and retirement mean to you. Do you like your work? Or are you eagerly awaiting your last day on the job? What are your expectations for retirement right now?

Your attitude about work and retirement will strongly influence how you approach retirement planning and what you see as being possible. Set aside your assumptions about yourself and your retirement. Give yourself the broadest possible perspective. Keep the door of opportunity open and create for yourself the most exhilarating, rewarding retirement you can imagine.

PART ONE

Your Lifestyle—
Now and Later

Retirement planning doesn't begin with estimating retirement income and expenses. In fact, such estimating cannot be done accurately until you make some important decisions about how and where you want to live in both the early and the later years of your retirement.

This section will help you identify your preferred retirement lifestyle: the roles you want to take on or expand in retirement, how you want to spend your new-found leisure time, and where you want to live—in what community, what neighborhood, and what kind of housing.

Chapters 1 and 6 will help you assess the nonmonetary benefits you receive from work and determine what retirement activities can replace those benefits.

The people in your life will take on greater importance in retirement. Your family, friends, neighbors, and acquaintances, from the person who cuts your hair to your accountant, contribute in many ways to your overall life satisfaction. For example, they provide recognition, companionship, and a sense of belonging. Before you retire, especially if you plan to relocate, assess all of your relationships. Chapter 2 will help you identify your personal support system of family, friends, and acquaintances and develop strategies for strengthening and expanding it now.

Two-income households are becoming the rule rather than the exception. The psychological ramifications of a wife, who typically is younger, continuing to work once her husband retires are discussed in Chapter 3.

With increasing longevity, many midlife adults preparing for their own retirements must factor in the social, emotional, and financial commitments they want to make to one or more elderly parents. This growing phenomenon is discussed in Chapter 4.

The success of your retirement will depend on your level of health and fitness, which in turn is determined largely by the lifestyle choices you are making today. Chapter 5 explores what you can do now to get in shape for your future.

Whether or not to work in retirement is both a lifestyle and a financial issue. Because we are living longer, healthier lives, more and more retirements are spanning twenty, thirty, or more years. Working in retirement can provide both psychological benefits and financial security during this vital time. Chapters 7 and 8 look at the work options that will be available to older workers and outline the steps an older worker can take now to remain in or return to the work force.

Once you have a good idea about how you want to live in retirement, it's time to explore where you want to live. Your retirement housing—your home, your neighborhood, and your community—should support and enhance your chosen retirement lifestyle in both early and later retirement. Chapter 9 provides useful information and exercises to help you organize your thoughts on this important retirement planning topic.

After getting a handle on your preferred retirement lifestyle, the next step is to determine whether you'll have the financial resources in retirement to finance that lifestyle. If you discover a gap between estimated retirement income and expenses, now is the time to develop strategies for bridging that gap while you're still working and more options are open to you. How to do all of this is explained in Part Two, "Financial Planning for Retirement."

1

LIFELONG RETIREMENT PLANNING

*Go ahead and dream, "What would I be
apart from my work?"*

Walter Kiechel III

*Editor's note: Although written for executives, this article addresses
important questions for anyone who has focused most of his or her
energies on work and has derived essential psychological rewards
from that work. "Who am I when the job ends? How will I obtain
those rewards—recognition, commitment, a sense of accomplishment in retirement?" After reading the article, take a few minutes to
do the exercise, "Who are you? Who would you like to be?" (Since
this article was written, mandatory retirement at any age has been
eliminated for most workers.)*

Imagine a test that would reveal how far you are likely to get in
your career, how enduring your accomplishments will be, what
you and your spouse really feel for each other, whether you have
any unexploited talents, and how large your position figures in
what others think of you and what you think of yourself. You probably will take such a test. It's called retirement.

Many—perhaps most—flunk, a fact that barely registers on
the rest of the population. Retired people certainly don't want to
talk about it. "The first thing retirees learn is to lie with a straight
face about how they're doing," says one human-resources type
who counsels such folks. Retirement, the experts say, seems to
bring an increase in the incidence of suicide, alcoholism, and divorce.

The experts also say that if you want to pass the test, you had better begin preparing early. Your employer may even be willing to help—these days more and more companies, including the likes of Ford, GE, and ABC, are offering so-called pre-retirement counseling. A typical program might consist of two days of sessions, covering not just finances and company benefits but also attitudinal adjustments, health, and housing; employees over 55 are invited and usually their spouses as well. While a company's motives for providing such counseling are not always simon-pure—sometimes employees are right in thinking that a program represents subtle encouragement to retire—for participants the exercise usually proves an enlightening first step in facing up to what may seem an approaching black hole.

At least two problems, however, weaken most pre-retirement programs. First, they are not offered early enough in an employee's career. Pay attention, all you baby-boom hotshots: There you are, getting ready to ditch Plod Co., your employer of several years, to take one of those high-visibility, hands-on-responsibility positions at another company. Do you know when your retirement benefits from Plod vest? If the answer is, "after ten years of continuous employment," and you have nine years and eleven months on the books, you might want to delay your departure slightly—this is called retirement planning.

Many conventional pre-retirement programs also fail to address the most important issues. Observes Joseph Perkins, corporate retirement manager at Polaroid, "The whole world thinks that the biggest problem for people facing retirement is money"—which corporate programs typically do cover—"but if you have enough to cover the necessities, money is the least of the problems." Executive types in particular have few worries on this score; other demons await them.

The toughest question that managerial types face in retirement—and one that it's especially useful to get an early start answering—is, "What am I apart from my work?" Philip H. Dreyer, a professor of education and psychology at the Claremont Graduate Schools in California and an authority on retirement, elaborates why successful executives have a particularly rough time with the issue: "These individuals have an enormous amount invested in their work. It's not work for them: they have been rewarded for it; the power they have, which they enjoy using, comes from it. The higher they go in the organization, the more they devote themselves to the well-being of the institution. It becomes their real self, maybe their only self."

Who are you?
Who would you like to be?

You are unique. No one else has your assortment of experiences, memories, characteristics, hopes, and expectations. Get to know yourself. On a separate sheet of paper, write the numbers 1 through 20 down the left-hand side. Now write twenty answers to the question "Who am I?" in terms of the roles you play. Consider your roles connected with work, family, and friends as well as social, civic, religious, and special-interest activities (for example, supervisor, co-worker, father, husband, bowler, election judge, choir member, gardener).

Now ask yourself:

1. Which roles are most important to me (really)? Why? What satisfactions do I receive from them (love, status, fun, involvement)? (See the first bulleted list in Chapter 6 for more possibilities.)
2. Which roles will change when I retire? How?
3. Which roles will disappear entirely when I retire? How can I obtain in retirement the satisfactions received from those roles?
4. What new roles do I want to take on in retirement? What can I do now to begin establishing myself in those roles?
5. What current roles do I want to expand in retirement? How?

Think about who you are and who you want to be in the years ahead and begin taking steps now to reach your goals.

After retirement you can't kid yourself any longer about how you're doing in the competition to get ahead, or console yourself with the thought that tomorrow is another day. As your gaze turns from the future to the past, you may not like what you see: new people running your old operation in new ways; your accomplishments becoming more evanescent as they become more distant.

Preparation against such epiphanies takes many forms. The most obvious is simply refusing to retire. Under federal law, a company can't force you to retire until you're 70. An exception is made for executives in so-called high policy-making positions who will receive at least $44,000 a year in benefits—the company can set the mandatory retirement age for them as low as 65—but the courts have defined the exception rather narrowly. A former employee recently won an age-discrimination suit against Union Carbide when the court ruled that his job as chief labor relations counsel was not elevated enough to qualify. If they want to, though, companies can make it awfully hard not to retire—offering packages that get less attractive over time, or gradually reassigning one's work to others.

Hence an increasingly common alternative—retiring from the old job and then, after a sobering glimpse of the void, taking on a new one. A recent survey of retired presidents and chief executives of the largest U.S. companies conducted by Russell Reynolds Associates, an executive search firm, found that 61 percent of the respondents had returned to work, the majority within six months of stepping down from the catbird seat. A third of these people worked full time. From a planning point of view, the lesson is as follows: You will probably want to launch a second career. Better to lay the groundwork early, and perhaps even start on that career, before you suffer a demoralizing brush with retirement.

If in taking the long view ahead you decide that you really, truly will want to retire, then take the advice of Davis W. Gregg, president emeritus of American College in Bryn Mawr, Pennsylvania: "Start early to disengage from work culture, which represents a great support system for most people. Look for substitutes." Think of it as putting together a post-retirement answer to that most American of queries, "What do you do?" If you hope to reply, "I am the world's foremost expert on sang-de-boeuf-glaze porcelains of the T'ang dynasty," immerse yourself in the subject while you still have another career. Recipe for despair: All your working life tell yourself, "Deep down, I'm really a novelist—I just work as a lawyer to put bread on the table." After taking early retirement, put in three agonizing months at the typewriter before finally figuring out that you have neither the talent nor the persistence.

Two further cautions are in order. First, do not confuse your present leisure pursuits with what you want to give your life to in retirement. Perhaps only the retired fully understand that the most satisfying round of golf is the round stolen from the press of business. This insight comes quickly. When recently asked how long it took him after retirement to realize that he didn't want to spend the rest of his life on the links, a former insurance company vice president replied laconically, "About two days." Second, don't rely on volunteer work, however charitable, to fill the whole void. Managerial types, accustomed to having the value of their labor measured in dollars, find the wages irritating.

You will almost certainly need some sort of activity outside the home to avoid domestic strife. What retirees often find out about the state of their marriage is summed up in a quip that drops from the lips of every retirement counselor: for better or for worse, but not for lunch. Women retirees may encounter less of a readjustment in this respect—throughout their lives, they've been needed in the home—but then, they suffer other pangs: Those who have returned to the work force late in life sometimes have their careers just up and running when the retirement bell rings.

The planning prescription? Get your house in order long before you and your spouse are sitting in it, facing each other over a lunch that seems like something out of an Ingmar Bergman movie. Find out what your spouse and children hope and fear, not just about your retirement but about their own lives as well. Listen, and don't treat what they say just as something to be managed as you manage the problems that creep up at the office.

Keep the not-so-old bod ready for the adventures to come. Probably the best way to forestall the health worries of retirement is to start living healthfully now. Give up smoking. Stand up straight. Start exercising. As you jog into the future, or swim that umpteenth lap toward glory, you can meditate on the summary imperative of lifelong retirement planning: When you retire, think and act as if you were still working; when you're still working, think and act a bit as if you were already retired.

2

DEVELOPING A STRONGER INNER-CIRCLE SUPPORT SYSTEM

Elwood N. Chapman

If you were asked to name your all-time favorite teacher, you would probably have little trouble doing so. If asked to explain why you selected that person over all others, the reason might be that the person encouraged you to accomplish something special.

My favorite teacher was Jean Wilson. She challenged me and inspired me to attempt college. Thirty years after being her student, I learned that she had passed away. Only nine of her former students attended her funeral. I wondered how this could happen after all she had done for students over the years. I learned the answer. Miss Wilson, after retirement, had become a recluse. She failed to maintain or build a human support system. When the police found Miss Wilson, she was surrounded by several hungry cats. Perhaps, for her own reasons, she preferred cats to people. But, it was sad to realize that at the time of her death no one was keeping in close touch with her.

Build a support system early

Without planning, it is possible, especially for those without family members close by, to wind up almost alone. By taking charge, you can create a human support system. A human support system consists of those who provide frequent spiritual, emotional, psychological, and, occasionally, financial support. This group constitutes your inner circle. They are the people with whom you have built the best reward systems.

The word *support* simply means that when you need help, these people will see you through your problem. You would probably not have to ask them, because they would voluntarily come to your aid in one way or another. They keep in touch and do things for you.

When it comes to human response, there are no guarantees, which is why any inner-circle system should include several people. It goes without saying that you must help earn any support you may require *before* you need it. This means you should start working now to build sustaining, mutually beneficial relationships. Often you will be on the support end more than on the receiving end. Love and compassion must be the bedrock of your support system.

Figure 1 shows Mrs. Reynolds's inner-circle support system.

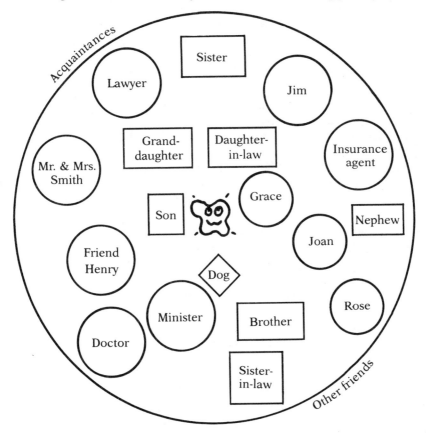

Figure 1.   Mrs. Reynolds's inner-circle support system.

Although recently retired, she began building a support system years ago. She is proud of her efforts. It gives her a feeling of security to know there are people who care about her. The system is uniquely hers, but it serves as an example, especially if you are working on one of your own.

The squares indicate family relationships, and circles signify friends. Not all family members qualify as inner-circle members. Distance often makes it impossible to include a relative, and sometimes an irreconcilable conflict is present. Even in ideal situations, a balance between relatives and friends is a good idea.

The closer a relative or friend is to the center of the circle, the more important the relationship. In the diagram, both Grace and Joan are friends of Mrs. Reynolds, but there is a stronger bond with Grace. As a result, Grace plays a more significant role in Mrs. Reynolds' life.

There are eighteen individuals in Mrs. Reynolds's support system. This is a large number. Generally, a system should have between five and twenty people. Mrs. Reynolds understands that her contemporaries may not outlive her, so she maintains some relationships with younger people. In addition to family members, she has developed strong relationships with her young lawyer and a neighbor named Jim. She is proud of these relationships.

Her closest relationship is with her son. This is understandable and, in her case, fortunate, because the relationship is mutually rewarding and loving. They enjoy being together. If help is required, her son would be called first and Grace next. Notice that her daughter-in-law and her only granddaughter are also close to the center. Mrs. Reynolds works hard to keep an excellent relationship with both.

Others in her circle are there for various reasons. Her minister plays a spiritual role in her life. Jim keeps an eye on her and helps with things needing to be done around her home. She pays him through her friendship and excellent baking skills. Her brother lives far away, so their relationship is maintained primarily by telephone. Mrs. Reynolds knows, however, that he would come to her rescue if needed. Her other friends are special in their own way. They are all concerned about her, and she knows they can never be fully replaced.

You will notice that her lawyer, her doctor, and her insurance agent are included. Although these are purely professional relationships, they provide necessary skills and contribute to her life. She feels more secure by having them in her inner circle and makes a special effort to keep close communication with all three.

They receive monetary rewards for their support, but they are also considered friends.

Her dog, Shady, is also in her support system. Pets can be very important.

Mrs. Reynolds is fortunate to have such a good support system at this stage in her life, but it did not happen automatically. She practiced Mutual-Reward Theory (MRT) in her relationships for many years. She worked at being an unselfish person. Also, she does not take her inner circle for granted. She knows that as she becomes older, the more important her system will be and the more difficult to maintain.

The Mutual-Reward Theory

If you accept the challenge of building better relationships, you should consider using the Mutual-Reward Theory. The Mutual-Reward Theory says that in a relationship both you and the other party must benefit somewhat equally. There must be a balanced reward system. You should get something you need from the other individual, and that person should get something he or she needs from you. In this way both parties come out ahead.

You have heard that it's better to give than to receive. Giving should be its own reward. This may be all that is needed by some people. Ultimately, however, the person who constantly gives without receiving starts to back away. Everyone needs something out of a relationship. MRT is a human-relations fundamental. Those who ignore it usually spend a lot of time alone.

Olive's realization

Everyone was kind to Olive after she lost her husband. Even two months later she had three or four callers each week. In time, however, Olive only got an occasional call. How quickly people forget!

Was it because she was negative, complaining about her problems? On the contrary, Olive was pleasant and positive. Then why did people back away? Without knowing it, Olive was not practicing the Mutual-Reward Theory. She was in a habit of accepting more than she was giving. Her friends were initiating all the contacts.

One day, while she was thinking about her friends, Olive realized she was not doing her share. She vowed to initiate more, and soon her friends and family were calling regularly.

Developing your own inner circle

If you like the concept of the inner-circle support system, you should evaluate what it will take to develop one or to improve one that you already possess. Mrs. Reynolds' system can be a guide, but your inner circle will be uniquely your own. It will have its own composition and design.

Start from the middle and work to the outside. If you are married, you and your spouse should consider doing one together. If you are alone and have only a few relatives to put into your circle, it will be necessary to build it primarily with friends and professional people. Whatever you eventually design should provide a new perspective on relationships and help you focus on the human side of your life.

After you choose those you want to include in your inner circle, you will occasionally add a person who has become special in your life. Don't, however, bring someone into your circle simply because you suddenly like him or her. A mature, durable, two-way relationship takes time to develop. In fact, when a new member is added, you should be proud because you helped it to occur by building a relationship.

With new members, you must ensure that you maintain each relationship. Ask yourself these three questions:

- Can you spend adequate time to keep the relationship alive and active?
- Can you take care of new members without neglecting older ones?
- Are you willing to provide, if necessary, the same kind of support you would anticipate receiving if you needed it?

Remember, it's usually better to have a small, well-kept garden than a larger one that you are forced to neglect.

Once you have completed your circle, it isn't necessary to broadcast the results. You might share the information with those closest to you, but generally it's best to keep it contained.

Building an inner circle may appear to be self-serving, but it isn't. It is nothing more than a way to help you focus on your most significant relationships. It is not meant to encourage an exclusive club that would cause you to ignore other friends. In fact, inner circles often motivate people to work toward building new quality relationships.

Sometimes circumstances make it necessary for an individual

to rebuild an inner circle almost from scratch. When this is required, all of your human-relations skills must be employed.

Retirement should give you time to strengthen present relationships, restore those that have been neglected, and add new friends. Those who have already established such a group have a jump on retirement, because once an individual leaves the work place, friends take on increased importance. Knowing those you want to spend more time with after retirement constitutes a human-relations plan. When new members are added, excitement is added. The nice thing about working on your circle is that you don't have to wait years for it to pay off. The rewards are immediate.

One nice thing about a paid-up financial endowment is that you can depend on it. A check will come every month. Wouldn't it be nice if we could depend on relatives and friends to provide human support in the same manner? Unfortunately, it doesn't work that way. Relationships are often capricious. For example, even when you have developed an outstanding relationship, that individual might move away. You could have a highly supportive child living nearby one day and across the country the next. People also have changes in their lives that can cause them to pull away. This is why you must work constantly on your inner circle. Then, if you lose members, for whatever reason, you will not be alone.

Some mental-health specialists subscribe to the idea that the best step to take when there is the loss of a pet or friend is to find a replacement. They feel a substitute is better than a vacuum. Replacement is not the best word, because it isn't possible to replace someone special, but it may help to partially fill the void. Retirees with a highly developed circle have less of a problem when it comes to replacing friends. Other are there to help.

Mrs. Hemingway

In preparation for retirement, Mrs. Hemingway sold her home and moved near the seashore—many miles from her old neighborhood. She was determined to keep her special friends (she didn't have any close relatives). She also was aware that she needed to add new members to her circle. Mrs. Hemingway took the initiative and within six months had made outstanding progress. Using MRT as a guide, she built a few new, exciting relationships with others living nearby. Within two years, she had a new inner circle. These were people willing to give her the kind of human support she was willing to give them.

Benefits of a support system

The process of developing a support system should produce many benefits. Here are a few:

- It should cause you to place more emphasis on the human side of your life.
- You will pragmatically study it as an insurance program against future situations.
- You may find you have neglected a few special people and do something about it.
- You may find you want more people in your life.
- You may discover you are spending too much time on one relationship at the expense of others.
- It should motivate you to work harder at building relationships outside your circle as potential future replacements.
- It may convince you to cultivate relationships with a few younger people now.

Other advantages and insights can occur. Best of all it is an intriguing exercise, and you should enjoy the process. (See Figure 2.)

Once you have completed the exercise, you will want to maintain it. Here are some tips you may want to consider:

- Think about the kind of rewards you want to provide to those important to you (both inside and outside your circle).
- Work to improve your communication. Make a special effort to upgrade conversations with those you care about.
- If you lose a member, find a new member.
- If appropriate, tell people that they are part of your inner circle. It is the greatest compliment you can pay them.
- Keep working to locate new friends so people will be available to move into your support system if necessary.
- Accept rewards (love) from others gracefully.
- Keep in mind that if someone is in your circle, you are probably in theirs. Make sure you deserve to be there.

Summary

The Mutual-Reward Theory is the key to building an inner-circle support system.

Loneliness is usually not planned. Retirees who wind up lonely often ignore building relationships until it is too late.

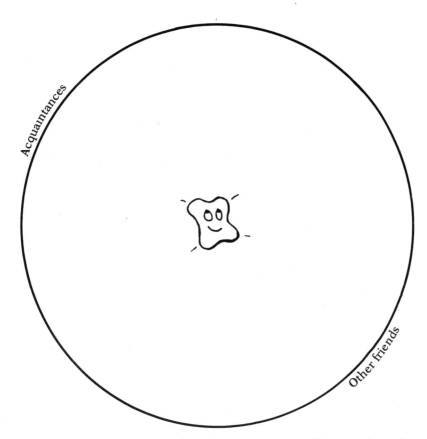

Figure 2.   Diagram your inner-circle support system. You now have the rationale with which to build a diagram of your own inner-circle support system.

No matter what kind of a support system you have, it can be improved. Now is the time to take action. No one can do it for you.

Properly implemented, an inner circle will enhance the quality of your life and the lives of those you love.

3

WORKING WIVES AND RETIRED HUSBANDS CAN MAKE GOOD MARRIAGES

Barbara Blossom

Editor's note: More and more women are entering or reentering the work force in midlife. Because wives typically are about eight years younger than their husbands, these families must plan carefully for both the psychological and the financial ramifications of two retirements, especially when they occur years apart.

Working couples now in their late thirties through late fifties will face a big decision in the next ten to twenty years: when the husband wants to retire, should his wife retire also?

This is a relatively new problem area in the ever-fragile couple relationship. Some couples say "yes," but surprisingly, not all do. It was those who say "no" that interested me. What happens when the "about-to-retire" husband is married to an "I'm-happy-in-my-job-and-don't-want-to-leave-it" wife?

Both positions are understandable. In many cases, the men have endured the stresses and strains of thirty to thirty-five years in their careers, and when their companies offer attractive incentives for early retirement, they're ready to jump at the opportunity. At the same time, many of their wives have entered or reentered the job market in recent years. Finding themselves in satisfying, fulfilling positions, they want to continue working. Retirement is low on their priority list.

The full impact of this dilemma hit me when my husband, after several years of saying he would do it, finally made the decision to take the next "window" (his employer's term for an early retirement bonus plan), retire, and do something else with his life. I had a job that I liked and had held it for thirteen years. The thought of leaving it was not appealing, so my husband's decision was a dark cloud on the horizon. The road ahead looked bumpy.

But surprisingly, my husband never suggested that I also retire. His basic assumption, it developed, was that I probably would go on working. (Since the women's movement came to full flower long after I had reached the age of "maturity," I felt grateful for my husband's attitude. I did want to continue my career, but not at the expense of his happiness.)

A few people, but only a few, seemed surprised that I continued my job. Some of these few, consciously or unconsciously, evoked twinges of guilt: Was I doing the wrong thing?

Two years have gone by since this new stage of our existence began, and it is working. The passage through the "white-water times" has been accomplished—the first months of any retirement situation require an adjustment period.

Our situation is not unique. Numerous couples have the same lifestyle. Many of the wives are in professional or white-collar occupations, but not all. Extra income does not seem to be a factor—the women stayed on for other reasons. I talked with some couples about the pains and pleasures of their nontraditional solution to this new predicament.

The husbands, almost unanimously, indicated their lives were more hassle free if their wives were working than if they weren't. Wilson B.'s wife Janet is a teacher. He said: "Janet really seems to thrive when she has a hundred things to see to. I'm more of a 'take it easy and one thing at a time' type. When we're in the same house for too long at a time—shall I be honest?"

He went on, "Too much togetherness, and our opposite personalities start chafing. That's not the best way to live."

Wilson's answer was frank. Others interviewed spoke with equal candor. This is a very difficult time of life, and yet we are told on every hand how wonderful it is. When former co-workers meet a recently retired person and ask the usual question, "How do you like your retirement?" it is heresy to reply with anything but "great." Husbands interviewed were well aware of the stress points in their new lives and felt that anything reducing pressure on them was beneficial. (Couples who have always done everything together seem to welcome the opportunity retirement gives to do even more together; but they do not constitute the majority.)

Janet, Wilson's wife, used to tell us that she probably would have a difficult time when she was too old to work because she just wasn't cut out to knit or paint or paste things together (our youthful idea of what "old people" did with their time!). Janet is still effervescent and has a particularly youthful quality, often a result of working with kids. Her words echoed the ones she uttered twenty-five years ago: "I know I'll have to face it someday, but I'm not ready yet. I love my work. I really don't feel fully alive when I'm away from it too long. I'm sure Wilson told you how much easier I am to live with when I'm working. It's true. We're both better off."

Rosalie M. is a receptionist in a busy insurance office. She disappeared from her post for almost two years and then came back. Her husband, a very active, energetic person, had retired at 57 from a job that was both physically and mentally demanding, so Rosalie—thinking it was the proper thing to do—left her position also. What had happened in the eighteen months between departure and return?

To quote Rosalie, "The frustrations built up. We're both active people, and the ends of our careers came too soon. We took it out on each other. That's no way to live." She went on: "Even though we took a few trips and caught up on a lot of projects around the house, we still had too much time with nothing pressing or important enough to motivate us. You can deteriorate very quickly in that situation."

Rosalie's husband made the first move to put purpose back in his life by finding a part-time job that used his talents. Rosalie had been valuable enough to her former employer that she was able to return. Bill, her husband, stayed with his new job about a year and then tried something else. Commenting on this, they say, "It's working a whole lot better than when we both tried retirement at the same time."

Another couple interviewed were Sarah and Len B. Their marriage has always been felicitous. Sarah heads up a large facility. She's highly respected, competent and well liked. People are impressed with her "style." Len, while sharing some of Sarah's attributes—he's well-liked and respected—is somewhat passive, but he, too, held a position of some substance, from which he retired as soon as his company allowed.

Len genially admitted that he'd have conscience problems he couldn't deal with if he stood in the way of Sarah's career. "She's so good at what she does, and she worked her way up from entry level to the top. It would be a crime to wipe that out because of some selfish desire I had. Our life is good," he continued. "Sarah has generous vacation time, we travel, and I have unencumbered days when I can pursue my business interests and my books and become completely absorbed in them without feeling I'm being unfair to someone. I know I'm easier to live with when I have a certain amount of time to myself."

Sarah confided in one of her free moments, "We've done this long enough that it's becoming a way of life. Sure, in the beginning we had a few gremlins in the works, but I can't even remember what they were now. Anyway, just what kind of lifestyle is without its problems?"

The stories are all similar. Each couple felt that for them the relationship was better if the wife continued in job or career as long as she wanted to. Certain recurrent strains emerged:

- Retirement, despite all the benevolent propaganda, can be a trauma for even the best-adjusted people. Easing into the revised lifestyle works better for many couples than going about it cold turkey.
- When a wife continues working, many husbands feel that although they might idealize what it could be like if it were otherwise, her working is probably good for them because it forces them to find productive activity and reduces considerably the tendency to depend too much on their wives.
- A couple's time together is of better quality and more appreciated when wives work.

Certain shortcomings in these arrangements exist. Travel time is limited (although the women interviewed had adequate vacation periods), and when the wives have early-morning departures, husbands wishing to sleep later must endure the disturbance of a 6:30 or 7:00 a.m. alarm, for example.

Many couples are happily living with this situation. Those facing the prospect of the husband's retirement in the next ten or fifteen years should include in their planning what his working wife will do.

4

PLANNING AHEAD TOGETHER

Katie Leishman

Editor's note: As life expectancy increases, more and more midlife adults are taking responsibility for helping their aging parents emotionally, socially, and financially. Your thorough retirement planning includes planning financially and psychologically for this possibility. (See also Chapter 20, "Insurance for Long-Term Care.")

The Junior League of Midland, Texas, recently sponsored a series of seminars titled "As Parents Grow Older." That experience differs dramatically, as the stories of those attending the seminars demonstrated. There was a couple in their early fifties. Both sets of their parents lived in a rural town 40 miles away. The wife's parents were failing, yet she and her husband had long ago agreed that their parents would not move in with them. A 37-year-old woman whose father had been stricken with Alzheimer's disease fifteen years earlier attended. There was a 55-year-old woman who had an extremely demanding mother; the mother didn't need physical help but constantly berated her daughter for not spending more time with her. A 37-year-old working mother was preparing to have her great-aunt move in. A 40-year-old woman whose mother had recently died was overwhelmed at the prospect of caring for her father and several aunts. Finally, there was one 34-year-old woman who announced at the first session, "My parents are still young and healthy, but I want to think ahead to the time when they may need me." Before the six-week course was over, her mother had died and her father had had a stroke.

It is never too early to discuss the future. Many books written about caring for parents seem to assume that the parents are quite elderly, enfeebled, and extremely dependent on their children. The literature sounds this way because, traditionally, many families have waited until a crisis to address the issue of parents' aging. Today, however, more and more people of all ages—baby boomers as well as people in their fifties—are thinking in practical ways about the realities of old age.

Across the board, American families are devoting more time, energy, and resources to caring for their elders than ever before. Last year The Travelers Corporation in Hartford, Connecticut, surveyed some 739 of its 10,000 employees, full-time workers all over the age of 30, who spend time caring for elderly relatives or friends. Seventy percent of the primary caregivers were women. Twenty-eight percent said they spent an average of 10.2 hours a week caring for elderly relatives and friends 55 years old and over. Eight percent spent 35 hours a week on such care. Forty-two percent had daily contact with their elderly relatives, and another 35 percent had contact several times a week. Sixty-two percent of the people receiving care were living in their own homes. Over half of the respondents provided household services, such as cooking or doing the laundry. Forty-four percent managed the elderly person's finances. Eighty percent said that caring for the elderly had interfered with other family, social, and emotional needs and responsibilities. About a third of the caregivers were between 30 and 40.

Lately, much has been written about working mothers and wives suddenly caught between the responsibilities of caring for their own families and for their aging parents or relatives. In fact, these women constitute only one part of the so-called sandwich generation. The fastest growing sector involves people of retirement age and older—people not long ago considered old—caring for their parents. At The Jewish Home and Hospital for Aged in New York City, the average age of admission is 85. "I recently got a letter concerning admission from an eighty-two-year-old woman, and I thought, Here's a young one," recalls Dr. Natalie Gordon, chief of social services at the home. "But, as I read more closely, I realized she wanted her ninety-eight-year-old mother admitted because she could no longer care for her herself." Recently she received a poignant letter from a 50-year-old woman dying of cancer whose greatest concern was the future care of her mother.

Americans need counseling and information services to help their elders. Although such services are cropping up and expanding everywhere, it is difficult to offer advice relevant to all families. Not only does each person age differently, but each person accepts the fact of aging in a unique way, which can determine his or her need for attention as much as any physical condition. "There are the people who want to do something but are no longer physically able to, but countless others who are in adequate physical shape but depressed and wanting to give up," says Kay Jones, instructor of the "As Parents Grow Older" seminar in Midland. The situation is shaped by a number of circumstances: the physical and mental condition of the parents; the points at which the adult child finds herself in the cycle of her own development—married or single, a

---

To help your aging parent

As the number of elderly people in this country grows, so too does the number of services and resources available to help them explore options for the future. Your local telephone book may be the best place to begin to gather information. The Blue Pages in the back contain the addresses and phone numbers of essential government offices: Medicare, Medicaid, and Social Security. You will find references to programs by looking under Aging, Area Council on Aging, Health Services, Social Services, Home Care, etc.

There are also a number of independent organizations to turn to for information and advice. Largest among them:

American Association of Retired Persons (AARP), 1909 K Street, NW, Washington, DC 20049; (202) 872-4700. Provides information and sponsors programs on a wide range of subjects. A $5 yearly membership fee grants access to all of their services.

National Council of Senior Citizens (NCSC), 925 15th Street, NW, Washington, DC 20005; (202) 347-8800. Offering programs and services similar to AARP's, NCSC also operates the Nursing Home Information Service, which distributes free, helpful pamphlets about nursing homes.

There are also excellent resource books for families:

You and Your Aging Parent: The Modern Family's Guide to Emotional, Physical and Financial Problems, revised edition, by Barbara Silverstone and Helen K. Hyman (Pantheon).

Caring for Your Parents: A Sourcebook of Options and Solutions for Both Generations, by Helene MacLean (Doubleday).

The Age Care Sourcebook: A Resource Guide for the Aging and Their Families, by Jean Crichton (Fireside).

Why Survive? Being Old in America, by Dr. Robert N. Butler (Harper & Row).

parent or childless, working outside the home or not; and the finances of both generations.

The single piece of advice experts most commonly offer caregivers is this: Accept your limitations. "The anxiety of adult children is that they can never do as much for their parents as their parents did for them," says Charlotte Kirschner, consultant for the Jewish Board of Family and Children's Services in New York City. There is a paradox beneath the anxiety. "The woman worries that she will have to be the primary caretaker—and that she won't be able to," says Dr. Mary Howell, director of the Kennedy Aging Project at the Shriver Center in Waltham, Massachusetts. "How can she care for her parent without destroying her own life?"

The cornerstone to helping aging parents is learning how to discuss the most sensitive and difficult topics in advance of an emergency. This means finding a way to ask, How do you want to die? Do you want to be in intensive care, on a respirator.? "It is never easy to ask such questions, but remember it only gets tougher to do so as parents get older," says Dr. Howell. It is easier to put off such discussions, especially these days, when on retirement so many parents move off to the sunbelt, looking and feeling great. But too often, years later, an emergency call comes and decisions have to be made hastily and unilaterally that could have been planned jointly in advance.

Many families are more comfortable talking about death than about money. Adult children often worry about offending or alarming parents by asking about finances and plans in the event of a sudden disability. Or the children themselves don't want to think of anything serious happening to their parents. They may also feel threatened by discussing money frankly with Mom and Dad. Money is something parents take care of, and many adult children still retain that perception in relationship to their own mothers and fathers. "Parents will very often drop clues about when they're ready to discuss this topic—kids often don't want to pick up on them," says Mary Egnor, associate director of Child and Family Services of Michigan. Every family has a different ethic about money, and the topic doesn't get discussed for all sorts of reasons. "Parents may not want children to know how little they're getting by on—or, conversely, they may want their children out there doing their own thing, not counting on inheritances," says Ms. Egnor.

Financially, older Americans fall predominantly into two groups. A great many are comfortable; they have made sound investments or had a decent pension plan and remained in relatively good health. Then there are large numbers of people who have no estate to speak of, who clearly qualify for public assistance and community-service programs. Perhaps the commonest mistake middle-class families make is to wait until there is an emergency to discover that their aging parents are underinsured. A careful review of parents' insurance policies is absolutely essential. Medicare pays approximately 40 percent of older Americans' health-care costs, yet, according to a recent survey of its members conducted by the American Association of Retired Persons, 79 percent thought that Medicare would take care of all their medical needs. And the program doesn't cover those who need some form of long-term, nonskilled nursing care. Wading through Medicare and Medicaid information is tedious but crucial.

The elders who may suffer the most are those just over the poverty line. "The marginally frail and the marginally self-sufficient are the ones most apt to fall between the cracks," says Natalie Gordon. These are the Americans for whom the specter of having to "spend down"—rid themselves of the assets they do have—to receive full Medicaid benefits is a daily reality. The notion violates so many values: People cling to the idea of leaving something behind, however modest, for their children. Many elderly people fear that, if they spend their resources, their young relatives will be less interested in them. It is a fear social workers hear voiced so often that people with relatives in this situation may want to find a way to bring up the subject. Often, it is the prospect of nursing-home placement that elicits the worry. Most nursing-home residents convert to Medicaid payment within two years of their stay.

The subject of nursing homes is anathema to most Americans, striking at their deepest fears of abandonment and isolation. Through the 1960s the myth prevailed that Americans were dumping their elders in nursing homes. Yet studies have shown that families are the central caregivers and turn to institutions only as a last resort. Studies in the 1970s conducted by Dr. Ethel Shanas, a sociologist at the University of Illinois, indicated that 83 percent of women and 66 percent of men age 80 and older live with their children or within ten minutes from them.

Too often Americans reinforce negative stereotypes of nursing homes by the way they think and talk about them, even at a time when there are more first-rate institutions than ever. "We constantly encounter the enormous disappointment an older person feels, their sense of failure that in having to enter a nursing home they have let their families down," says Natalie Gordon. Adult children, too, can feel as if they have failed their parents when the decision must be made. Yet some of the most comfortable elder Americans are those who thought ahead, "shopped" with their children for a nursing home, the way one might for any home, and signed on in advance for the one that suited them best. "A woman who came to this home over twenty years ago recently died here at one hundred and two," recalls Natalie Gordon. "She had had no physical disabilities but had outlived family and friends and wanted the comforts and social contacts such a home can offer."

According to Helen MacLean in *Caring for Your Parents*, only 5 percent of people over 65 live out their lives in a nursing home; their median age is 81, and two-thirds of them are women, almost half of whom are childless. However, these statistics will change as the cohort of Americans over 80 continues to grow. Some 12 to 15 percent of these people are expected to get Alzheimer's disease, which almost invariably results in nursing-home placement.

The scenario that distresses families and experts is obviously not one in which a nursing home is the most appropriate source of care, but one in which nursing-home placement occurs only because it is not possible to arrange for, or receive reimbursement for, the few hours of daily nonskilled nursing or housekeeping services that would allow an elderly person to stay in his or her own home. As it emerges that home care is usually cheaper than nursing-home care, the government is reassessing compensation for home health services. In the meantime, families may consider pooling resources with other families or neighbors, whose elders also need only part-time care. "Everybody should be socking away relationships, especially ones that cut across age groups. They become invaluable," says Dr. Gordon. "Sometimes all that's needed to let Mom stay in her home is someone to check in on her and make sure she's gotten—and eaten—the Meals on Wheels."

Most families make every effort to help elders stay in their own homes, if they wish to, until it is no longer in the elders' best interest. At that point, families often worry about whether they should invite a parent to live with them. Occasionally this works out well for everyone—parents, children, and grandchildren. More often, it does not. Most social workers and gerontologists agree that, unless parent and child, usually mother and daughter, lived together peacefully for years, they shouldn't try it now. "People wishfully think there will be some new closeness and the emotional baggage of the past will disappear. They should know it isn't going to get any better than it ever was, and may get more difficult," says Kay Jones.

The concept of changing needs is a crucial one. Parents' needs

---

Living together again

For economic, health, or other reasons, it may one day seem sensible for you to consider having an elderly parent (or an adult child) move in with you. The questions below will help you consider various aspects of the situation before making a decision.

1. What is my current relationship with my elderly parent (adult child)?
2. Can my parent and I discuss a variety of subjects without becoming embarrassed or angry?
3. Who will have to give up what (for example, a bedroom) if my parent moves in with me?
4. Would everyone have some privacy?
5. Could we adjust to each other's way of life?
6. Will my parent be dependent on me for a social life?
7. Would I be "in control"?
8. Could we work out a way to share expenses?
9. Could we establish clear and fair "ground rules" regarding such matters as selecting TV programs, shopping, and preparing meals?
10. Could I avoid overprotecting my parent and vice versa? Could we relate to each other as adults?

---

can change very gradually or overnight. "Sometimes you will have to do something you once said you wouldn't, perhaps even promised not to do. You may not be able to keep the promise, but understand—and help a parent understand—that you said something under one set of circumstances, but the circumstances have changed," says the Reverend Bruce Sylvester, a minister in Plainfield, Illinois, who has counseled parishioners concerning aging parents.

No matter how circumstances develop or alter, families should always hold on to the concept of partnership. "Even when you have to make a decision for a parent, involve him or her in it. Never discuss a parent, or let any one else discuss him, in the third person when he is right there," says Mary Egnor. Doctors and lawyers often try to address the adult children rather than the parent, discussing "what she needs." Such professionals should be called in advance of an appointment and told to speak directly to the parent. "Even if their actions have become childlike, parents are not children and never should be treated that way," say Ms. Egnor.

Society's model for caretaking *is* that of caring for the young. The outcome of such care is, of course, that the child becomes stronger and more independent. This is not the outcome of caring for elderly parents. Even knowing so, many people still experience a sense of guilt, frustration, and sadness that, with the best care, older parents inevitably grow frailer. Certainly some of that sadness has to do with what is, for many people, the first real intimation of their own later years. Yet even when adult children can't guarantee parents lifelong independence, they can safeguard their continuous dignity. Planning for old age is one of the last experiences parents and children will share. It should be as meaningful as all the others.

5

How You Age
Is Your Choice

Doralie Denenberg Segal

"We're moving toward an age-irrelevant society." So says Bernice
L. Neugarten, Ph.D., aging expert and sociologist at Northwestern
University. Dr. Neugarten is referring to an abolition of age in
determining our worth in the work place. We should not be hired,
fired, retired, passed over for promotions—or discriminated
against in *any* way because of our chronological, or calendar, age.

Nevertheless, we are required to compete in the work place,
and Dr. Neugarten assumes that we are physically able to do so. If
we are plagued with the chronic, disabling diseases that often accompany aging, it may become almost impossible for us to travel
to our office, no less to be productive once we're there. In other
words, what's important is not our age measured in years, but our
age measured by our capacity to function.

It's an obvious observation, but one worth repeating, that
some people are old at 50 while others are young at 75. Arthur S.
Leon, M.D., is director of the applied physiology/nutrition section
and research cardiologist at the University of Minnesota and a former vice president of the American College of Sports Medicine. He
tells us it's not unusual for active women in their sixties to have
higher aerobic power than inactive women and even men in their
twenties. Dr. Leon cites a study that he helped to conduct at the
University of Minnesota that was designed to measure physical

performance and life satisfaction in women over age 65. One 80-year-young woman in tennis shoes, who walked about ten miles a day inside shopping malls, had the cardiorespiratory fitness, that is, the endurance and vigor, usually seen in sedentary men in their twenties!

Some scientists studying the aging process claim that our true biologic potential is around 110 years rather than the life expectancies we know today—on average around 75 years. In other words, we are felled prematurely by all the personal and environmental weapons that we aim at ourselves.

Actually, our potential lifespan really hasn't changed, but our life expectancy has been progressively extended over the centuries. If only our ancestors knew then what we know now about infectious disease control, sanitation, and healthy nutrition, they might well have lived a longer life than we, given their cleaner environment and more exercised bodies.

Many of the problems that we associate with aging are not necessarily caused by aging. Dr. Robert N. Butler, former director of the National Institute of Aging, and now chairman of the department of geriatrics at Mt. Sinai Medical Center in New York, tells us, "Diseases must be distinguished from the effects of the aging process itself."

For example, coronary heart disease, high blood pressure, stroke, adult-onset diabetes, osteoporosis, certain respiratory problems, and various types of cancer become more prevalent in our society as we age. "It's not the years that cause these problems; rather, it's the *years of neglect*," cautions Dr. Leon. We abuse our bodies and sacrifice our optimal health by indulging in damaging health behaviors such as smoking; overeating; not eating enough of the "right stuff" and too much of the unhealthy, high-risk other food; and abusing alcohol and drugs. Individually, we can control these factors, but we must depend upon our society to cleanse our impure and sometimes toxic environment: the air we breathe, the water we drink, the water that supports our fish supply, the soil in which our foods are grown, the foliage on our trees and plants, and even animal feed that affects our food supply and ultimately our health and life expectancy.

Nor is there any doubt that we jeopardize our bodies by our sedentary existence. Our ancestors, don't forget, were *constantly* on the run—in chase or being chased—carrying, lifting, pushing, climbing, swimming, and jumping, in order to survive. Bruce Springsteen reminds us, in song, that we were "Born to Run." By sitting life out, we gather cobwebs that clog our human engines.

Dr. Walter M. Bortz II, a gerontologist at the Palo Alto Medical Clinic and co-chairman of the American Medical Association's Committee on Aging, tells us, "In reviewing the changes commonly attributed to the process of aging, I was struck by the coincidence of many of these changes that accompany physical *inactivity*." Interestingly, experiments with animal subjects reveal that females allowed "ad lib" exercise lived 11.5 percent longer than their cage-bound counterparts, while males lived 19.3 percent longer than their caged counterparts.

The age delay for the hearty

The health of our heart and blood vessels can be life saving or life threatening. And the studies demonstrating protective effects of exercise against heart disease are now so convincing that we are gambling with our health if we ignore the message. (We're talking about aerobic or endurance exercise—during which our large muscles are working in a continuous and rhythmic pattern, using oxygen for energy release. Bicycle riding, vigorous walking, swimming laps, aerobic dancing, skipping rope, rowing, jogging, folk dancing, and cross country skiing all qualify.)

When we become physically conditioned or "trained," we are less susceptible to blood clotting problems than if we are untrained. In fact, the entire cardiovascular system becomes more efficient. Even our red blood cells improve their ability to release oxygen into the active muscles. "The resulting improvement in cardiovascular efficiency may be the most important way in which exercise training reduces heart attack risk," states Dr. Leon. If we can prevent diseases of our heart and blood vessels, we can, perhaps, extend our years of good health—and maybe even our total years!

Professor Ralph S. Paffenbarger, Jr. of the Stanford University School of Medicine and his colleagues report the positive effect that *sustained* exercise has on cardiovascular health and reduced mortality rates. They tracked the health, mortality, and activity records of some 17,000 Harvard alumni over many years. Those alumni who expended 2,000 or more calories a week in exercise had *less than half the risk* for coronary heart disease than did those who utilized fewer than 500 calories. (Roughly: jogging one mile slowly or walking one level mile requires 100 calories.) The more active group also was less likely to develop hypertension (high blood pressure) than the less active.

Dr. Paffenbarger's findings, published in the *New England*

Journal of Medicine, report that exercise reduces not only the number of deaths due to cardiovascular disease but deaths from all causes—heart and lung disease, cancer, natural causes, and trauma—if the exercise is performed regularly. Alumni who walked, climbed stairs, or played sports increased their life span, on average, by one to more than two years when compared to their more sedentary counterparts. Further, the more they exercised— up to 3,500 calories a week—the better their longevity score. After that amount, however, the benefits seemed to turn around.

And, just in case you're still a smoker, the Paffenbarger data showed that exercise can reduce your disease/mortality risk. Also, the hypertensives who exercised had half the mortality rate of their inactive peers.

We tend to think of coronary artery disease, the cause of most heart attacks, as a "mostly male" problem. After menopause, however, women become susceptible to this killer—our country's number one—and statistics for incidence of the disease begin to mimic the males'. The obvious explanation has been that estrogen provides some type of hormonal protection that helps to keep female coronary arteries "clean and young." But recently, G. Harley Hartung, Ph.D., research associate professor at Baylor College of Medicine in Houston, reported some intriguing findings about the relationship between exercise in women and levels of HDL-C, or high-density lipoprotein-cholesterol—popularly known as the "good cholesterol" because it carries and clears cholesterol out of the arteries and toward the liver, where it is degraded. Dr. Hartung found that "Low HDL-C levels are an extremely good predictor of coronary artery disease in women; but those women who engage in regular endurance exercise, both before and after menopause, clearly have higher HDL-C levels—which protect against heart disease—than do inactive women."

Perhaps the greatest benefit women may derive from exercise is that it helps prevent a decline in HDL-C and other associated favorable risk factors that usually occur following menopause. After menopause, a vigorous life style can override the decreased estrogen levels and offer the protective cholesterol profiles that younger women enjoy.

Overhauling our engines

As we get older, our tissues become more insensitive to insulin, and it becomes more difficult for our muscles to utilize glucose, our blood sugar, for energy. Eventually, we have develop a glucose intolerance. This condition is known as "adult-onset diabetes." It concerns us because high insulin levels in our blood cause hardening and narrowing of coronary arteries, or *atherosclerosis*.

About 80 percent of the diabetics in our society are over 40 years of age. When the disease develops in adulthood, it is highly associated with physical inactivity and an overweight condition. Douglas R. Seals, Ph.D., and coauthors from the section of applied physiology in the department of medicine at Washington University, St. Louis, report in *JAMA*, the *Journal of the American Medical Association*, that ". . . older athletes (i.e., older than 60 years) who have performed endurance exercise regularly for years exhibit the same glucose tolerance and sensitivity to insulin as younger endurance athletes. . . . Exercise has a powerful insulin-like effect on glucose uptake by muscle, which can persist for a prolonged period."

Dr. Bortz makes a power-packed statement: "Obesity can be viewed as premature aging. The fat person deteriorates in the same way as the slim person, only the deterioration comes at an earlier age." There is no doubt that endurance exercise promotes weight control and in conjunction with a prudent diet, is the most effective, safest way to burn fat, not muscle or other organ tissues.

Skeletons—Out of the closet!

The time-honored adage, "use it or lose it, but don't abuse it," applies to all our body parts and systems! Actually, the best prescription to prevent a creaky, prematurely old skeleton is to keep our joints exercised through their full range of motion. There is absolutely no evidence that moderate exercise will wear out our joints. In fact, we're more likely to "rust out from lack of exercise," warns Dr. Leon. We actually "nourish" our joints when we're active by increasing their blood supply. The joint cartilage may become thicker and we develop better lubricated, more healthy, and "younger" joints.

Two separate studies that emphasized the benefits of exercise on our joints recently appeared in *JAMA*. In one study, researchers at the University of Florida compared a group of 17 male runners, ages 50 to 74, with a similar group of 18 nonrunners. The runners, 53 percent of whom were marathoners, ran on average about 28 miles a week for 12 years. The comparisons of many joints, made by x-rays, clinical examinations, and physical histories, disclosed no significant differences in joint disease between the two groups. The authors claimed, ". . . long duration, high-mileage running need not be associated with premature degenerative joint disease in the lower extremities."

In the second study reported, researchers at Stanford University School of Medicine compared 41 long-distance runners, aged 50 to 72 years, with 41 "matched" nonrunners or occasional runners. Again, the results showed no difference between the two groups in the prevalence of osteoarthritis, or degenerative joint disease. However, both male and female runners had 40 percent higher bone density than their counterparts. Incidentally, the average weight of the runners was 14 pounds less than their matched controls.

Osteoporosis, the condition that results when bones become weakened and porous from a loss of minerals, occurs in both men and women, although women are much more subject to this condition. Even after a trivial injury, their demineralized "bone shells" become prone to fracture. This incapacitating and often crippling condition can play havoc with one's rate of aging, especially if activity is restricted out of fear.

As women's estrogen levels decline after menopause, they become susceptible to osteoporosis. New evidence, however, puts more responsibility back onto their weakened shoulders. At the Spring 1985 meeting of the American College of Sports Medicine, several authorities reported that the *primary* cause for bone loss is *inactivity*, which decreases our ability to use calcium. After periods of bedrest or weightlessness, we feel weakened and we excrete calcium. Astronauts must perform resistance-type exercises in space to prevent this loss.

The report concluded that "[the] data support the role of exercise in the retardation of bone loss with aging. . . . For women, weight-bearing exercise, in addition to estrogen and calcium therapy, may retard the phenomenon of bone loss with aging."

As we age, our intestines do not absorb calcium from our food and supplements as readily as when we were younger. Other factors contributing to osteoporosis are inadequate calcium intake, excess protein intake, smoking, alcoholism and, of course, heredity.

Everett L. Smith, Ph.D., director of the biogerontology laboratory in the department of preventive medicine at the University of Wisconsin, reminds us that we can prevent 75 to 80 percent of the spine and hip fractures that result from osteoporosis. Dr. Smith emphasizes that bones are living tissue, like muscle, and they respond to stress with a weight-bearing load at any age. (Note: swimming does not qualify!) He has done extensive studies with older women and has reported that his active subjects in their eighties actually increased their bone mass in response to a physical activity program, while the sedentary women lost more bone.

Mental fitness

When we lost interest and involvement in our surroundings, we become bored, apathetic, and even more sedentary. No wonder that some older adults become less alert, their memory fails, and they react more slowly. At least some of this behavior is thought to result from cultural influences and expectations.

Is the loss of some mental capacities, then, not inevitable? We know, for example, that studies reveal older individuals who are highly fit score better on tests of "fluid intelligence" (spontaneous decision-making ability) than their less fit counterparts; also, older men who keep up actively with racquet sports and running show faster response times than do their sedentary, age-matched controls.

Now a group of investigators at the neuropsychology research laboratory and VA Medical Center in Salt Lake City report in the journal *Neurobiology of Aging* that after previously sedentary older adults (aged 55 to 70 years) trained aerobically for four months, they scored significant improvements in a variety of mental abilities, such as response time, memory, hand-eye coordination and speed, and mental "flexibility." Another notable result: An exercise control group that performed only strength and flexibility exercises also improved on these psychoneurological tests, but to a much lesser extent than the aerobic group. A nonexercise control group showed no improvement.

The authors of the report are cautious in offering an explanation. Perhaps, they suggest, the aerobic exercisers developed better oxygenation in brain tissue as well as in other body tissues. Oxygen assists the metabolism of certain brain chemicals, called *neurotransmitters*, such as norepinephrine, serotonin, and dopamine. Each of these neurotransmitters plays a role in our behavior and each also declines with advancing age.

The improved biochemical functioning in the brain as a result of physical conditioning is thought to improve our attention span and concentration. These, in turn, may help improve performance on the various mental ability tests. We also know that endurance exercise is an excellent therapy for treating mild and moderate depression, a condition characterized by a disturbance in the neurotransmitter levels. Our mood improves after exercise, and we decrease our anxiety and tension levels. Perhaps these secondary changes also have favorable effects on our memory and intelligence.

The best defense is a good offense

Our immune system becomes less effective as we age. Can we "rejuvenate" this defense mechanism by adopting and maintaining an active life style? According to research performed at the University of Michigan, the physiological responses to exercise and to infection are remarkably similar—each produces a protein known as *interleukin-1*. When blood containing this protein was taken from normal women and men who worked out for one hour on a stationary bicycle and injected into rats, the animals developed a fever—and fever, we now know, helps us fight bacterial and viral illnesses. Blood injected from nonexercising controls had no effect upon the animals. Results from other animal studies also look promising.

Sixty-three percent of polled runners claimed that they had increased their resistance to ailments such as colds, asthma, flu, and hay fever; and they attributed the improvement to their running. Whether this was the "power of positive thinking" or real physiology can't yet be determined for sure—maybe a little of both is involved.

The bottom line

When Dr. Leon was asked, "If you want to age as rapidly as possible, what would you do?" He replied, "Go to bed. Don't talk to anyone. . . . This leads to a rapid deterioration of both physical and mental status."

We have many as yet unanswered questions about the process of aging. We still cannot completely prevent aging, but we can take measures to promote our "aging in the slow lane."

So invest in some healthy strategies *now*—it's never too late to begin. Become aware of healthy foods and eat low-fat, high-complex carbohydrate meals. Substitute olive oil for other kinds of oil and fat whenever possible; eat dark-meat fish (salmon, tuna, mackerel, swordfish, rainbow trout, etc.) and poultry instead of fatty meats; use no-fat- or low-fat- instead of whole milk; say no (most of the time) to fatty rich desserts; concentrate on fresh fruits and veggies, high-fiber, whole-grain cereals and breads, potatoes, brown rice, pasta, and nuts.

Find those activities that you enjoy and can do on a regular basis. Alternate between different choices if possible (swim one day, bike the next, etc.) Walk instead of ride. Climb stairs instead of taking the elevator. (Even if you can't make it up all ten flights on your first try, go as far as you can and ride the rest; eventually, if you add one more flight at each, or every other, attempt, you'll own the whole ten flights!) Walk briskly, walk often, and, perhaps, graduate into jogging if your doctor agrees.

Sign up for a class in something that sounds very intriguing or exotic, or take a course that you've always thought about but never had time to pursue. Learn a new foreign language; then go to a country where it's spoken and try your luck. Experiment. Find a new hobby. Plan an adventure.

Stay active, stay alert, and stay healthy. It's the way to age well and youthfully.

6

THE TIME IN YOUR LIFE

Worker Equity Department
American Association of Retired Persons

Too often, people approach retirement without at least a tentative plan for reallocating the time in their life. Many people actually resist the idea of planning, preferring instead to entertain vague pipe dreams about sleeping in, fishing, golfing, or traveling. These activities are all well and good, but even the most avid golfer can't spend one-fourth to one-third of his or her life on the golf course. And with early retirement and longer life expectancy, that's just what your retirement can be—fully one-third of your life.

Thorough retirement planning involves identifying your needs and desires and then finding activities that help you achieve them. This is especially important if most of your key needs have been met through work.

Which of the following needs are most important to you? How are you currently meeting those needs? How can you meet them once you retire?

- Commitment, involvement
- Recognition
- Friendship
- Structure to daily living
- Personal or intellectual growth
- Self-esteem

- Creativity, productivity
- Development of new skills
- Adventure, fun
- Relaxation, recreation
- Health and fitness
- Service to others.

In his book, *Growing Old, Staying Young*, Christopher Hallowell states: "The key to successful aging is involvement. People who age the best tend to be involved in various interests; they are involved with people; they are curious and they are flexible."

In his studies of the life satisfaction of retirees, Dr. Daniel Ogilvie, a psychologist at Rutgers University, found that "a powerful factor in satisfaction is how much time a person can spend doing those things that he does best, enjoys the most, and finds most meaningful."

Researchers have also found that how people spend their free time can make a real difference in their health. It's commonly agreed that being in good health will make you more satisfied with your life. But "being more satisfied with life, and so being in positive moods more often, seems to be good for your health," says psychologist Ed Diener, of the University of Illinois.

The information and ideas in this chapter will help you begin now to do the following:

- Identify your key needs and desires.
- Identify possible activities that will help you achieve those needs and desires.
- Obtain further information on these activities through literature, people, and organizations.
- Get started "testing the waters," that is, trying out these activities before you retire, for several reasons: (a) to see if you really like them, (b) to find out how much each activity will cost and then figure that cost in your tentative retirement budget, and (c) to aid your transition to retirement by having some structure, commitment, and companionship to replace what you will be losing when you stop working.

To help you begin, here is advice from successful retirees:

- Consider variety, since few people can engage in even the most absorbing activity all day, every day.
- Plan some activities you can do alone and some to do with other people. Everyone needs private time, but social contact is vital too.

- Commit yourself to an activity. Experts say it helps to involve others, not only because company adds zest to what you're doing but also because you'll be embarrassed to quit if you've "dragged" friends along.
- Make sure that some of your activities are demanding enough so that they're not too easily mastered and provide the challenge of increasing levels of difficulty.
- Consider activities that offer you the sense of contribution to others that is vital to a feeling of self-worth.
- Don't overextend yourself. In spite of all our exhortations to keep active, consider quality rather than quantity as your main criterion for choosing activities.
- Consider the possibility of some physical slowdown in later years. Again, a variety of activities—some physical and some creative or intellectual—is the key.

Time for others is time well spent

"No one is useless in this world who lightens the burdens of another." This quotation of Charles Dickens sums up the essentials of the case for volunteering in terms especially appropriate for retirees, who report that among the greatest threats to their happiness is a sense of loss of identity, a lack of self-worth—a feeling of uselessness.

Those who begin volunteering on a regular basis before they retire, however, find the transition to retirement much easier because volunteering helps them maintain a sense of accomplishment and involvement with the world. As post-retirement volunteers, they go right on putting their skills and talents to good use.

And consider the other advantages of volunteering. You'll meet new people and expand your social network, enhance your identity by taking on a new role, and begin to structure your time to fight that tendency to drift that comes with idleness. You may also be able to acquire new skills and gain experience that will be useful in obtaining paid employment in the future. This may be especially true for women reentering the work force or entering for the first time in later life.

How to choose a volunteer activity   In choosing a volunteer activity, select something you firmly believe in—something to which you are committed. Convince yourself that you can indeed make a difference in this world. But don't overextend yourself. Devote your energy to one, maybe two, causes instead of parceling yourself out in little bits to every organization that calls. Otherwise, you'll find yourself missing that feeling of a job well done because you won't have had time to do it.

How do you find the organization or cause that warrants your devotion? Approach your search with all the care you'd give to finding a paid job. After all, this is a job you're seeking—an important one.

Thus, some serious self-evaluation is in order. Start by writing a brief description of yourself, listing your present and past occupations, your interests, and your talents. Then ask yourself the following questions, designed to reveal preferences that might point to a volunteer position.

1. Can you work well by yourself, or do you function better with a group?
2. Do you like children, and do you know how to relate to them? tutor them? play constructively with them?
3. Do you prefer being with adults? Can you work well with people younger or older than yourself? with the very old?
4. Can you work well with persons with physical or mental impairments?
5. Are you good at clerical work, or do you prefer more creative endeavors?
6. Do you prefer to work in the background, or do you want to be seen and heard?
7. Do you prefer to be in the same place, or are you willing to go to different sites?
8. Are you able and willing to extend yourself physically?
9. Is public acknowledgment of your efforts important to you?
10. What interests you most? The troubles of people in your own age group? Teenage conflicts? Child abuse? Abuse of the elderly? The drug problem? Homeless people? Women's rights? Some other aspect of life in your community?

Think of what you have to offer to each interest you identify. Are you a patient teacher? a good listener? a born salesperson? a talented carpenter? Every ability or gift has a volunteer application. Now that you have some idea of the direction in which your inclinations lie, you must find the cause, project, or organization whose needs match your talents and interests. A good place to start looking for openings is at your local voluntary service bureau or volunteer clearinghouse. Look it up in your phone book under any of a variety of names beginning with *Volunteer* or *Voluntary*, or try looking under United Way, Community Chest, Council of Social

Agencies, and so on. You can also ask about volunteering at your city hall, your chamber of commerce, or a religious center.

Make an honest commitment   When you think you've found the place for yourself, be honest with yourself and the organization about how much time you're willing to put in. It also helps—and this was part of the point of your self-evaluation above—if you can be fairly specific about what you want to do. "I'll be happy to do anything," although meant sincerely, is rarely the case in the long run, and voluntary agencies know it. People differ in what they enjoy doing, and it's to the agency's advantage to find the right job for you.

Be realistic in your preferences. You're unlikely to be running the show in the first two months, and there's no point in expecting to—especially if you're working for one of the larger service organizations.

Where to volunteer   What follows is a brief list of volunteer possibilities—a complete list would look like the Manhattan Yellow Pages! It's just to start you thinking creatively about your options.

Education   This is one of the most fruitful fields for retired persons because schools, public schools in particular, are often in need of people to take some of the burden off hard-pressed teachers and administrators. According to the National School Volunteer Program, about 4.3 million adults of all ages are participating in some 3,000 school volunteer projects today. What can you do? You can grade papers, design bulletin boards, monitor the lunchroom or playground, help in the school office or library, be a crossing guard, assist in dramatics programs, tell stories, and much, much more. See your local school board or go right to the school principal.

Literary Volunteers of America (see sidebar) is a nationwide organization that is training volunteers to teach adults to read. A number of the teachers have joined the projects through employer volunteer programs—a good way to begin volunteering before you retire.

Culture   Museums, art centers, theater groups, opera and ballet companies, and orchestras all need help to get started and keep going. Needed services range from fund raising to typing subscribers' lists, from making posters to acting as a guide or an usher. One man specialized in tracking down hard-to-find props for his local repertory theater.

Voluntary action resources

Write or call the following organizations for more information:

ACTION, 806 Connecticut Avenue, NW, Washington, DC 20525. Or call toll-free 800-424-8580. Administers VISTA, RSVP, Foster Grandparents Program, and Senior Companion Program.

AARP Volunteer Talent Bank, AARP, 1909 K Street, NW, Washington, DC 20049. Matches volunteers with AARP programs and programs of other national voluntary organizations.

Volunteer: The National Center, 1111 N. 19th St., Arlington, VA 22209. 703-276-0542. A clearinghouse for information on volunteer programs throughout the country.

National Park Service, Office of Information, U.S. Department of the Interior, P.O. Box 37127, Washington, DC 20013-7127. Contact the park you're interested in or write for a brochure on volunteering in national parks.

National School Volunteer Program, 701 N. Fairfax Street, Alexandria, VA 22314. 800-992-NSVP. Information on how to start or join a school volunteer program.

SCORE/ACE (Service Corps of Retired Executives/Active Corps of Executives), 1129 20th Street, NW, Suite 410, Washington, DC 20036. 800-368-5855. Information on how to use your skills to help new and struggling businesses.

Peace Corps, The Peace Corps, Washington, DC 20526. 800-424-8580, extension 93. Recruits older Americans with skills to share.

Veterans Administration. Maintains a large volunteer program in its various locations. Contact the Office of Voluntary Service in the VA center near you.

VITA (Volunteers in Technical Assistance), 1815 North Lynn Street, Suite 200, Arlington, VA 22209. 703-276-1800. Provides volunteers to help in developing countries.

Literacy Volunteers of America, 5795 Widewaters Parkway, Syracuse, NY 13214. Or call toll-free Contact Literacy Center at 800-228-8813. Helps adults learn to read.

Hospitals and other health services   Hospitals need volunteers to act as receptionists, nurse's aides, gift shop attendants, file clerks, or friendly visitors to patients who want someone to talk with. Most hospitals have a director of volunteers who will be glad to explain their volunteer program and get you started.

There are, of course, many health-related jobs to be done outside the hospital, and your local chapter of the Red Cross is a good place to find them. Everyone thinks of the Red Cross in connection with rescue work during disasters, but the organization provides other much-needed services. These include instruction in first aid, water safety, and baby care. Red Cross volunteers also serve in rehabilitation centers and nursing homes.

And don't forget the critical area of mental health. Your local mental health association can tell you where you can help. For example, you could work on a telephone hot line, talking to people in trouble and steering them to those who can help them.

Politics and civic affairs   Working for good government can take many forms. You can serve the party of your choice, getting involved in the excitement (and hard work) of a local, state, or national campaign. You can even run for office. Surprisingly, a number of low-level positions sometimes go unfilled for want of someone to run for them! Or, if you're not sure where you stand politically, you can join a nonpartisan group such as the League of Women Voters. [Editor's note: Men are equally eligible for membership.]

Civic affairs is an umbrella label for the work of any number of organizations ranging from the chamber of commerce and service organizations to committees focusing on specific environmental, consumer, or political concerns. For example, if you like children, consider the Boy Scouts of America, the Girl Scouts of the U.S.A., or the Big Brothers/Big Sisters of America.

Services to the aging   You may find it fulfilling to help older people by performing such needed services as visiting nursing homes, providing transportation, delivering meals to shut-ins, and telephoning persons who live alone to be sure they are all right.

Moreover, fighting for the rights of the aged is a cause retirees, in particular, can readily endorse. There may be a local senior activist group in your community, or you can join a national organization with local affiliates, such as the American Association of Retired Persons (AARP).

Government programs   The federal government sponsors a number of volunteer programs, some especially geared toward older volunteers. The ACTION agency administers VISTA (Volunteers in Service to America), RSVP (Retired Senior Volunteer Program), the Foster Grandparents Program, and the Senior Companions Program. Volunteers in these programs may receive a small stipend. The National Park Service has volunteer openings, as does the Veterans Administration. Volunteers for SCORE/ACE (Service Corps of Retired Executives/Active Corps of Executives) use their skills to help people starting their own businesses. To contact these groups, see the sidebar "Voluntary action resources."

International opportunities   The Peace Corps is very interested in recruiting older Americans willing to share their skills and experience. VITA (Volunteers in Technical Assistance) is a private, nonprofit organization that provides technical assistance to people and groups in more than one hundred developing countries. To contact these groups, see the sidebar "Voluntary action resources."

Do-it-yourself service   You may prefer to think up your own way of serving the cause of your choice. Often, individuals come up with remarkably creative ideas when they perceive an unfilled need. For example, the retired owner of a kitchen and bathroom fixture business designs safe kitchens and bathrooms for elderly people, free of charge. A retired personnel officer realized her community needed a counseling service for women trying to enter or reenter the job market, so she set up such a service on her own.

Volunteer now, before you retire. You may be surprised at the number and diversity of employed persons who are volunteering these days. So start now, even if you can only give one or two hours a week. Soon you will have acquired the volunteering habit.

The time to learn is any time

A 50-year-old New Jersey salesman—a high-school dropout—enrolled in college full time, earned a bachelor's and a master's degree in German, and now teaches at the college that took a chance on him.

A 55-year-old housewife went to school to become a practical nurse after working as a hospital volunteer for several years.

A 63-year-old Fort Lauderdale grandmother earned her pilot's license, the fulfillment of a lifelong dream.

The three cases above are but a tiny sampling of the adventures in the world of learning awaiting midlife and older adults these days. The examples only hint at the variety of motivations at work, the myriad directions the search for knowledge is taking, and the richness of opportunity available for learning new skills, exploring new interests, or pursuing a never-completed diploma or degree.

The thousands of older adults who sign up for courses and become experts on everything from collecting antiques to the Franco-Prussian War don't believe that they lose their ability to learn as they grow older. And they're right. Research has shown that healthy people can continue to learn up to and beyond their nineties. In fact, studies have indicated that using the mind preserves it.

Many people find that social contact is a bonus that comes with participating in educational programs. For some retirees, cut off from their business acquaintances, meeting people with similar interests is the main attraction of returning to the classroom.

The reason adults study, the subjects they choose, and the sites of their educational efforts are almost as numerous as the students themselves. Where do you fit into the educational picture?

We urge you to investigate the possibilities mentioned below and others that may occur to you. Embracing the concept of lifelong learning will immeasurably enrich your pre- and post-retirement years.

High-school diploma   If you want to complete your high-school education, contact your board of education or a local public high school for information. Both can also provide information on how you can earn a diploma by taking the General Educational Development (GED) examinations and on special courses to help you prepare for the tests.

Community colleges   Community colleges usually emphasize technical and vocational training and offer two-year programs leading to an associate of arts degree. They also frequently offer special degree and nondegree programs for adults, with classes held at convenient day and evening hours and often at convenient off-campus locations. Contact the college's admissions office for more information.

Four-year colleges and universities   If your goal is to attend regular college classes, don't be concerned about sitting there with all those kids. Many older adults are doing it; you'll be surprised at how well you'll get along.

A number of colleges offer reduced tuition to older adults in regular undergraduate and graduate programs. You can either take classes for credit or audit them, that is, attend without being required to take tests or submit assignments.

You may be able to use the knowledge you've acquired over a lifetime to earn college credit through the College Level Examination Program (CLEP). Check first to see if the college or university you plan to attend accepts CLEP credits.

For more information on undergraduate and graduate programs, contact the school's admissions office.

Adult continuing education   Credit and noncredit courses are being offered in high schools, community centers, college and university extension centers, community colleges, religious centers, and museums all over the country. Adult continuing education has become big business.

Through these offerings, you can earn an undergraduate degree, sharpen old skills, learn new skills, or simply pursue a favorite subject. For example, you could take shorthand and typing courses to get a secretarial position, a real estate course to prepare you to obtain a license, or marketing and accounting classes in case you plan to start your own business. Or you could pursue a hobby such as woodworking or pottery, learn to play a musical instrument, take a course in how to stop procrastinating, or learn how to make home or car repairs.

For more information, contact the institution's continuing education office.

Correspondence courses   Correspondence courses are offered by colleges, universities, and private organizations on a variety of topics to help you earn credit toward a high-school diploma or a college degree, to help prepare you for a new career, or simply for your enjoyment. Some institutions may offer televised courses in conjunction with their correspondence courses. For more information on correspondence courses, see the listings for the National University Continuing Education Association and the National Home Study Council in the sidebar "Education resources."

Vacation schools   One way to find out if you want to go back to the campus is to take one of the noncredit week-long summer "vacation college" courses being offered by several institutions. One such program is Elderhostel, which offers liberal arts and science courses to people age 60 and over. (A younger spouse or companion can also participate.) Courses, which are normally one week long, cover a broad spectrum of subjects from literature to marine

Education resources

For more information, write to the following organizations:

College Level Examination Program, CN 6600, Princeton, NJ 08541-6600. 215-750-8420. Write for free brochures: *CLEP Colleges* and *Moving Ahead with CLEP.*

Elderhostel, 80 Boylston Street, Suite 400, Boston, MA 02116. Will send catalog describing their low-cost, short-term academic programs held in colleges and universities in fifty states, Canada, and abroad.

Institute of Lifetime Learning, AARP, 1909 K Street, NW, Washington, DC 20049. Provides activities kits for mini-courses on a variety of topics.

National University Continuing Education Association, One Dupont Circle, NW, Suite 420, Washington, DC 20036. 202-659-3130. For a list of member universities that offer independent study programs through extension services, send $8.95 plus $1.75 for postage and handling to Peterson's Guides, P.O. Box 2123, Princeton, NJ 08543-2123. Or call 800-225-0261.

National Home Study Council, 1601 18th Street, NW, Washington, DC 20009. 202-234-5100. Provides a free *Directory of Accredited Home Study Schools.*

biology. Classes are supplemented with field trips and social events. To obtain more information, write to the address listed in the sidebar "Education resources."

Self-study   You may be one of those people who don't go in for organized programs. If so, you'll find plenty of intellectual stimulation in libraries and museums. You can embark on an individualized study program in anything from the Victorian novel to ornithology. Of course, to enjoy reading, you don't need a programmed study plan; one of the greatest joys of being retired is finally having the time to real all the books you've been stockpiling over the years.

There are other, slightly more directed, ways to learn on your own. In recent years, several university systems have begun individualized courses that allow students to study on their own, at their own pace, with guidance from faculty advisers.

Other options   People are also acquiring some rather specialized skills before and after retirement. Witness the Fort Lauderdale flying grandmother mentioned earlier. If you want to become a pilot, a trail guide, a deep-sea diver—whatever—don't let your age discourage you from investigating. Check the Yellow Pages and find out how to get started in your community.

A new idea in adult education is the "swap meet," a gathering where retirees teach one another. For example, a person who is an expert weaver will exchange lessons with another who is fluent in Spanish. Or consider organizing an informal discussion group to meet regularly to talk about a subject of mutual interest. To find other interested people, post signs on bulletin boards, run announcements in community newspapers, or ask friends if they know someone already involved in the topic of interest.

Having a wonderful time

Time is definitely on your side when it comes to travel in retirement. You now have the flexibility for travel you've never had before. You can choose your seasons, and you can move at a more leisurely pace while you take advantage of special package deals and group charters aimed at those with time to spend.

Today, travelers can choose from a variety of tours, modes of travel, and places to stay. And the cost can be remarkably flexible too, if you plan your trip carefully. Below is just a sampling of some of the ways people are finding to get away these days.

Travel choices

Home exchanges   Trading homes with someone is a great way to really get the feel of a place and save on hotel, restaurant, and, often, auto rental expenses. Veteran house exchangers don't worry much about the care their house is receiving, but for your peace of mind, you can agree on mutual deposits against damage.

To arrange an exchange, you can register with organizations that maintain exchange lists; advertise in a newspaper or magazine or use a directory to set up your own swap directly; or work privately through social, business, or professional organizations.

Cruises   A luxury cruise can be the ultimate way to relax. Although cruises range in duration from a three-day "cruise to nowhere" to a round-the-world voyage, most last from seven to eighteen days. Even though cruises can be expensive, remember that all your living expenses are included in the fare.

Today many cruises highlight a certain theme: fitness and

sports, Big Band music, murder mysteries, or brushing up on everything from bridge to the stock market.

Theme tours   If you prefer to pursue a favorite subject on dry land, you can find a group tour that follows in the footsteps of a famous person, samples gourmet food and drink in the various regions of France, or observes the archaeological wonders of Greece. Ask your travel agent or contact the relevant group or club about a particular theme tour you are interested in.

Farm and ranch holidays   How about taking your vacation on a working farm or ranch? You can get involved in the daily chores or just sit back and enjoy the scenery and clean air. You can also participate in easy to strenuous trail rides. You need not be an expert rider for most rides; just be able to stay on a gentle horse.

Travel by recreation vehicle (RV)   Is mechanical horsepower more to your taste? RVs have become extremely popular with midlife and older travelers because they offer independence, flexibility, and usually cost savings. Buying an RV can be a substantial investment; a wise way to find out if you like this mode of travel is to rent one for your first trip or two.

Travel by bus or train   If you'd rather leave the driving to someone else, look into special train and bus passes that allow unlimited travel for specified lengths of time. Overseas there are Eurailpass and BritRail Pass, among others. Here, Greyhound (Ameripass) bus line offers similar deals. Such passes are economical only if you'll be traveling long and far enough to make them worthwhile. The overseas passes must be purchased in the United States before you go. If seeing the United States by train interests you, call Amtrak (800-USA-RAIL) for information on discounts.

Do your homework   Planning is the key to a successful trip. Decide first what interests you, what you can afford, and what level of comfort you require. Then see a travel agent, whose advice and services are usually free. But don't stop with an agent. Write to appropriate organizations and tourist offices (most countries have offices in New York City); ask friends and friends of friends; read books and articles (the *Reader's Guide to Periodical Literature* lists magazine articles about particular destinations and modes of travel).

Before you sign up for anything, study the fine print. With tours and airfare packages, be certain you understand all the terms. You might even call the Better Business Bureau of your local consumer office to see if the tour operator has an established reputation.

You can enhance your enjoyment of future retirement trips by attending travelogs, studying the art and culture of countries you'd like to visit, or acquiring hobbies (photography or a foreign language, for example) that can be furthered by travel. Then, as soon as you have the flexibility to go the way you want to go, you'll be prepared to get the most from your travels.

Travel tips Most of the following advice from seasoned travelers is along the money-saving line:

- Use public transportation. You'll save money and get to know the territory better.
- Investigate less-expensive tourist homes, guest houses, bed-and-breakfast accommodations, and no-frills budget motels. Most foreign and many domestic cities have tourist bureaus—often located in airports or railroad stations—to help you find accommodations to suit your budget.
- Use toll-free 800 numbers when making hotel reservations in the United States. You can usually obtain these numbers from telephone information.
- When traveling overseas, use credit cards infrequently. They may place you at an exchange-rate risk because the rate is figured the day your bill is processed, not the day you used the card.
- Single persons should investigate "shared accommodations" arrangements on tours and cruises to avoid the considerable single supplement charged by an industry that is based on double occupancy.
- Numerous airfare deals are available today. Be sure to ask your travel agent or the airlines about the best terms for you.
- "Tip packs" of foreign coins can be bought here for immediate needs on reaching your destination.
- Travel light. Pack everything you think you'll need; then remove half of it. There'll inevitably be times when you'll have to carry your own bags. And you may want to do some shopping on the trip.
- Carry copies of prescriptions, extra pairs of glasses, and a medical information sheet if you need special care of any

Travel resources

For more information on some of the travel opportunities mentioned on these pages, contact the following organizations:

House exchanges
Vacation Exchange Club, 12006 111th Avenue, Youngtown, AZ 85363. 602-972-2186.

Land and water travel
BritRail Pass, c/o BritRail Travel International, Inc., 630 Third Avenue, New York, NY 10017. 212-599-5400.

Eurailpass, c/o French National Railroad, 610 Fifth Avenue, New York, NY 10020. 212-582-2110.

AARP Travel Service, 5855 Green Valley Circle, Culver City, CA 90230. 800-227-7737. Domestic and foreign escorted tours for AARP members.

Bed and breakfast country inns
The Globe—Pequot Press, Old Chester Road, Box Q, Chester, CT 06412. 800-243-0495. Publishes listings of bed-and-breakfast homes and country inns for various regions in the United States and for certain foreign countries.

Single travel
Gramercy Singleworld, 444 Madison Avenue, New York, NY 10022. 800-223-6490. Organizes singles groups of all adult ages and arranges shared accommodations.

The great outdoors
National Park Service, Office of Information, U.S. Department of the Interior, P.O. Box 37127, Washington, DC 20013-7127. Obtain information about Golden Age (62+) and Golden Eagle (under 62) passes and about the national parks.

Farm and Ranch Vacations, Inc., 36 E. 57th Street, New York, NY 10022. 212-355-6334. Publishes *Farm, Ranch, and Country Vacations; Adventure Travel North America;* and *Adventure Travel Abroad.*

Woodall's Campground Directories, Woodall Publishing Company, Lake Bluff, IL 60044. 800-323-9076. Annually publishes the *National Directory*, $12.95; *Eastern Directory*, $8.95; *Western Directory*, $8.95. Also check bookstores and local RV dealers.

Medical assistance overseas
Intermedic, Inc., 777 Third Avenue, New York, NY 10017. 212-486-8900. Members receive a listing of English-speaking doctors in foreign countries.

Guides
For more travel information, see the Fodor, Fielding, Frommer, and Mobil travel guides, all of which should be available in local bookstores.

kind. You may wish to join an organization that provides names of approved English-speaking doctors overseas.
- Finally, get in shape before you go. Start walking!

What about travel for the single older person?   You can have your choice of group and escorted tours, or you might want to travel alone. If you are considering a trip alone, ask yourself the following questions. They should help you decide whether it's a good idea for you.

1. Are you gregarious? Can you talk to strangers easily?
2. When you encounter problems, can you assert yourself?
3. Are you a self-starter? Can you plan your days?
4. Do you have a good sense of humor?
5. Can you read a city map? Do you have a good sense of direction?
6. Can you afford to stay at first-class hotels? (They usually have their own dining rooms, should you choose to stay in for dinner.)
7. Can you go into a hotel bar alone, sit down, and order a drink without pain and suffering?
8. Are you flexible?
9. Do you enjoy your own company?
10. Can you get to the train or plane on time?
11. Can you limit your luggage to what you yourself can carry?
12. Are you in good physical health?
13. Can you handle solitude?[1]

Perfect pastimes

Experienced retirees say that it's great to have a hobby in retirement but that you must not count on it to provide full-time satisfaction. You should be able to spend as much or as little time on your hobby as your other interests allow, keeping in mind that too much of even a good thing will probably make its charms fade fast.

Now we hasten to add that there are always exceptions. People have been known to become so passionately involved, in, say, beekeeping, that all else ceases to interest them. But we tend to feel that this is no longer a hobby; it's an occupation.

The word *hobby*, for us, encompasses not only craftlike activities but also collecting of all kinds, dramatics and music, writing—in fact just about any pursuit that offers you the following:

- Relaxation and absorption

- Satisfaction in doing and accomplishing
- Involvement in productive or simply pleasurable activities
- Expansion of your knowledge and skills.

Thus, the list that follows is far from complete and is only provided to start you thinking about what might interest you. Your next step is to follow up on your ideas. Get a good hobby book or ask about a class at your community center, "Y," or adult continuing education center.

Arts and crafts   This category deserves a chapter of its own. In fact, there are dozens of crafts books that you may want to consult. Here are just a few of the more popular activities in this category:

Mosaic art   Creating designs using tiny pieces of glass, pebbles, tiles, or seeds is an ancient art that is once again thriving.
Pottery and ceramics   Creating something from the raw earth, experimenting with shape and color, is enormously satisfying; consequently, pottery making is one of the fastest-growing crafts.
Jewelry making   Using your imagination to create works of art out of a variety of raw materials is an ancient art form.
Woodworking   Here's a craft choice that has income potential, since skilled woodworkers, carpenters, and furniture restorers are much in demand.
Sewing, knitting, crocheting, and weaving   As pastimes, these handicrafts have the virtue of being readily started and stopped as time permits, and the products make greatly appreciated gifts.
Drawing, painting, and sculpting   Look into these arts even if you think you have no talent. Sign up for lessons. You may be surprised at the results. You'll acquire an increased sensitivity to shape and composition and possibly discover a rewarding pursuit to enrich your life.
Music   Learn to play an instrument; collect or make folk instruments; attend concerts; add to your record and tape collections; join a chorus or orchestra, or form your own. Music is an ideal interest because it lends itself to both solitary and social enjoyment.
Theater   Don't just attend the theater—join it! Participating in amateur theater groups is a great way to meet people, and you don't have to act. There are dozens of jobs to be done, from props to publicity.
Writing   The old saying that we all have at least one novel in us may or may not be true, but how about a short story? A journal? A family history for your grandchildren? Even if you've never

published, putting your observations and feelings on paper will help you gain a fresh perspective on yourself and your world.

Nature   This category encompasses a variety of interests from bird-watching to fossil hunting to astronomy. A perennial (and economical) favorite is gardening, whether you're farming the back forty or raising some herbs on your windowsill. People who love to grow things never quite get over the thrill of the season's first zinnia or red tomato. Gardening can be good exercise too.

Collecting   What do you treasure? Porcelain-faced dolls? Victorian washstands? Stamps? Whatever it is you value, you can be sure that someone, somewhere, has a collection. What about cup and saucer sets, thimbles, teddy bears, or paperweights? Collecting is a flexible pastime; you can pick up an item here and there for fun, or you can make a lifework of researching, enlarging, cataloging, and maintaining your collection. A few suggestions for would-be collectors follow:

1.   *Collect only what you love.* Your collection may well increase in value, but if you love what you're collecting, the monetary return or lack of it will be a secondary consideration.
2.   *Collect only what you can take care of and have room to store.* You may love antique cars, but your neighbors may object to your backyard parking lot!
3.   *Collect only what you can afford.* Only you know what a particular collectible is worth to you. But just the same, it's wise to do the necessary research. When you're facing the auctioneer or shopkeeper, you'll feel secure in the knowledge that you won't be overcharged.

Libraries, bookstores, and local and national collectors' clubs can provide you with information about how to get started and how to evaluate and sell your collections.

Reading and library activities   Retirement is a great time to catch up on all the reading you've been meaning to do. In addition to books, your local library may provide an assortment of other materials and services:

- Special events such as book discussions, film forums, lectures, and poetry readings
- Specialized newspapers and magazines

- Records; audiotapes of music, speeches, and books; and instructional videotapes and feature films.

Sports   There has been a burgeoning of opportunities for older Americans to pursue sports and fitness activities through organized programs. If you are age 50 or older and are interested in competitive or recreational sports, contact the National Senior Sports Association (317 Cameron Street, Alexandria, VA 22314, or call 703-549-6711). The association sponsors golf, tennis, and

---

Start thinking creatively right now about what you'll be doing with those years of opportunity. Then make plans to explore specific activities that appeal to you.

Aside from 70 hours spent sleeping and eating, you probably will have about 98 hours a week free time during retirement. How do you want to fill those hours? Consider hobbies, religious activities, sports, exercise, community service, family, clubs, learning, travel, earning money, and quiet time.

Now think about what you can do today to test out some of your ideas about how to spend your free time.

Sleeping and eating   70 hours/week

Total	168 hours/week

Figure 1.   The post-retirement time in your life.

bowling tournaments at major resorts worldwide at economical rates through group purchasing power.

Social clubs and special-interest organizations   Participating in clubs can provide you with the opportunity to socialize and to pursue a special interest of yours with people who share your enthusiasm.

Television   According to the 1986 *Nielsen Report on Television*, women 55 and over watched television more than any other age group—42 hours a week; men 55 and over came in second—38 hours. Television offers many entertaining, interesting, and educational programs. But it can be an addictive activity, especially for homebound or otherwise isolated persons. People of all ages should guard against substituting too much television for more worthwhile and challenging activities.

Pets   People can gain a great deal from animal companionship. Pets can provide acceptance, amusement, attention, unconditional love, and a sense of purpose and commitment. The emotional and physical therapeutic effects of pets have been scientifically proven. Pets can also help break the ice when a person moves into a new area. Take your dog for a walk; you're sure to have at least one or two people strike up a conversation about it.

Contemplation   Midlife is an appropriate time to spend some time reviewing our lives. Doing so can be good for both physical and psychological health. Quiet time alone can help alleviate stress and put problems in perspective. And it gives us a chance to identify our many accomplishments over a lifetime and pat ourselves on the back from time to time.

Socializing   Unless you have the instincts of a hermit, you're going to want and need to spend some of your retirement time with other people. We're not suggesting a constant social whirl. As we just mentioned, everyone needs some time alone—time to think and reflect. But the company of others is one of the best ways to keep yourself both interested and interesting.

In retirement, you might have to work a little harder than before at having a social life because, for many people, work is the chief source of friends and acquaintances. Of course, a few of these job-related friendships may endure, but once the common interest of work is removed, contacts with people from the work place tend to diminish.

So, it may be necessary to cultivate social contacts outside of work, and the time to start is now, before you retire.

How do you go about it? Your attitude is crucial. You must be friendly to make friends. Look for interesting people at the local church bazaar, at the community center, or on the golf course. Seek out activities that will put you in contact with others. Take courses; do volunteer work; join clubs.

When you've met people you think you'd like to know better, invite them to your home. You have to extend invitations to receive them. Of course, not everyone you seek out in this way will become a close friend, but you're bound to form some new associations to enjoy in retirement.

1. Reprinted with permission from Rosalind Massow, *Travel Easy: The Practical Guide for People over 50* (an AARP Book), 11. Copyright 1985 by the American Association of Retired Persons, Washington, DC, and Scott, Foresman & Co., Glenview, IL.

7

THE SHAPE OF
WORK TO COME

Caroline Bird

We love our work and hate our jobs. We say we would work even if
we didn't need the money, but more and more of us quit as soon as
we qualify for a pension. Work is doing something outsiders value
(as in water*works* or the *works* of Shakespeare), but a job is drudg-
ery we don't do if we don't have to.

The factory whistle is what we want to retire from, like the
fellow who set his alarm clock as usual for the joy of going back to
sleep after turning it off. Some of us would like to stay on if the job
were more interesting or less demanding, if we could do it part
time, or if retirement hadn't been anticipated.

Will our jobs continue to prevent us from working? Is the government right in projecting fewer and fewer workers over age 55
in the future? To find out, we pored over scores of studies, talked
with authorities in business, higher education, and government
and put challenging questions to a little band of visionaries who
specialize in the future.

The issues stir up a hornet's nest of hidden political agendas.
Computer manufacturers with an eye on the stock market quote
the optimists; liberals and labor union lobbyists, the pessimists.

A lot depends on what you mean by work. To 78-year-old John
Kenneth Galbraith, the feisty liberal economist, "There's work,
and then there's work that isn't work, like what you and I do." A

good Calvinist at heart, he doesn't count it as work if you enjoy it, like the handful of artists and writers who have the good luck to get paid for what they would do anyway. "People who leave the Ford plant for the last time are extraordinarily glad never to see it again." Pessimistically, he predicts jobs will be fewer and worse, and all but the happy few like himself will "sure as hell quit as soon as they get Social Security."

But it's not that simple. On the north side of Chicago, a 77-year-old woman works mornings as what McDonald's calls a "lobby hostess." She has a following. Old friends who live in the area stop by when they know she'll be on duty. Very few people at McDonald's know she owns three buildings on Michigan Avenue and could live comfortably without earning a penny.

It's not always easy to know what people get from their work. Everyone likes money, but the social scientists find it isn't the most important thing people want from their jobs. A substantial minority of people say they would take a pay cut to switch to a job they liked better; even more would turn down a raise if it meant less-interesting work.

Control, or freedom to avoid control by silly rules, is high on everyone's list of what makes a job good. "Head of own business" is the leading dream job of both men and women, followed by "professional athlete," "president of large corporation," "forest ranger" and "test pilot" for men; "tour guide," "flight attendant," "novelist" and "photographer" for women.

The best bosses know what people want in a job and find ways to give it to them: self-expression; self-esteem; a job worth doing; recognition for doing it well; co-workers who like each other; a chance to learn and advance; a sense of achievement; and challenge. In one survey, 78 percent of those responding said they wanted a job that wasn't too easy!

Nonmonetary rewards mean even more to older workers. In a 1982 Public Agenda national survey, 69 percent of people over 55 said they had an "inner need to do the very best I can, regardless of pay," compared with only 48 percent of those younger. There were majority votes for continuing to work even if you could get enough money to live comfortably for the rest of your life and for continuing to work in some way or other after age 65. When asked why, 94 percent checked "I like working."

We put four questions to all the people we interviewed.

1. Will jobs be good enough that older people will want to do them? Best-selling futurists promise that work will be fun in the coming postindustrial, information economy. "The human effort now spent on keeping things going will be unnecessary," says Isaac Asimov, the 67-year-old science and science-fiction writer. "With computers, robots and automation, a great deal of the daily grind will appear to be running itself." He thinks home computers tapping into central libraries will make more work for writers, artists, researchers, administrators, scientists, philosophers, and others who do the kind of work from which neither he nor Galbraith wants to retire.

"High-touch" as well as "high-tech" is the way John Naisbitt describes future work in his books and lectures. Automation will give us more time for working one-on-one with other people.

"Demassification" is Alvin Toffler's term for the "third wave" we are diving into. "Instead of millions of people all doing similar work, there are going to be many more varied slots in the system," he tells his eager audiences. There are few typists in his office of tomorrow. Machines will respond to the sound of your voice and print what you speak on a screen.

Gone too will be the boss as we know him or her. Naisbitt warns chief executive officers that organization charts will look like networks instead of pyramids. We'll work in friendly small teams, like spaceship crews or scientific researchers. Toffler thinks traditional roles will blur at work as well as at home, and people will take turns being boss, depending on who has the critical skill needed at a particular moment.

On the theory that nobody cares, the Census Bureau doesn't tabulate the detailed occupations of workers over 65, but a breakdown done especially for MODERN MATURITY suggests that people already work past retirement age in jobs that give them freedom, challenge, creativity, and all those other good things workers want at least as much as money.

Architects, musicians and composers, editors and reporters, doctors, lawyers, judges, legislators, real estate brokers, accountants, insurance agents, religious workers, farmers, and especially those who have realized the dream of a business of their own: All are unusually well represented among workers 65 and older.

These are the happy few who are already working in the postindustrial future. All but the farmers and some of the business proprietors are knowledge-workers. They don't punch time clocks. They are paid for results instead of attendance, and they influence when, where, and how those results are accomplished.

Harvey Sterns, Ph.D., an industrial gerontological psychologist at The University of Akron, thinks advances such as word processing and containerized shipping have made jobs easier, cleaner, safer, and more attractive to older people, and workers directly affected say technological advances may make their work more interesting and give them more control over it. A bank teller interviewed on one survey said the automatic cash machine has liberated her for the more exciting work of tracking down stolen paychecks.

Better yet, the factory whistle itself has been retired. A rising number of workers are on flextime, and employers are easing up on work rules that cause resentment.

Ronald C. Pilenzo, president of the American Society for Personnel Administration (ASPA), thinks employers will be doing more to give workers greater control over their jobs, because better-educated young workers expect it and new technology won't work without their cooperation. Some are sharing power already. Motorola competes in the semiconductor market by putting every employee in a group that sets its own goal and earns a bonus for fulfilling it.

Old-fashioned liberals with labor-union ties suspect this happy talk. Labor economist Sar Levitan of George Washington University likes to point out that jobs don't change very fast, and there's a limit to what can be done to improve them; word processors may be more efficient than typewriters, but he doesn't think Toffler's voice-activated machines will—in the foreseeable future—eliminate the need for humans to spell and type.

Sociologist Arthur Shostak, Ph.D., of Drexel University finds a few of the new high-technology jobs "spirit enlarging and mind challenging" but says most are "incredibly mind stunting and mind dulling."

Finally, say the pessimists, automation is supposed to keep labor costs down, and so far it has succeeded. Stanley Seashore, Ph.D., a University of Michigan sociologist, likes to point out that real pay hasn't improved since 1980. Displaced auto workers can't pay off their houses on what they can earn at McDonald's.

Short-term, transitional problems, retort the optimists. If it's stressful, boring or repetitive, a machine will be invented to do it, just as robots now do the assembly-line tasks that trapped Charlie Chaplin in his classic old movie *Modern Times*. They sometimes talk as if dirty work will just disappear; and of course some of it has. Self-service systems, loose-fitting one-size-fits-all fashions, and permanent press have enabled us to do with fewer waitresses, grocery clerks, alteration hands, and ironers.

2. Will there be enough jobs for all the older people who will want to work? Futurists predict a chronic shortage of workers for the labor-intensive new jobs they see ahead in teaching, training, coaching, healing, counseling, communicating, comforting, and creating. Naisbitt tells business leaders they are on the brink of a postindustrial revolution that will create jobs on a scale that can only be compared with the onset of the Industrial Revolution.

Liberal economists worry about what's happening on the way to those jazzy new jobs. The Social Security Administration reports that most men take their benefits before they are 65. About one-quarter don't receive their first Social Security check for more than six months after leaving their last job. Are some of them retiring early because they can't find the work they've always done?

Economists outside government don't believe there will be as many new jobs in 1995 as the Bureau of Labor projects on the basis of past experience. Last year, 1973 Nobel Prize-winning economist Wassily Leontief estimated that new technologies already in use are displacing workers so fast we could make everything we made in 1980 with 11 million fewer workers in 1990, 20 million fewer in 2000. The way he sees it, more jobs will be lost in offices than in factories.

Futurists stick by their guns. Naisbitt concedes that the new work won't arrive in a month or a year but over a transitional decade. According to him, we're in that decade now because of the rate at which enterprisers are starting new little businesses; firms with fewer than 100 people now employ half the work force and create 85 percent of the new jobs.

Everybody can think of new jobs ahead that will be especially attractive to older people. The big growth will be in familiar human services rather than in the high-tech industries themselves. "Financial services, health care, retailing, restaurants," says Peter Francese, president of American Demographics. "You're talking about tens of millions of jobs, and fewer young people to do them."

Francese thinks older workers will be especially welcome because the people they are serving are older, too. Pharmacies and clothing retailers have already found that older customers are more comfortable with older salespeople; so have the mutual funds and financial institutions catering to the growing number of retired people with money to invest.

The job outlook seems dim now, the futurists argue, because most people will be working at jobs that haven't yet been invented. Asimov reminds us that nobody in 1933 had ever heard of a television anchor man, a jet pilot, a computer programmer, a molecular biologist, or an astronaut. "In the 21st century, older people may be teaching calisthenics on the moon, where they won't have to contend with gravity."

More immediately, the transition itself will create jobs for older people. More knowledge-workers will be needed, but we have fewer young people and since 1970 are getting fewer of those we do have through high school.

Shostak suggests that older people could work as "techno-guides," testing new high-tech advances, suggesting how they can be made practical for consumers, and helping consumers use them. These workers will be especially needed to implement advances that will improve the quality of life for older people.

3. Will there be more work on the flexible schedules most older people like?   The futurists promise that all workers will have a choice of terms. "Not because bosses will become nice guys," says Toffler, "but because the work itself will require that each one be treated as an individual." Perhaps because he likes to work that way himself, he fancies "electronic cottages" in which families will work with a helper or two wherever they find it pleasant to live, keeping in touch by computer with customers and co-workers all over the world. According to a projection quoted by Marvin Cetron, president of Forecasting International, by the year 2000, 22 percent of the entire workforce won't ever set foot in an office or factory.

Naisbitt's dream is a bit more sociable: He thinks the computers will be in small satellite offices where we'll work with our neighbors. Those who object because they "work to get out of the house" miss the point: There'll be no single "right" way. What there will be is room for a wide range of preferences—good news for older workers, whose preferences run a wider gamut.

You can see this individualization coming now, although, as Toffler admits, "you sometimes have to look with a microscope." Middle managers axed from big companies are selling their skills to small firms on whatever terms make sense for the work that needs to be done. There are more part-time, home-based, temporary, contract, and other arrangements alternative to the traditional 9-to-5 career ladder, as well as more job- and field-switching.

New evidence shows that the retired aren't staying put either. An increasing majority of men can now expect to retire more than once, says Mark Hayward, a researcher tracking second careers at the Battelle Memorial Institute in Seattle.

You see it all around you. A detective investigator for the New York City District Attorney who thought he was retiring to the country started working part time for the local sheriff's office; when he didn't like what he saw, he quit to pump gas; then the court hired him away from that to fill a job similar to the one he

---

These jobs attract more older women

Because they have been restricted to fewer and less rewarding occupations, women over age 65 retire earlier than men if they possibly can. Houseworkers can't because few of them have been covered by Social Security.

Just three occupations employing more than 35,000 women over 65 are estimated to have an age index higher than one.

An occupation has an age index of 1.0 if it has its fair share of workers over age 65. Thus an index of 1.5 means the occupation has one and one-half times its share, 2.0 means twice its share, and so forth.

Occupation	Age index
Private household workers	5.5
Saleswomen, unspecified commodities	1.9
Bookkeeping, accounting, and auditing clerks	1.5

---

retired from in New York. Did he retire once, twice, three times, or never?

Look at the sidebars. You'll notice that not all the jobs are exciting. People over 65 are working as security guards, house workers, janitors, and cleaners. Some desperately need the money. But all are in jobs that are part time, temporary, or on negotiable schedules. Talk to the people doing these jobs and you discover retired teachers and executives among them. Like college students, they are willing to take what looks like a step down in the world just long enough to earn the money for a trip.

McDonald's makes a special effort to accommodate such older workers. Its McMasters Program recruits people over 55 by giving them their choice of hours, days of the week, and jobs on a list that includes community-relations representative, drive-through ordertaker, maintenance worker, hostess.

Temporary agencies are another straw in the wind. They used to funnel students and housewives to factories and offices that needed occasional unskilled workers, but now they are placing accounting, legal, computer, and marketing help. Business trends analyst Jeff Hallett sees the professionals who go from one temporary job to another as pioneers of the project-oriented future work.

Traditional labor economists see nothing good about this trend. They suspect alternative work styles. Part-time, temporary,

These jobs attract more older men

This chart shows occupations that are estimated to employ the highest proportion of men over age 65. We disregarded detailed occupations employing fewer than 35,000 men over age 65 since the Census sample of 59,000 households isn't big enough to break down their ages accurately.

An occupation has an age index of 1.0 if it has its fair share of workers over age 65. Thus an index of 1.5 means the occupation has one and one-half times its share, 2.0 means twice its share, and so forth.

Occupation	Age index
Farmers (except horticultural)	5.3
Guards and policemen (except public service)	3.2
Janitors and cleaners	2.1
Groundskeepers and gardeners (except farm)	2.1
Sales supervisors and proprietors	1.2
Sales representatives, mining, manufacturing, and wholesale	1.1
Managers and administrators not elsewhere classified	1.1

and home-based work have traditionally exposed workers to exploitation; and small, informal settings are where labor laws are violated. But what they see as bad fits the lives of students and parents in the work force, as well as the retired.

4. Will we change policies that keep older workers out? Alan Pifer, editor of *Our Aging Society*, thinks the big and politically savvy generation of baby boomers, who revolted against adult authority when they were teenagers, won't stand for policies that put them down because they're middle-aged or older.

Age discrimination in employment makes no sense in the postindustrial economy, and such discrimination is crumbling already. With a few exceptions, it's now illegal to retire anyone on the basis of age alone. Social Security is reversing its tilt toward early retirement: You'll shortly be able to earn more without losing benefits and gain more by delaying retirement, and for those now under 47 the traditional benchmark age for retirement will begin to rise.

We have just begun to think about ensuring older workers' access to training; the barrier to training is of growing importance. Excluding workers over 50 is not only illegal but a waste of precious human capital. If everyone is going to have to be retrained every seven years, the cost can be recouped on a 55-year-old.

The stumbling block is the industrial career-ladder ethic, which says you should start out in a good steady entry-level job with a big company that will promote you regularly until you reach the preset age at which it retires you on a fat pension. To keep the annual raises coming, the company underpays you when you're young and overpays you later.

As you climb the ladder, you may become more valuable to the company but not necessarily to anybody else. Even if you are valuable to others, you won't move for fear of losing your pension.

This industrial model fills good companies with restless, burned-out 50-year-olds shackled to dead-end jobs by golden handcuffs. ASPA president Pilenzo thinks a majority are dreaming of doing something else and would quit if they could take their pensions with them. And though their spouses might demur, some would be willing to start out all over again at lower pay.

They'll soon be put to the test. When pensions become more portable under a provision of the new Tax Reform Act and when related new legislative initiatives take hold, Pilenzo expects a significant trend will develop toward older workers leaving to start up their own companies. At the same time, opportunities will develop within larger companies for those the companies want to keep.

For those who don't rebel, the only way out of a dead-end job is early retirement. In these lean days, financial officers with sharp pencils can figure exactly how much the company can save by paying overpaid older workers to retire early, but many top managers complain that the few they don't want to lose are just the ones who jump at the opportunity.

If only to salvage company loyalty, firms like Honeywell, Lockheed, Grumman Aircraft, and Travelers are experimenting with alternatives to the career-ladder model. Some are designed to give valuable older people the freedom they want, others to try out tasks and terms that give company retirees the participation in the world of work denied them by total leisure.

Professionals working past age 65 show us how this off-the-ladder work can be structured. Lawyers and accountants may limit their practices to long-time clients they happen to like. Retired clergymen may help their young successors out by calling on parishioners. At age 86, Representative Claude Pepper of Florida continues to champion older people, with the help of a big, competent staff, larger than many congressmen have had a chance to assemble.

People tied to the ladder aren't so lucky. "That's a job I could do," a successful business executive on the eve of retirement said to his son as they nodded to the apartment-building doorman. Like the McDonald's hostess, this man was through climbing ladders. He didn't need pay or prestige, but he wanted to do something worth pay in a place where the world went by.

Paying jobs reward us in more ways than we know, and freedom on the job is the promise of the information economy ahead.

Will more older people want to work in the future?

Our answer is yes.

8

WORK IN THE FUTURE

*Staying on the job
may require a careful game plan*

Patricia Walsh

Editor's note: The preceding chapter focused on work options for older persons in the future. This chapter examines the options and challenges facing older workers today as our economy moves through a transition period comparable to the Industrial Revolution. It suggests strategies older workers can adopt now for finding the kind of work they want before or after retirement.

Older workers today are caught between two major, conflicting trends. After forty years of policies that encourage retirement, Congress is enticing older workers to work longer.

Mandatory retirement has generally been eliminated, and employers soon will be required to accrue pension credits for employees over 65. The age for drawing full benefits from Social Security will rise after the turn of the century from 65 to 67. And the credit a worker receives for each year he or she delays collecting benefits after the normal retirement age is being increased, from 3 percent today to 8 percent in the year 2008.

But while government now sees older workers as part of the solution to anticipated labor shortages in the future, many business and industries are still acting as if they're part of the problem. Using early-retirement incentives and other tactics, employers continue to push workers in their fifties and sixties out the door.

Reprinted with permission of the author from the *AARP News Bulletin*, July-August 1987, 13–14. Copyright 1987 by Patricia Walsh.

Other disincentives to a longer worklife—such as the Social Security earnings limitation—continue. And the unhappy state of affairs between many employers and their older employees is illustrated by the 100 percent increase in age discrimination charges filed with the Equal Employment Opportunity Commission between 1981 and 1986.

Things *will* get better. Simple arithmetic tells why: With 18 million new jobs being created over the next thirteen years, older workers will be in great demand. In addition to a predicted shortage of skilled workers within the next two to three years, fewer young people are entering the work force. In the 1990s, 1.1 million young people are expected to enter the work force each year, down from 3.3 million in 1960.

According to Secretary of Labor William Brock, "We are simply going to run out of people with the skills to hold the jobs that are being created." The solution: Use the people who have the skills for a longer period of time.

There is a problem, however. In predicting work patterns of the future, experts have glibly matched the growing pool of older workers to the large number of new jobs, without noting that, in many cases, the "fit" of people and positions is wrong.

Economic forecasters say that demographic shifts, changing consumer tastes, new technology, and intense international competition are eliminating old jobs and creating new ones. But not necessarily in the same places, or on the same skill and pay levels as before.

Although older workers will be able to work longer, experts agree, it may be at jobs that require trade-offs: relocation, smaller paychecks, changes in career directions.

Good job options will exist, but "taking advantage of them will require a hard look at your experience and your expectations for the future," says David Gamse, director of the American Association of Retired Persons (AARP)'s Worker Equity Department. The first thing an older worker should do, according to Gamse, is estimate just how long he or she will need to work. "Most people underestimate the time they've got. A 55-year-old worker should assume he'll have to support himself another 25–30 years."

Gamse also advises older workers to think the unthinkable. "Plan for being unemployed in the near future for one or more of these reasons: poor health, downsizing of your company, or the [negative] attitude of your employer [toward older workers]."

A strategy for staying in the work force should consider what's happening in the marketplace. The National Alliance of Business reports that "1.5 million workers are already permanently displaced, their skills obsolete due to the shift from manufacturing to high-technology and service industries and to international competition."

Also, various forces—from changing consumer tastes to increased competition—will likely telescope the average product life to about five years. The effect on workers, according to Brock: people will be switching jobs and careers repeatedly over the course of their lives "not by choice but because the jobs will be changing right underneath their feet." Brock feels workers will change jobs four to six times over their work lives and may have two to three careers.

Other factors to consider as you plan:

- The Bureau of Labor Statistics says nine of ten jobs created in the next thirteen years will be in the service industry. Service means more than dishing up fries in a fast food restaurant: it includes transportation, communications, information, trade, finance, real estate, government, health care, travel, and recreation.

  While many of the new service jobs are cleaner, safer, and less physically demanding than the manufacturing jobs they are replacing, Department of Labor figures for 1986 indicate that generally speaking they pay less, too. Thus, an unemployed auto worker who made $14 an hour, or an unemployed engineer who made $23 an hour, may find that his or her choice comes down to retraining for a service job paying $8 an hour—or staying unemployed.

- Gerri Garvin, assistant manager of AARP's Work Force Education Section, advises older workers to "brush up on their basic literacy skills—and use them. They are an important asset that may give the older worker a competitive edge in the labor force. Older workers will need to be flexible and willing to learn new technical skills. Develop your job search skills before you need them. And save for education and retraining."

  Garvin says, "The majority of new jobs will require experience, knowledge, basic literacy skills, problem solving skills, and highly developed 'people' skills.

  "This is good news for older workers," she adds, "because they often excel in these areas."

- While most new jobs won't be "high tech," new technology

will influence how the jobs get done. Garvin suggests that older workers "master at least the principles of computers, perhaps taking a basic course. This will provide the experience and confidence to learn other technology as it evolves."

(One way to pick up computer literacy skills may be through volunteering. Garvin gives the example of the Colorado Springs, Colorado, Police Department, which trains volunteers to enter crime statistics into its computer system.)

- With large companies cutting back on the number of full-time workers, experts forecast the growth of smaller, younger, highly innovative businesses to provide services to large companies on an as-needed basis—everything from accounting to repair work. These small businesses may be a key source of many new jobs in the near future.
- Consider alternatives to your current career, especially if you want to stay in the community in which you now live. Says Gamse, "If relocating is out of the question because of family obligations or other reasons, take out some 'insurance' to prepare yourself for change. Look around while you have a job. Check the classifieds to get a general idea of the types of jobs and skills businesses in your area are looking for. Call to get an idea of the hourly rate being paid" for different occupations.
- Identify local employment resources *before* you need them. Community colleges often have close ties with local business and industry and thus offer technical courses that reflect the local job market. And they may offer skills assessment, job search and career exploration courses, and apprenticeship programs. Some serve as small business resource centers for would-be entrepreneurs.
- Don't overlook help offered through state employment offices, religious centers, senior centers, and local public service agencies.
- Build and maintain networks of family, friends, and work associates. Stay active and in touch with your field through the local chapter of your trade or professional association.
- Find out about the Job Training Partnership Act (JTPA) in your area. It provides job training to economically disadvantaged persons, displaced workers, and others who face significant employment barriers (such as age discrimina-

tion). Your governor's office can refer you to the agency overseeing the program in your state.

- Learn to spot signals of change in your community and nationwide by reading business journals, magazines, and newspapers. Other sources of information about economic change include the local chamber of commerce and your city's and state's high-tech councils.
- Finally, know your rights under the Age Discrimination in Employment Act (ADEA) and assert yourself. You have a right to equal opportunity.

9

CHOOSING WHERE TO LIVE

Elwood N. Chapman

Editor's note: We recommend that married couples do the exercises in this chapter separately and then compare the results. This will bring to light differences in expectations about retirement that should be discussed and negotiated. See also Chapter 17, "How To Retire on the House."

One of your biggest retirement decisions will be where to live. Do you stay where you are? Move to Florida? Have a mobile home in Oregon or a condo in California? Rent an apartment in your home town? Move into a retirement center or a full-care facility? There are many options, and many factors—finances, leisure plans, and so on—are involved in your decision-making process.

Exciting possibilities, but there is a disturbing finality about it all. Once you sell a home, you might not be able to buy it back. Once you move to a retirement center, there may not be an easy way out. So, as you read this chapter, the primary word is *caution.* Try not to make a move until you are sure. Make your investigation a personal one. As you accept or reject possibilities, keep in mind that what makes sense for some people might not work for you. You are an individual, and you must make decisions about where and how to live based on your background—your comfort zone*

*Your comfort zone is the range within which your personal values and beliefs fall. Your comfort zone comprises your standards and principles.

and what makes you happy. The quality of your retirement years can depend on your decision.

Your first choice is geographical

Ah, exotic Hawaii! Or what about sunny Florida? Perhaps a retirement home in Arizona (Sun City)? Or California (Leisure World)? It's fun to talk about faraway places and to dream. This is especially true before retirement, because you can prepare for your move through pre-retirement financial planning. There is time to make enough money to facilitate your dream move.

After retirement your choices may be more limited, because your income will probably be more stabilized. Geographical choices may still remain, however. People of all income levels still move from colder climates to Florida or Arizona.

Retirees migrate like birds. The journey can be fatiguing, and sanctuaries are difficult to assess. For many, it will become a permanent migration, since only wealthy birds can maintain two homes.

Migrating can be a mistake   Although most dream of a distant retirement paradise, some retirees, after careful analysis, wisely opt to stay close to their roots. They discover paradise is in their own backyard.

I know a woman whose personal paradise is in Newton, Kansas. Her life is wrapped up in the town. She has adjusted to the climate. Her church and her friends are there. It would be a mistake for her to move.

A member of my family, a surgeon, has spent her adult life practicing in San Francisco. She owns a lovely home, and her many friends are there. She has had a love affair with the Bay Area for more than forty years. It would be a mistake for her to move.

What about you? Do you already live in paradise or is it time to consider a new location? Should you move to a warm climate? Should you compare advantages and disadvantages of where you now live with what is available? The following exercise may be helpful. It presents ten factors that you should take into consideration before making any geographical move.

On a separate sheet of paper set up three vertical columns. Head the first column "Where you live now." Head the second column "Option #1 (city)," and head the third column "Option #2 (city)." Next, write numbers 1 through 10 vertically in each of the three columns for each of the ten factors listed below.

Step 1: Rate all factors on where you now live. Write a number from 1 to 10 next to the appropriate factor number (10 is the highest rating; 1 is the lowest).

Step 2: Select two other locations you have considered in the past or have investigated. Write these locations under options 1 and 2.

Step 3: Rate each of these locations and compare them to the rating of the place you now live in. (Before doing this step, you may want to accumulate more information about your other locations. You can do this by writing the city's chamber of commerce, subscribing to the local newspaper, or visiting and talking to people who live there.)

Step 4: Keep in mind that some of the ten factors could be far more critical to your needs than others and should therefore be given more weight in your personal analysis.

Step 5: Total the scores for each of the three columns.

Factors to be rated

1. *Climate from a health point of view.* Is the climate good for you? Less demanding, with less chance of illness? Might it extend your life? A rating of 10 would be the most healthy of all climates.
2. *Climate from a cost standpoint.* Would it reduce your utility bills? Are clothing costs less? Under this category, it is probably, more expensive to live in Michigan than in Texas.
3. *Does the geographical area fit your comfort zone?* Do you enjoy changes in seasons? Are mountains more attractive to you than beaches? Would you fit the local culture? West Palm Beach, Florida, is vastly different from Albuquerque, New Mexico. Give high ratings to those areas that best fit your personal comfort zone.
4. *What about housing?* Could you afford the kind of housing you want? How do costs compare to where you are now? What would it cost to move? Preliminary housing-cost comparisons may be made by writing for a local newspaper. Make certain you have accurate data before rating this significant factor.
5. *What about other expenses?* Do you know the cost of consumer goods or tax rates? Prices vary. Some states do not have income taxes. Sales taxes are lower in some areas. A high rating indicates lower prices. Local newspapers can

provide data in this area. Your library or chamber of commerce can provide even more information.

6. *Are your kinds of leisure activities available?* Can you enjoy them year-round? Do they cost less? The quality of your retirement years can depend heavily on your leisure activities.

7. *What about medical facilities?* Would you be close to the best possible help? If you belong to a health maintenance organization (HMO), does it have a facility at the new location? Would your present medical plan be totally operational? Would you need to change doctors? Do you have a special health problem?

8. *Would you be able to build a new inner circle easily?* Would you be with your kind of people? People in New England can be different from those in California. Would you be quickly accepted in a new environment?

9. *What about transportation?* Is public transportation available if you need it? Would transportation in the new location be rated low or high?

10. *Other factors?* Would you be near friends and relatives you would choose to be with? Would you be closer or farther away from your special vacation spots? Would you be too isolated for friends to visit? Give this a general rating based on what has not already been covered. A high rating indicates you are still enthusiastic; a low rating indicates you may be changing your mind.

If you rated where you live now higher than your options, you are saying there may be more advantages in staying where you are than in making a move. If either option is rated higher, this signals that more investigation would be desirable, including perhaps a trip to make specific comparisons.

A geographical move is a decision that should be made only after lengthy, careful, and complete analysis. Several months' time is recommended, including visits during different seasons so you can verify all significant factors. Many retirees recommend living in a new area for several months as renters until you are sure.

Understanding yourself better

Once your geographic preference has been selected, what kind of housing or living environment is best for you? What can you afford? What is your comfort zone? Here again, make sure of your decision—a mistake could be costly.

It may help to position yourself on the scale in Figure 1. To accomplish this, first complete the continuum exercise by circling the appropriate numbers. This may help you understand your needs better in deciding what direction to take in the future. As you complete the exercise, keep the following in mind:

Your own comfort zones
The state of your health
Whether or not you live alone
Your age

Total your score for all items and divide by 20. If you scored 100, for example, you should circle number 5 on the continuum scale at the bottom of Figure 1. If you scored 60, you should circle number 3. The number you circle indicates how much you want independence versus protection. The left side means you want to assume responsibilities; the right suggests you are comfortable turning responsibilities over to others. As we become older, there is often movement toward the right—but not always.

Understanding your position   If you averaged 8 or above on the continuum, this probably suggests you should not move from your home (or present living facility) at this time. You want to take care of yourself and remain in charge.

If you score in the middle—between 4 and 7—you seem to indicate you don't want the responsibilities of home ownership, but you want independence. Many facilities can provide this, including adult parks, condominiums, and retirement centers. It will require investigation of your part to decide.

If you score 3 or below, you seem to desire a more protected living environment. You will probably be happier with protection and health care close to you. A full-service retirement center might fit your needs better than simply owning a condominium in a protected environment.

Some general rules for choosing where to live

Following is a discussion of seven living-environment choices. The possibilities, of course, are vast. Covering these broad choices may help direct you to additional investigation. As you consider which path to take, keep these general thoughts in mind:

- It is usually a good idea to stay where you are happy, comfortable, and near your inner-circle support system.

Continuum exercise

Left	10	9	8	7	6	5	4	3	2	1	Right
I'm fiercely independent and need space.	10	9	8	7	6	5	4	3	2	1	I'm highly social—give me people.
I'm happiest alone.	10	9	8	7	6	5	4	3	2	1	I'm happiest with others.
Risks of living alone do not bother me.	10	9	8	7	6	5	4	3	2	1	I want all the protection I can get.
I want pets around me.	10	9	8	7	6	5	4	3	2	1	I'm happier without pets.
I'm happy at home; traveling is not my thing.	10	9	8	7	6	5	4	3	2	1	I love to travel and be free to leave at anytime.
I love gardening and caring for my home.	10	9	8	7	6	5	4	3	2	1	I want to be free of all home responsibilities.
I refuse to give up my possessions to move into a smaller place.	10	9	8	7	6	5	4	3	2	1	I no longer want the responsibility of possessions.
I have a high neighborhood and community identity.	10	9	8	7	6	5	4	3	2	1	I have no deep roots and can live anywhere.
Money is not a problem—I can maintain my home.	10	9	8	7	6	5	4	3	2	1	Money is a problem—I need a cheaper place.
I make friends slowly.	10	9	8	7	6	5	4	3	2	1	I make new friends quickly and love it.
I don't want to be around other older people.	10	9	8	7	6	5	4	3	2	1	I want to be with those my own age.
I hate group efforts.	10	9	8	7	6	5	4	3	2	1	I would ask to be on a committee.

I can take care of my own recreation.	10 9 8 7 6 5 4 3 2 1	I need and love group activities.
I will drive my car until my license is taken away.	10 9 8 7 6 5 4 3 2 1	The less I drive and the sooner I give it up the better.
I intend to take care of my own health as long as possible.	10 9 8 7 6 5 4 3 2 1	Being close to medical help is vital to me.
I'm not concerned with lifelong care.	10 9 8 7 6 5 4 3 2 1	Lifelong care has great appeal.
I love having children around.	10 9 8 7 6 5 4 3 2 1	Give me a pure adult community.
A changing neighborhood doesn't bother me.	10 9 8 7 6 5 4 3 2 1	I can't handle neighborhood changes.
Freedom, to me, is living away from others.	10 9 8 7 6 5 4 3 2 1	Freedom, to me, is not having to worry about tomorrow.
A home of my own is part of my identity.	10 9 8 7 6 5 4 3 2 1	Give me comfort, protection, people, and less responsibility.

Total score _____

Continuum Scale

Private homeowner, fully independent	10 9 8 7 6 5 4 3 2 1	Retirement center, full-care facility

Figure 1. Continuum exercise for measuring your future from independence to protection. See text for instructions.

- Before deciding to move, make sure that advantages measurably outweigh disadvantages.
- You alone should make the final decision. Do not be overly influenced by relatives, friends, or promoters. (Remember, the grass always looks greener on the other side.)
- Protect your freedom with a passion. Any move that will cause you to lose freedom or make your world smaller may not be worth the apparent security it brings.
- Take culture shock seriously. Culture shock—the disorientation that occurs when moving from one country to another (e.g., United States to Japan) or one part of the country to another (e.g., Knoxville to Los Angeles)—requires adjustment. There is also a necessary adjustment when you move from your private home to a different living environment. There will be new neighbors, new social situations, and new rules to follow. This culture shock is possible in your own community when you move from your home into a retirement center.

Check the appropriate boxes as you analyze the possibilities.

Is your home still your castle?   If you own your home, you might be happier staying there. More and more gerontology specialists advocate this, and there seems to be a trend in this direction. There can be a lot of happiness in your own backyard. Sometimes, though, it is wise to move: neighborhoods change, or we change. Study the following advantages and disadvantages of living in your own home, and check items important to you. Write in any you feel are missing.

Advantages
- ☐ Your image is tied to your home. People you love identify you as living there.
- ☐ You feel more in charge in your own home.
- ☐ You have more privacy and space in your own home. You don't have to listen to someone else's plumbing.
- ☐ You retain more of your possessions.
- ☐ You can keep your pets.
   Other: _____
   _____

Disadvantages
- ☐ Home ownership is often more expensive (taxes, maintenance, etc.).

☐ Maintenance takes time, and you may do too much yourself
  or worry about it.
☐ Security risks may be higher.
☐ It may be more difficult to take trips.
☐ Until you sell your home, you can't take advantage of the
  once-in-a-lifetime $125,000 tax break on capital gains.
  Other: _____

☐ My decision is to stay   ☐ I need to seriously investigate
  put, for now   other options

Would you be happier renting?   Some retirees are very happy in
rented apartments. The reason is that they are not tied down with
homeowner responsibilities. They can select the neighborhood
they prefer in the community they like. They can also stay close to
their inner circle without the problems of maintaining their own
home.

Advantages
☐ Moving to a new apartment is usually easy.
☐ Apartments don't have maintenance problems.
☐ Apartments require no capital investment.
☐ Credits are available for tax purposes.
☐ Apartments with special facilities (swimming pools, health
  clubs, etc.) are often available.
  Other: _____

Disadvantages
☐ Landlords can be uncooperative and difficult.
☐ Rent increases are always possible.
☐ Neighbors living too close can be a problem.
☐ Apartments build no equity.
  Other: _____

☐ No thanks—apartment   ☐ I have an open mind and
  living is not for me   will investigate

What about a condominium?   If you own your home, you might
be able to sell it, buy a nice condo at a lower price, and invest the
difference. Many do this and feel they have done the right thing.
Condominium life can have style!
  Maintenance is normally not required. You are responsible

for things inside your unit, but nothing on the outside. You will have deed and/or mortgage and pay real-estate taxes. But you join with other owners to pay for outside maintenance, including recreational areas, landscaping, and even roofing. There are many elegant condominium facilities in the United States. All have a homeowner's association in which you automatically become a member.

Advantages

☐ Usually safer than an isolated, private dwelling.
☐ Easier to leave for long trips because there is less to care for.
☐ Special facilities are often available—pool, sauna, recreation rooms, tennis courts.
☐ More likely to have neighbors of your own age and social level.
☐ Easier to make new friends.
Other: _____

_____

Disadvantages

☐ There are rules to follow and association involvement.
☐ Normally you have less room, which may force you to sell some of your possessions.
☐ Your assessment fees can increase.
☐ Your neighbors are not always compatible.
☐ There are often restrictions on pets.
Other: _____

_____

| ☐ Condominium is best bet | ☐ Much more investigation is called for |

Mobile home living can be nifty   A growing number of retirees are living happily in adult mobile parks, some of which are quite elegant. The homes are really prefabricated houses, and some have two or three bedrooms. Mobile homes normally cost less than condominiums or single-dwelling houses. Often you can sell a private home, buy a mobile home, and bank the difference.

Advantages

☐ Less capital investment is required.
☐ There are many parks from which to select.
☐ Security protection can be excellent.
☐ Your neighbors are often in your comfort zone.
☐ There can be excellent recreational facilities or locally sponsored social events.

Other: _____

_____

Disadvantages
☐ Neighbors can be too close.
☐ Usually some restrictions prevail—for example, pets may not be permitted.
☐ Park owners can raise rent on space.
☐ Like neighborhoods, parks can deteriorate.
☐ Sometimes it is difficult to get into good parks.
Other: _____

_____

| ☐ Mobile home living is not my cup of tea | ☐ I need to investigate this option |

Retirement centers are in vogue Many retirees are so enthusiastic about retirement centers that they have closed their eyes to other possibilities. Retirement centers can come in all sizes, varieties, and prices. Many have medical centers. Large ones often have churches, organized social activities, golf, swimming, and tennis. Compared to adult condominiums and mobile-home parks, retirement centers are more self-contained.

Advantages
☐ Retirement centers offer greater protection.
☐ More facilities are available, especially medical.
☐ You have less worry and feel more secure as you grow older.
☐ You have easier access to inside facilities.
☐ Different centers fit most pocketbooks.
Other: _____

_____

Disadvantages
☐ There are many restrictions.
☐ Generally no pets are allowed.
☐ Centers are like a closed world.
☐ There are fewer young people around.
☐ Sometimes it is difficult to get out.
Other: _____

_____

| ☐ I'm not the retirement center kind | ☐ I'm going to do a complete investigation |

Should you apply for government-sponsored housing? If your income is modest, government housing could be the best step to take. If you can find a place and the list is not too long, you might want to act in a hurry.

Advantages
- ☐ Lower costs are often adjusted to your income.
- ☐ Each facility must meet government specifications.
- ☐ There are few responsibilities.
- ☐ Government housing is usually close to public transportation.
- ☐ Government facilities are normally secure.

Other: _____

_____

Disadvantages
- ☐ Being accepted can be difficult.
- ☐ Like most things connected with government, there are many restrictions.
- ☐ Rooms are usually small.
- ☐ There is often a hotel atmosphere.
- ☐ There is some loss of freedom.

Other: _____

_____

☐ Government housing   ☐ I'm going to look into this
   is not for me

Life-care centers have special attractions There are centers that provide full or life care. This usually means that, with a sizable investment, you can enter a community with the intention of staying there the rest of your life. You may be totally able when you enter; but later, when you need greater—even custodial—care, the facility is prepared to care for you. Some are very attractive, and often they are connected with a religious denomination.

Advantages
- ☐ You can receive the greatest possible care and security.
- ☐ Life-care centers can provide peace of mind.
- ☐ The other residents are usually in the same comfort zone.
- ☐ The centers potentially eliminate future difficult decisions.
- ☐ Often less concern is required by your family.
- ☐ Activities may fit your needs better than other retirement options.

Other: _____

_____

Disadvantages
- ☐ Centers cost money. Often a sizable investment is required.

In some cases you turn over a part of your estate.
☐ The age level is usually more advanced.
☐ Often people lose more freedom than expected.
☐ The decision can be almost irrevocable.
☐ It is difficult to find the perfect center.
☐ There is a possibility of default.
   Other: _____

_____

☐ I could become interested   ☐ I'm going to spend
    at a later date   some time investigating

Take your positive attitude with you

If you decide to make a major move, take your positive attitude
with you. Pack it with your most priceless possessions and hand-
carry it to your new environment. More than anything else, it will
help make your move successful. Here are some further tips:

- Within reason, take your prized possessions with you. They
  quickly help make a new location seem more like home.
- Once settled, engage in a number of civic, athletic, social, or
  church activities.
- The sooner you make new friends or rebuild an inner-circle
  support system, the better.

People you meet will do more than anything else to make your
new environment a happy one.

Summary

The most difficult decision facing those who retire is where to live
and what kind of housing facility or living environment to select.

When the advantages of one geographic area over another become
apparent, a move should be seriously considered, finances permit-
ting.

It is helpful for people to position themselves on a continuum between having their own home or joining a full-care facility.

Comfort zone is an important consideration in the choice of any
living environment.

Housing decisions are not always revocable.

PART TWO

Financial Planning for Retirement

Once you have a good idea about how and where you want to live in retirement (Chapters 1–9), it's time to look at the financial side of the equation. Can you afford the retirement lifestyle you want? What can you do now to ensure your financial security in retirement?

The first step in financial planning is to figure out your current financial status. Chapter 10 explains the importance of preparing an annual net worth statement and using an annual budget to guide your spending. The annual net worth statement will help you determine if you are making progress toward your financial goals or falling behind. A current budget will also help you identify where your hard-earned money is going and what funds can be reallocated into savings and investments to meet your financial goals.

The next step, discussed in Chapter 11, is to estimate retirement expenses and income. An important part of this is factoring in the effect of inflation on purchasing power and estimating how much you'll need to maintain your standard of living throughout your retirement years.

Next, Chapter 12 outlines basic financial strategies for achieving your retirement goals. How many of these strategies are you already employing?

(For growing numbers of retirees, work in retirement will play a key part in financing their retirement years. Chapters 7 and 8 in Part One discuss work options and how to find the kind of work you want in retirement.)

The remaining chapters in this section provide valuable information and insights on other key financial planning issues: What you should know about Social Security (Chapter 13); the value of personal tax-deferred compensation programs to the retirement planning of local government employees (Chapter 14); whether, under the tax reform law of 1986, IRAs are still a good investment (Chapter 15); whether life insurance should serve both as family protection and as a tax-deferred investment (Chapter 16); and how to draw on the equity in your home to help finance your retirement (Chapter 17).

Protecting your hard-earned wealth now and passing it on later according to your wishes are the subjects of Part Three, "Protecting What You've Worked For."

10

SIZING UP
YOUR FINANCES

Jack Egan

How do you stack up financially? If you're like most people, you have only a vague idea. But it's hard to set goals, much less meet them, unless you know where you stand. An annual fiscal checkup helps you plan your financial future and gauge your progress, whether your goal is to come up with a down payment for a home, send your kids to college, or retire early. Here are some ways to tell if your savings and investment programs measure up to your objectives.

If you feel a bit queasy about where you're headed financially, join the club. Most Americans think they're getting by for today but are chewing their nails over what tomorrow will bring. They feel beset by monthly bills. They worry about the steadily rising cost of medical care and college tuition. By 2 to 1, they say their net worth isn't what they'd like it to be. The sluggish national economy is making it hard for them to save, now and in the future. And 2 out of 5 people fear, above all else, that they will outlive the funds earmarked for retirement.

This pessimistic portrait, based on a survey conducted for the International Association for Financial Planning, should not be surprising. Americans live in a debt-burdened society that depends on vigorous consuming to keep the economy humming. The old virtues of scrimping and saving have been replaced with plastic gratification—thanks to the credit card. As a consequence, the personal savings rate keeps dropping. "Most people are making more money than ever but claim they are not making much progress in getting ahead," says financial planner David Dondero of Alexandria, Virginia.

This pervasive sense of financial unease reflects the haphazard approach the average person tends to take where money matters are concerned. If you're like most people, getting your finances in shape may be a top priority but one that's frustratingly elusive. Most likely you have only a fuzzy sense of your current net worth and how it has changed over the past year. Your main financial goal—whether it's accumulating a down payment on a house, sending your children to college, or achieving financial independence—is probably a vague aspiration rather than a clearly articulated objective. If you have a strategy at all, it's likely to be a hodgepodge rather than a well-thought-out plan of action.

Know what you've got

If that describes you, the first step in remedying it is to take a close, hard look at every facet of your financial standing. "You should have an annual fiscal checkup for the same reason you have an annual physical," says Lewis Walker, head of Walker, Cogswell & Company, an Atlanta financial-planning firm, and president of the Denver-based Institute of Certified Financial Planners. "The problem is that most people don't run their personal affairs like a business," says Graydon Calder, president of Financial Planning Consultants of San Diego. "If you're a business, you draw up an annual income—or profit and loss—statement and a balance sheet. We encourage our clients to do the same." The P&L statement is a record of what's coming in and going out. Compiling a balance sheet is a way to see if your net worth is increasing and if you're making progress in meeting your financial goals.

With a little effort, you should be able to come up with your own accurate income statement, which paints a picture of your cash flow over an entire year, and a balance sheet, in effect a snapshot of your assets and liabilities taken at one point in time. Worksheets are provided in Figure 1 to help you assemble an income statement; a balance sheet is provided in Figure 2.

Besides letting you get a grip on your finances, such a review is a starting point for setting basic goals and for drawing up a plan to turn them into reality. "Planning is a process; it's a way of problem solving," says Carol Nathan, president of MetroWest Financial

Group of Framingham, Massachusetts. "It gives people more control over their lives and lets them get better use out of their assets."

Before you tackle the worksheets, you'll have to pull together the relevant financial records. These include recent tax records, bank statements, canceled checks, credit-card information, other itemized living expenses, brokerage-account and mutual-fund records, mortgage payments, pension-account records, and loan-repayment schedules for your auto and other goods purchased on credit.

Coming up with all of this documentation may seem daunting, but is a highly instructive exercise by itself. "Because of poor record keeping, many people don't have any idea of what progress they're making financially," says Calder. "Many clients tell me that clarifying where they stand is the biggest benefit they derive from the financial planning process."

Besides sweeping away some financial cobwebs and making sure you can readily lay your hands on your most important papers, the specifics in these documents permit you to quantify your goals. "I once got a plaque from a client that said, 'Picky, picky, picky,'" says John Sestina, vice president of SMB Financial Planning in Columbus, Ohio. "But the key to finding how someone can succeed financially depends on getting a lot of details."

Once you've pulled together the relevant papers, a good place to start is with the income statement (see Figure 1). "Probably the most important piece of information is an individual's cash flow," says Sestina. The income statement tells you how much of your income is already earmarked for fixed financial commitments, such as monthly mortgage and automobile payments, and how much is discretionary and therefore can be squeezed to fund major expenditures or to boost savings.

You can also use the income statement to help draw up a budget. But to do a thorough job, you should probably augment the spending information from your financial records of the past year for a couple of months by keeping a diary that details exactly what you spend, no matter how minor. That way, you can identify just how much money leaks out of your pocket for odds and ends of all kinds.

The income statement also can be the cornerstone for an enhanced savings plan, since new savings can come only from higher income or lower expenditures. There's no precise rule on how much you should be saving, but most planners suggest that at least 10 percent of pretax income should be socked away each year—more if possible. Savings is a habit that, developed early, goes a

long way toward letting you achieve a high degree of financial security. Says planner Calder: "It matters less how much you make
than how much you save. If people start young enough, they can
accomplish virtually all of their financial objectives by saving 10
percent a year."

Budget your savings

You should think of savings as a fixed expense, say planners, not as
a self-congratulatory and infrequent exercise. "People in this
country have not clocked in with the idea that they must pay themselves first in the form of savings in order to ensure their own financial security," says Mark Bass, president of Pennington/Bass
Companies, a Lubbock, Texas, financial-planning firm.

On top of regular savings, Sestina tells his clients to create separate savings reserves for the periodic replacement of big-ticket
items like a car or a refrigerator. "If you're living to the hilt on
what you make and one of these items breaks, that's the kind of
surprise that cripples you financially," he says. "Then you have to
go into debt to pay for a replacement. That's why people complain
they're not getting ahead."

For those contemplating retirement, even if it is years away,
the income statement can serve as a bench mark for what it will
cost to keep up a desired lifestyle when one is no longer working.
Most advisers counsel that you need 70 to 80 percent of your pre-
retirement income. Inflation, of course, has to be factored in. Over
the past twenty years, inflation as measured by the consumer price
index has averaged 6 percent annually.

On the balance sheet, (see Figure 2) it's best to break assets
and liabilities into categories, as done on the work sheet. On the
asset side, first list those that are fairly liquid, or readily converted
into cash, such as what you have in your bank or in mutual-fund or
money-market accounts. This is money you can lay your hands on
readily. Separate out balances in regular accounts from those in
pension-related plans, such as individual retirement accounts,
Keogh plans, and 401(k) plans. List the current cash value of any
annuities, life insurance policies, and employer profit-sharing
plans.

A third category of fixed assets includes your home, other real
estate, personal property such as a car, boat, motorcycle, or works
of art, and ownership interests in a small business. Enter only the
amount that you could realize if you had to sell any of these items
currently—and be conservative in your estimates. For many people, the equity value in their home is the biggest component of

their net worth. However, they should look at it differently. From, say, their holdings in a portfolio of stocks and bonds. "For most people, a house is part of their lifestyle and not an investment per se," says Nathan. "If you sell your house and move, you've got to buy something else."

Now that you've totaled your assets and liabilities, the difference between the two is what you'd be worth if you were to turn everything into cash and pay off all you bills. "More than anything else, a balance sheet, even an unsophisticated one, lets you measure in a consistent manner where you stand every year," says Nathan.

A year-to-year change in financial assets on the balance sheet indicates two things: How many new dollars have been put to work, and the annualized investment return achieved. Setting realistic growth targets for investments is a problem these days, says Nathan. "I feel that I can get a return of 10 to 12 percent year after year, then I'm doing fabulously. A lot of money managers for large financial institutions set goals of 2 to 3 percent over the consumer-price-index inflation rate and are delighted to get that over the long term." In 1986, the CPI rose 2 percent, and estimates for this year range from 4 to 6 percent.

Go for the long haul

Individuals too, should strive for long-run consistency and the avoidance of large losses. Big gains one year can be erased, and then some, by equally big drops the next. After all, it takes a 100 percent gain on a share to make up for a 50 percent decline.

If you have complex finances or feel intimidated by the prospect of sorting out where you stand, there are lots of financial planners around to help you out. Fees can range from a few hundred dollars for a standard workup to several hundred dollars an hour for individual consultation on estate, tax, and investment matters. Beware of salespeople in planners' clothing who offer free or cheap advice but are being compensated through the sale of insurance, mutual funds or some other product.

But whether you do it yourself or seek help elsewhere in achieving most financial goals, it is a patient eye, fixed on the long term, that ultimately makes the difference. Spending hours poring over income statements and balance sheets and filling out long lists of goals and objectives will produce paltry results without a consistent follow-up and a diligent repeat of the process over a number of years. Says financial planner Bass: "It's easy to get all fired up about a plan—and then nobody does anything about it."

So how am I doing? How to find out?

To see how a company is doing, shareholders turn to both the income statement and the balance sheet in a firm's annual report. These two documents are also key in assessing your personal finances. The income statement tracks your cash flow over a twelve-month period—what you took in from salary, investments and other sources, where it all went, and anything left over. The income statement shows you whether you're teetering precariously at the edge of your resources or can put money aside for the future. The balance sheet, which can be thought of as a snapshot of your assets and your liabilities at one point in time, lets you determine what you're worth. By comparing one year's balance sheet with the next, you can see how your savings and investments are performing.

What comes in and goes out

Start by gathering your check stubs, your most up-to-date bills, and other records, and fill out the income statement. Unpredictable expenses, such as auto repairs, should be entered under "variable," while mortgage payments and other regular bills belong under "fixed." Use the current year's figures wherever you can. Don't worry if you have to estimate.

Current year's income	
Salaries and wages	
Husband	_____
Wife	_____
Self-employment income	_____
Dividends and interest	_____
Capital gains and losses (e.g., from sale of stock)	_____
Rents, annuities, pensions	_____
Alimony, child support	_____
Tax refunds	_____
Bonuses, gifts, misc. income	_____
Total income	_____

Figure 1. Income statement.

Current year's outgo	Fixed	Variable
Federal personal income tax	_____	
State and local income taxes	_____	
Social Security and disability taxes	_____	
Housing		
Yearly mortgage payment $_____(12 × per mo.)	_____	
Yearly rent $_____(12 × per mo.)	_____	
Utilities		
Electricity	_____	
Oil or gas	_____	
Water	_____	
Maintenance and repairs	_____	
Insurance		
Homeowners	_____	
Property	_____	
Mortgage	_____	
Taxes	_____	
Real estate	_____	
Personal property	_____	
Groceries (52 × $_____per week)	_____	
Restaurant meals		_____
Clothing		
Clothing purchases		_____
Laundry, dry cleaning, repairs		_____

Figure 1, continued.

Current year's outgo	Fixed	Variable
Transportation		
Auto payments		
Monthly payments ($_____ × 12)	_____	
Purchase		_____
Auto insurance	_____	
Gasoline	_____	
Maintenance and repairs	_____	_____
Auto licenses	_____	
Medical		
Health insurance	_____	
Doctor, dentist		_____
Medicine		_____
Child-care expenses	_____	
Education: College, school tuitions	_____	
Life-insurance premiums	_____	
Major appliances and other significant purchases		_____
Alimony, child support	_____	
Vacations	_____	
Entertainment	_____	
Other		_____
Total fixed expenses	_____	
Total variable expenses		_____
Total living expenses		_____
Total income	_____	
Less total living expenses	_____	
Total remaining for savings or investment	_____	

Figure 1, continued.

What you're worth

Now enter the value of your assets and liabilities. The bottom line is your net worth. Especially if you own a house, it may surprise you.

Monetary assets		**Liabilities**	
Cash		Short-term liabilities (outstanding bills)	
On hand	_____		
Checking and money-market accounts	_____	Federal, state, and local taxes	_____
Passbook savings account(s)	_____	Insurance premiums	_____
Money loaned to others	_____	Rent or mortgage	_____
		Utilities	_____
Investments:		Charge accounts	_____
Profit sharing	_____	Other	_____
Stocks and bonds	_____	Total short-term liabilities	_____
Keogh, IRA, 401(k)	_____		
Mutual funds	_____		
Cash value of life insurance	_____	Long-term liabilities (loan balances)	
Cash value of annuities	_____	Bank	_____
Total monetary assets	_____	Education	_____
Fixed assets		Home, other mortgage	_____
Market value of home	_____	Auto, other	_____
Other real estate	_____	Total long-term liabilities	_____
Other investments (gold coins, stamps, etc.)	_____		
Automobiles	_____	**Total liabilities**	_____
Ownership interests in small business	_____	Total assets	_____
Personal property (artwork, furniture, etc.)	_____	Less total liabilities	_____
Total fixed assets	_____	**Net worth**	_____

Figure 2. Balance sheet.

11

CAN YOU AFFORD
TO RETIRE?

Marie Hodge

Editor's note: Chapter 10 helped you assess your current financial status. This chapter will help you estimate the cost of your desired retirement lifestyle. After figuring these costs, do the exercises at the end of this chapter: "Are you on your way to a comfortable retirement?" and "How much you must save to maintain your lifestyle." Strategies for meeting your financial goals for retirement are discussed in Chapter 12.

It's been said that early retirement is the new American Dream. In fact, statistics show that 45 percent of all men and 32 percent of all women between the ages of 55 and 64 are already "at leisure."

Perhaps you've toyed with the idea of retiring early but aren't sure whether you will have enough income to support the lifestyle to which you intend to become accustomed. According to the American Council of Life Insurance, "an individual household needs 75 to 80 percent of current income to live comfortably in retirement," but since that rule of thumb doesn't apply to every individual, you may want to invest a simple hour in paperwork to size up your own unique situation.

In order to determine whether you'll have "enough," you must make fundamental decisions (in some cases, little more than guesses) about the quality and direction of your future life: where you want to live, how often you wish to travel, what your daily ac-

Reprinted by permission of the author from *50 Plus* magazine, December 1986, 29–33. Copyright 1986 by Marie Hodge.

tivities will be, what kind of health you can reasonably expect to enjoy, etc. Start by assessing your expenses now, while you're working. (If you haven't formally budgeted in a while, you will probably find some surprises in how your daily income is apportioned.)

Expenses in retirement

Most daily expenses will either increase or decrease in retirement, but few will remain the same. Follow Figure 1, and calculate your current expenses on a separate piece of paper, then add or subtract according to your anticipated needs in each category, placing the final figure on your worksheet. Put a check mark next to the categories that are vulnerable to inflation (e.g., fuel costs are, but fixed mortgage payments aren't), and we'll figure in inflation's probable effects at the end. (You may want one worksheet for each year.)

Housing

1. This should be a "good news" category, since about 80 percent of 50-plussers own their own home and will undoubtedly find remaining mortgage commitments minimal or even nonexistent. Don't forget to add in repair and maintenance costs, particularly if you're thinking of using retirement as a time to remodel or make long-awaited additions to your home.

Even if you rent, you may need less living space, which will have an effect on housing costs, utilities, and maintenance and repair costs.

2. Utility costs will increase as inflation increases (see "Inflation"). However—and here's where accurate projections about future plans count—if you expect to move to a warmer climate, you'll decrease heating costs substantially. (On the other hand, your electricity costs for air conditioning might increase.) If you're likely to make more long-distance telephone calls to relatives or friends at peak daytime hours, that would clearly be an expense to budget.

Food and clothing

3. Some say that your food costs in retirement should decrease, since calories are rather like sleep: The older you get, the less you need. Of course, if you're likely to eat out more often, or if you expect to spend your days whipping up one culinary delight after another, make sure this is reflected in your food budget.

4. Clothing costs may decrease substantially as you spend more

---

Income

1. Social Security (self)   _____
2. Social Security (spouse)   _____
3. Private pensions   _____
4. Savings and investments   _____
5. Part-time work   _____

     Total income   _____

Expenses

1. Rent or mortgage   _____
2. Utilities   _____
3. Food   _____
4. Clothing   _____
5. Drugs, eyeglasses, dental care   _____
6. Health insurance, Medicare costs   _____
7. Medigap and long-term-care insurance   _____
8. Life insurance   _____
9. Auto and homeowners' insurance   _____
10. Leisure and hobbies   _____
11. Federal taxes   _____
12. State taxes   _____
13. Property taxes   _____
14. Job-related expenses   _____
15. Family obligations   _____
16. Debt repayment   _____
17. Inflation   _____

     Total expenses   _____

Total income   _____

Total expenses   _____

Excess or deficit   _____

Figure 1. Retirement planning worksheet.

time at leisure and less in a work environment, where a certain standard and variety of dress often demand large expenditures. Also, if you do move to a warmer climate, some high-ticket items (coats, boots) will drop out of your wardrobe.

Health care

5. Unless you have a paid prescription plan that will carry forward into your retirement, you can anticipate twice the drug bill you had when you were younger. If your eyeglass prescriptions

---

Are you on your way to a comfortable retirement?

By age 50, most people are planning seriously for retirement. But younger people often lack a specific strategy. If you are under 50, this quiz will tell you whether you are doing enough for your retirement. Give yourself a point for each yes answer.

1. If you are under 40, are you saving 10% of your annual salary? If you are 40 or older, are you setting aside 10% of your salary specifically for retirement?
2. Is part of your savings in a tax-deferred account, such as an Individual Retirement Account or 401(k) plan?
3. Do you have three to six months' worth of living expenses in a cash account available for use in emergencies?
4. If you are under 35, do you own growth investments that you plan to leave untouched for at least a decade? If you are 35 or older, do you have a well-diversified portfolio that includes cash, bonds and real estate?
5. If you have children, have you established a college tuition fund? (If you have no children, count this as a "yes.")
6. Do you own your own home? If not, and you are under 35, are you saving to buy a home?
7. If you are under 35, do you work for a company with a pension plan? If you are 35 or older, do you have a vested pension?

How you rate

1 point or less: You are in the pits when it comes to retirement planning. Start putting money away using techniques such as payroll deductions.

2 to 4 points: You're off to a good start. Once you have an emergency fund, invest for long-term growth.

5 to 7 points: Pat yourself on the back. After filling in any cracks, all you will need is the discipline to stay the course.

Source: Prepared by Jeanne L. Reid. Reprinted with permission from *MONEY* magazine, April 1988, 76–77.

and dental costs were previously covered but will not be in retirement, estimate at least the cost of eye and dental checkups, and allow a generous amount for possible occasional work that goes beyond the checkup.

6.   If you will be retiring before age 65 and won't have health insurance from your employer, you must plan to pick up your own premiums—possibly as a continuing member of the group health insurance plan at your former place of employment.

On the other hand, if you will be at least 65 when you retire, you can anticipate having some health needs covered (at a current monthly premium of $17.90) by Medicare—but not as many as you may have assumed. Medicare covers only about half the medical costs of the elderly. Though there is no foolproof way to plan for a catastrophic illness that could drain your savings, it may be appropriate to augment your health insurance.

Insurance

7.   As the information about Medicare implies, people over 65 will probably need a good medigap insurance policy. Price the premiums for these before you calculate retirement expenses. You may also want long-term-care insurance, but be advised that it's very expensive.

8.   Assuming that most of your dependents have left the nest, and that mortgage payments on the house have decreased or ceased altogether, you may want to cut back on life insurance, which will decrease premiums. Or, your life insurance premiums may be finally paid up. In either case, there's probably reason to make conservative expense projections here.

However, if you have a spouse whose income would be substantially reduced by your death (for example, if there were no "survivor benefit" to your pension), then full-scale life insurance may still be in order.

9.   Assuming that you plan to continue owning your own home and your car in retirement, add in your homeowners and auto insurance costs.

Leisure activities and hobbies

10.   No matter how modest your means, chances are that expenditures for your leisure activities and hobbies, as a proportion of your expenses, will increase once you've retired. Activities that once were sandwiched in during odd moments may become the mainstay of your daily life: traveling, golf, crafts, fishing, gardening, gourmet cooking, home decorating, etc. Allow a generous amount for these activities—at least at the start of the budgeting process—because your degree of enjoyment in retirement may depend heavily on them.

Taxes

11.   Whatever your tax bite now, it should be substantially less in retirement. (Only one in four people over 65 pays any income taxes at all.) Make a projection of future federal taxes on the basis of your diminished income. You may want to check with the IRS for details about which benefits (Social Security, pensions, annuities, etc.) are taxable in retirement, and under what conditions. For more information, pick up the free IRS publication "Tax Benefits for Older Americans" at IRS or Social Security offices.

Unfortunately, as a result of tax reform, people over 65 will no longer be able to take one extra exemption for themselves plus another exemption for a spouse filing jointly. (Their standard deductions, however, will increase.)

12.   Many states give special deductions or reductions on state tax to retirees. Check with your state income tax department before you budget.

13.   Older people often get a break on property taxes, too. Check in your locality.

Job-related expenses

14.   Unless you are planning a part-time job, you can say goodbye to the costs associated with working: commuting, eating lunch in restaurants, and—as already mentioned—some kinds of clothing. However, if you are used to having an expense account that covers say, some of your meals, paying for those meals will pose an additional expense beyond your current outlays.

Family obligations

15.   Almost everyone who is retired has children or older parents. Many 50-plussers are sandwiched between obligations—financial and otherwise—to both groups. If you anticipate financial liability to either group somewhere down the line, treat this as a possible expense for which you have to plan.

Debt repayment

16.   Add in this category the annual totals of outstanding loan and credit-card payments, either current or projected. If your car is about to wheeze its last, or if you think you'll need two cars once

How much you must save
to maintain your lifestyle

Your investments will probably have to provide a third of your income after you retire. This worksheet will help you calculate how much you should be saving if you want to maintain your present standard of living. (The notes and the four tables will help you complete the worksheet.)

Line 10 shows the amount you should save this year; in future years, you should increase your contribution to keep pace with inflation. If you are just starting out and cannot put away as much now as you would like, try to save a regular percentage of your income each month.

1. Annual income you would need if you retired today (80% of your current income) $_____
2. Assuming a 5% inflation rate, the annual income you will need to retire at a future date (line 1 times multiplier from Table A)   _____
3. The amount your pension will provide   _____
4. Social Security income you will receive (the current benefit for your income level times multiplier from Table A)   _____
5. The income you will need from your investments (line 2 minus lines 3 and 4)   _____
6. The capital you should have at retirement to provide enough investment income to last for your expected life span (line 5 times multiplier from Table B)   _____
7. Value of your current invesetments   _____
8. What your current investments are likely to be worth when you retire (line 7 times multiplier from Table C)   _____
9. Additional capital you will need to provide sufficient investment income (line 6 minus line 8)   _____
10. Annual amount you should be saving to reach your retirement goals (line 9 divided by divisor from Table D)   _____

Notes

Line 3. Ask your employer's benefits office to project your pension assuming inflation runs 5% annually—as many economists forecast—between now and when you retire.

Line 4. If you retired today, Social Security would pay you a benefit based on your salary history. If your salary is $45,000 a year or more, you probably would qualify for the maximum benefit of $10,056 a year. If you earned less than that, assume you would get the average annual benefit of $7,512. To calculate what your benefit could be when you actually retire, multiply the benefit you would get today by the appropriate figure from Table A. This calculation assumes that the Social Security Administration will increase benefits by 5% a year to cover inflation.

Line 6. The multiplier you choose from Table B depends on what type of portfolio strategy you prefer. The Income multiplier assumes you invest in high-quality intermediate-maturity fixed-income assets and average a 7% annual return over time, which is reasonable by historical standards. If you are comfortable with more risk, you might opt for the Equity multiplier, based on a portfolio of blue-chip and growth-oriented stocks that could earn 10% a year on average. The multipliers also assume that, given a 5% rate of inflation, you will need to withdraw more income each year to maintain your standard of living.

Line 7. Current investments include those that you have earmarked for retirement, such as corporate savings plans, Keoghs, Individual Retirement Accounts and the cash value of life insurance policies.

Line 8. Choose the multiplier that corresponds to your portfolio strategy.

Line 10. Choose the divisor that corresponds to your portfolio strategy.

Table A.

Years to retirement	Multiplier
5	1.3
10	1.6
15	2.1
20	2.7
25	3.4
30	4.3
35	5.5
40	7.0

Table B.

Years capital must last	Multiplier	
	Income portfolio	Equity portfolio
20	16.8	13.3
30	23.1	16.6
40	28.3	18.6

Table C.

Years to retirement	Multiplier	
	Income portfolio	Equity portfolio
5	1.4	1.6
10	2.0	2.6
15	2.8	4.2
20	3.9	6.7
25	5.4	10.8
30	7.6	17.4
35	10.7	28.1
40	15.0	45.3

Table D.

Years to retirement	Divisor	
	Income portfolio	Equity portfolio
5	6.8	7.4
10	18.1	21.2
15	36.4	46.2
20	65.1	89.6
25	109.2	163.9
30	176.0	288.8
35	276.1	496.9
40	424.5	840.8

Source: Prepared by Jeanne L. Reid. Reprinted with permission from *MONEY* magazine, April 1988, 76–77.

there are two people home all day, be realistic and add in the likely monthly payments once you buy.

Inflation

17. The last ten years have been an inflation roller coaster, which makes planning a bit more difficult. But over a period of years, you might project an annual average of 5 percent as a figure to work with, advises New York financial consultant Lawrence P. Eichler, C.P.A. So at this juncture, take those expenses that you have checked off as vulnerable to inflation, and increase their total by 5 percent for each year. Total all figures.

This is your "ideal" expense profile, as nearly as you can determine it, and should be updated every year as your life situation changes—when kids graduate college, *you* go back to college, buy a new car, etc.

Income

Americans hoping to retire with an income of $20,000 or more a year should not count on Social Security to provide very much. Here are the current sources of income for retirees with that level of income:

Investments	34%
Earnings	24%
Social Security	22%
Pensions	18%
Other benefits	2%

Now comes the task of matching income to expenses:

Social security

1. You will be eligible for Social Security checks as early as age 62, but the earlier you retire, the less the benefits will be. Check with your local Social Security office for a projection of benefits if you retire at 62 and one for retirement at age 65. Or ask for their booklet, "Estimating Your Social Security Retirement Check."

A person who retired at age 65 in 1987, at an annual salary of

$20,000, could expect a monthly stipend of about $702. Cost-of-living adjustments (COLAs) are now automatic and are tied to the inflation rate. (For 1987, it is 1.3 percent.)

2. If you are married, your spouse is eligible (at age 65) for at least 50 percent as much as the benefits you're entitled to (more, if your spouse's worklife entitles him or her to more), so count that in projected household income, too.

Private pensions

3. Private pension benefits in retirement must be discussed with your benefits specialist at work. Find out how much you can expect to receive if you retire before age 65 and how much you stand to gain by waiting. Often, such plans do not adjust when the cost of living goes up, but it's a question you should ask.

You should also find out whether your pension benefits will be "integrated" with Social Security benefits in retirement—i.e., whether the amount you're entitled to will be reduced by some portion of the Social Security benefit you'll be receiving simultaneously, because that will have a strong effect on your monthly benefits figure.

Savings and investments

4. Depending on how much you draw from savings and investments to supplement other monthly retirement benefits, your savings can last virtually indefinitely, with any kind of modest interest rate. Table 1 projects the amount you will be able to withdraw from savings deposits of up to $50,000, at the modest interest rate of 5¼ percent, over 5-, 10-, 15-, and 20-year periods.

5. When attempting to guess how long your savings and investments will have to last—and therefore how much you can safely withdraw each month—keep in mind that a man retiring at age 65 can look forward to an average life expectancy of another 13½ years, and a woman can expect to live an average of nearly 20 more years.

Part-time work

6. If you anticipate working at least part time in retirement, calculate what you can realistically expect in the way of monthly income. But include this amount only if you intend to count it as spendable income. You may want to deposit a portion of such income in an IRA to make it tax deductible. If so, don't count that amount as "spendable."

Table 1.   How long will your savings last?

Assuming interest at 5.25%, these are the monthly amounts that can be withdrawn over 5-, 10-, 15-, and 20-year periods.

Amount deposited	5 years	10 years	15 years	20 years
$ 5,000	$ 95.11	$ 53.84	$ 40.41	$ 33.92
10,000	190.22	107.69	80.82	67.85
15,000	285.45	161.54	121.23	101.77
20,000	380.45	215.39	161.64	135.70
25,000	475.56	269.24	202.06	169.62
30,000	570.68	323.09	242.47	203.55
35,000	665.79	376.93	282.88	237.47
40,000	760.91	430.78	323.29	271.40
45,000	856.02	484.63	363.71	305.32
50,000	951.13	538.48	404.12	339.25

Source: Bowery Savings Bank of New York and International Foundation of Employee Benefit Plans.

If expenses exceed income

You can wait to retire, and save in earnest. Or you can cut back on expenses and talk to a financial adviser about investments that maximize income, through monthly interest and dividends. Or you may wish to step up part-time income in retirement. Whichever way you choose, you will have the security of knowing that you have made the best possible financial evaluation of your prospects.

12

TWELVE STEPS TO FINANCIAL SECURITY

Jeanne L. Reid

First, bonds took a beating. Then stocks collapsed. Now from the crow's nests of many economists comes the shout, "Recession dead ahead!" It's enough to make the saltiest investor reach for the Dramamine. Yet becoming more cautious about your finances does not mean selling investments in panic or hastily retrenching within your household. Rather, it means adopting prudent financial habits as a permanent strategy. The high risk of setbacks in any economic climate demands it. As documented in a two-year study of family economics by the University of Michigan Survey Research Center, 31 percent of Americans take a big financial hit—from the loss of a job to the loss of a breadwinning spouse—at least once in a decade, and a third of that group fall below the poverty line as a consequence.

We offer the following twelve steps to protect your present wealth, drawn up in consultation with scores of investment advisers and financial planners.

1. Pay off your credit-card debt

A primary symptom of a bull market hangover is swollen credit-card debt—when investment profits are pouring in, it is easy to justify the most impulsive buying. As part of a pandemic of borrowing since 1982, outstanding credit-card balances have tripled. In the same period, balances owed by Americans to creditors other than mortgage lenders have gone from 15.2 percent to 18.6 percent of the nation's after-tax personal income. And despite a general decline in interest rates, the cost of carrying credit-card debt has not eased much. While 20-year Treasury bond rates have fallen from 13 percent to 9 percent since 1982, credit-card rates have hovered near 18 percent. Therefore, paying off your credit cards is equivalent to earning about an 18 percent return, free of taxes and risk.

The squeeze you may feel now from liquidating your credit-card debt is nothing compared with the pressure you will feel if your income drops. Nor can you count on tax breaks anymore to ease the burden. In 1988, only 40 percent of interest payments are deductible. The amount drops to 20 percent in 1989 and 10 percent in 1990 and then vanishes. With the top marginal tax rate falling to 33 percent in 1988, $1,000 of interest now costs $868 after taxes, up from $750 in 1987.

Many advisers say the ratio of your nonmortgage debt payments to your after-tax income should not exceed 20 percent, and the more conservative ones prefer 15 percent of less. Elgie Holstein, director of Bankcard Holders of America, a nonprofit consumer education organization in Washington, DC, cites four other symptoms of addiction to plastic:

- You pay only the monthly minimum of 2 percent to 5 percent of your outstanding balances.
- You use cash advances from one card to pay the minimum on another.
- You use plastic to pay for everyday expenses such as food and utilities.
- You apply for higher limits or new cards so that you can continue borrowing.

In some people's lives, the ease of credit-card use leads to absurd financial maneuverings. Not long ago, a middle-aged, $30,000-a-year clerical worker in New York City told her credit counselor she needed help paying off her credit-card debts. On further questioning, she disclosed that she had run up $15,000 in cash advances on her cards over the previous five years, partly to fund her Individual Retirement Account. "How else can I ever hope to retire?" she complained.

When it comes to emergency borrowing, instead of relying on

cards, consider applying for a home-equity line of credit. "Open credit lines when times are good," advises Alexandra Armstrong, president of her own financial planning firm in Washington, DC, "so that you can draw on them if problems arise."

2. Become a regular saver

You don't need a guru to tell you that stockpiling some money every month is the best way to build a storehouse of wealth. Yet, as IDS financial planner Jim Siggens of Seattle says, "Many people live from paycheck to paycheck and find there is too much month at the end of their money."

Siggens' antidote: "Adjust your cash flow." What he means is find out where your money is going and redirect a reasonable portion of it to savings. Start by itemizing your monthly fixed costs: income and FICA taxes, mortgage or rent payments, property taxes, car payments, insurance premiums, utilities, commutation, alimony if you pay it, and salary withholding for retirement and savings plans.

Then rough out your variable expenses for, among other things, groceries and restaurant meals, clothing, telephone calls, automobile maintenance and fuel, medical bills, travel, recreation, hobbies, education, and gifts. Such outlays are called variable because you can usually reduce them.

Counterpose against living costs your monthly wages and other earnings, not including income from investments. If earnings exceed costs, you've got a surplus worth saving. If they don't, they should. You are likely to find that a mélange of miscellaneous expenses is the black hole in your budget. Controlling this leakage does not require a draconian regimen, just the tedious task of keeping a running tally of your spending habits for three months or so.

Once you have identified the splurges that are consuming your savable cash, you can turn a deficit into a surplus by controlling your worst extravagances and putting the proceeds in a savings account. Most people can comfortably afford to save 5 percent to 10 percent of their gross income, in the opinion of Steven Enright, director of financial planning at Seidman Financial Services in New York City. The secret, he says, is to "put money aside before you even think about spending and investments." The reward will be some financial breathing room and, much more important, the formidable potential to build wealth.

3.   Set aside an emergency fund

Don't start committing your newfound surplus just yet to stocks, bonds, real estate, or other investments that are subject to market fluctuations. Put all of it in a more impervious repository such as a bank until you have accumulated three to six months' worth of living expenses. Every household needs at least that much in an emergency fund to see its members through rough times. "The cash is there so you won't have to sell investments when their prices are down," says planner Armstrong.

The University of Michigan's ten-year study of family economics exposed the most common causes of financial setbacks. Of the people who reported financial hardships, 9 percent suffered the loss of a job, 7 percent went through a divorce or separation, 5 percent retired or were permanently disabled. 3 percent lost a parent or spouse, and another 3 percent were sidelined by sickness or injury. Some financial crises are less dire, such as a tax-planning glitch that requires an unexpectedly high payment.

Where should you keep your emergency fund? Because you may need to get at it quickly, deposit the money where it is safe and almost instantly obtainable but still gives you a large enough return to keep pace with inflation. That generally limits your options to federally insured money-market accounts at banks or savings and loans (recently yielding 6 percent on average), three- to six-month certificates of deposit (6.8 percent) and taxable or tax-free money-market funds (6.4 percent and 4.5 percent).

To be extra cautious in uncertain times like these, many planners suggest letting your cash pile up beyond the usual three to six months of living costs. "When the markets are as volatile as they are now, individual investors should sit on the sidelines," advises Bob Martel, president of Financial Planning & Management in Lexington, Massachusetts. Then, when the economic outlook gets clearer and makes you feel comfortable about jumping in, you will have the wherewithal to seize an enticing investment.

4.   Insure your family adequately

Nobody likes paying for insurance, but few people can do without some. There are, after all, some types of emergencies that you *can* insure against. The key is to cover only financial losses so large that you could not cope with them and remain financially fit. Nothing more, nothing less.

If you can afford to repair a $500 fender bender, for example, you don't need insurance for it. By raising the deductible (the amount you pay from your own pocket before the policy kicks in) from $100 to $500 on a collision policy, you knock about 35 percent of the dent out of your annual premium. In the same spirit, don't waste money insuring personal belongings that you can afford to replace. Avoid narrowly defined policies such as those limited to cancer or airplane crashes. They aren't worth the cost.

You don't want to skimp on life insurance. But remember that children and others with no dependents don't need it. To gauge how much a policy should provide, you need to estimate your family's living expenses if you were to die and how much income they would have without you. The difference is the amount of coverage you should carry. Consider renewable term insurance. It lacks the cash buildup of whole and universal life policies, but it usually provides coverage at a far more affordable cost.

One insurable hazard that many Americans neglect is loss of salary because of sickness or injury. Disability insurance can cover that risk. "If you have very limited money for insurance, spend it on disability before you spend it on life," advises David Kennedy, author of *Insurance: What Do You Need? How Much Is Enough?*[1] He explains: "The chances are much greater that you will be totally disabled for several months before you turn 65 than that you will die before that age."

Don't count on Social Security disability benefits to carry you through. To qualify, you must not be able to do *any* kind of work. Group and private disability policies may have the same restriction, warns Katherine Sandberg, president of her own financial planning firm in Houston. The best individual policies pay if your disability prevents you from pursuing your own occupation.

Disability coverage should replace 60 percent to 70 percent of your gross income for as many months or years as you are out of commission. Only about one in five people in group plans gets this much protection. To keep an individual policy affordable, increase the period you must wait before the insurance company will start sending monthly checks. You can usually hold out until your sick pay stops and, beyond that, until you exhaust the emergency funds that you tucked away for just such a pinch.

Finally, shop around. "Most of us are sold insurance. We don't buy it," says Kennedy. For a quick review of the basics, read the thirteen-page *Buyer's Guide to Insurance.*[2]

5.   Buy a house if you haven't already

Close your eyes and picture the American Dream. Smack-dab in the middle of it is probably a house. For most people a home is far more than an investment. But you can take comfort from knowing that in the long run your house may well be one of the best investments you will ever make. Since 1968, the median price of single-family houses has gone up more than 300 percent, according to the National Association of Realtors.

You should not expect property values to blast off like that again anytime soon. For 1988, for example, many real estate analysts expect single-family homes to appreciate little more than 6 percent to 7 percent unless something happens to rekindle inflation fears. Furthermore, if consumer retrenchment reduces the demand for housing, driving down prices, buyers who have been priced out of the market in recent years may soon find a window of opportunity at least briefly thrown open to them.

Home ownership also yields one of the few juicy tax breaks that survived reform. Mortgage interest payments on first and second homes remain fully deductible—a welcome relief from even today's lowered income tax rates, which, in any case, are hardly guaranteed to stay down.

In defense against a possible recession, don't commit more current income than is absolutely necessary to mortgage payments. Give preference, for example, to a good old 30-year fixed-rate mortgage over a 15-year loan. Says Katherine Sandberg: "Although your interest cost is higher, the lower mortgage payments—which can never rise—put less pressure on your cash flow." For example, borrowing $60,000 at 11 percent for thirty years requires monthly payments of $571, compared with $682 on a 15-year loan. If you think you might be able to pay down the principal in less than 30 years, look for a lender who won't charge prepayment penalties, Sandberg says. "Then, when you can afford it, make a principal-only payment on top of your regular payment."

6.   Take advantage of tax-deferred savings plans

If your employer offers a 401(k) retirement savings plan, grab it. Often he will match every dollar that you contribute with 25¢ or more of his own—a gift you should not pass up. No taxes are due on what either of you kicks in or on investment earnings until you start tapping your account for retirement income.

Individual Retirement Accounts (IRAs) don't do half as much for you. The reasons: In a 401(k) you can put away as much as $7,000 a year versus an IRA's $2,000. Further, IRA contributions are not deductible any longer if you or your spouse is eligible for a pension plan and your salaries exceed prescribed limits. Under current tax law, for single filers deductions start phasing out at earnings of $25,000 a year and disappear at $35,000. For joint filers the phaseout occurs between $40,000 and $50,000.

But both savings plans offer one big boon: tax-deferred growth. Sheltering your investment from the tax man allows earnings to compound uninhibited. Consider this: If you put $2,000 a year in an IRA and it earns eight percent annually, in 15 years you would have $54,300. Put the same $2,000 a year in a taxable account and in 15 years it would grow, net of taxes, at 28 percent, to only $45,700. Contribute for 35 years, and you would have $344,600 in the IRA but only $211,800 in the taxed account.

Do not, however, commit money to an IRA or 401(k) that you may need before the year you turn 59½. Until then, you must pay a hefty 10 percent penalty plus income tax on any withdrawal. IRAs have another drawback for people whose contributions are taxable: All withdrawals will be partially taxed according to how much of your contributions were deductible (those made under the old tax law) and how much were not (those made under the new law). "The paperwork of trying to keep track of which contributions were and were not deductible is a headache," says Steven Enright.

7.   Figure out how much risk you can stand

The late, lamented bull market lulled tyros and experienced investors alike into an ever-upward mentality. One lesson to be learned from Black Monday (October 19, 1987, when the stock market took a nose dive) and its aftermath is to evaluate your risk tolerance frankly and not abandon your native caution. "People forgot their goals during the run-up in the stock market," says Elliot Raphaelson, a vice president at Chase Manhattan Bank and an instructor in personal finance at the New School for Social Research in New York City.

Before you sink money into any investment, consider whether you could live with the worst-case scenario. If one of your goals is short term, such as sending a child to college soon, you cannot take the chance that stocks in a depressed market won't pan out by then. But if your goal is farther away, such as early retirement in twenty years, you have the time to withstand the fluctuations of a volatile investment like stocks.

Once you know what kind of investor you want to be, stick to your style. "Decide whether you are a short-term trader or a medium- to long-term investor, and don't switch boats in midstream," says Henry Montgomery, an investment adviser at Planners Financial Services in Minneapolis. Likewise, don't take on more risk than you really need. If safe intermediate Treasuries yielding 8 percent will get you to your goal, say "no" to junk bonds yielding 12 percent.

8.   Diversify your investments within markets

Betting all your money on one stock that looks like the next IBM could bring stellar returns, but it could just as easily wipe out most of your capital. The stock market is risky enough as it is. By investing in only one or two stocks, you take a much higher risk: that the company behind your shares will do poorly. Buying stocks in several different companies and industries saves you from resting your fate on the fortunes of a single enterprise or sector. It is the classic diversification strategy.

How widely to diversity depends, again, on your tolerance for risk. Investors with strong convictions and even stronger nerves may live comfortably with a three-stock portfolio. Investment advisers insist, however, that you need ten to twenty stocks, in almost as many industries, for a solid portfolio. Similarly, cautious investors should not concentrate all their money on one type of real estate investment or in high-risk bonds. (For more on bond diversification, see Step 10.)

Selecting and monitoring a dozen or so stocks, or an array of bonds or real estate holdings, demands the kind of attention to business developments that few investors can muster. If you haven't the time or inclination to manage a diversified portfolio, consider buying shares in a mutual fund or real estate investment trust. Fund and REIT managers do the job for you, usually at an annual cost of 0.5 percent to 2 percent of your share holdings.

9.   Allocate your assets broadly

Diversifying within one market does little to cushion investment hazards when the market falls apart, as any investor heavily loaded with stocks learned from the October 1987 debacle. "You need different types of investments, not just different forms of the same investment," says Elliot Raphaelson.

Investors who had their capital divided among stocks, bonds, real estate, precious metals, and cash before Black Monday are now wearing a dirty little grin: they know the joys of asset allocation. When stocks took a dive, bonds rallied. Gold held firm and later took off, edging toward $500 an ounce in December, from $465 or so in early October.

Marilyn Capelli, president of Forest Financial Advisers in the Chicago suburb of Naperville, Illinois, explains: "In your twenties, you have time to ride out short-term fluctuations and wait for equities to grow." Even then, however, she would temper the risk of stocks with heavy cash holdings, because "when you are young, you often have unpredictable expenses such as job changes or children."

As people near retirement age, Capelli would have them emphasize fixed-income investments, such as bonds and certificates of deposit, to help replace salary with investment income. That by no means rules out stocks. "It is realistic to expect that you will have twenty-five years of healthy retirement, so you have to keep some of your money growing," she says.

Ready-made asset allocation of a sort can be had through certain types of mutual funds. Balanced funds, for example, typically maintain proportions of 60 percent stocks to 40 percent bonds in their portfolios. As a group, balanced funds fell 8.6 percent from October 16 to October 22, 1987, compared with 16.6 percent for the funds holding mainly stocks.

10. Stagger your bond and CD maturities

A third type of diversification reduces your portfolio's sensitivity to interest-rate swings. When rates rise, the value of existing bonds falls, while owners of certificates of deposit get stuck with below-market yields. Whether to commit money to these investments for several years or only a few months hinges on whose interest-rate forecast you believe. As a defensive investor, you can decide not to decide who is right. Instead, spread your investments over several maturities. Then if rates go up, you can reinvest your principal at higher rates as your short-term bonds mature, partly offsetting the longer-term bonds' drag on your total return.

Katherine Sandberg advises clients to invest in maturities from one to ten years. "There is no reason to go out beyond ten years," she says. "The extra yield does not make up for the risk that rates will rise substantially." Since 1977, according to a study by Back Bay Advisers in Boston, bond maturities of one to ten years have returned on average 10.6 percent, compared with 9.7 percent from longer-term bonds.

11.   Use dollar-cost averaging when you invest

Timing is all, but trying to time the stock market with any precision is like training a plant to grow away from the sun. Too many investors get swept into panic selling when prices are down and into panic buying when prices are up. A levelheaded alternative is a long-term defensive strategy known as dollar-cost averaging. If you follow it, you won't become the next Wall Street hero on ABC's *Nightline*, but you may well achieve celebrity in your own household.

To dollar-cost average, you invest a set amount at regular intervals, say $100 every three months. You buy fewer shares when prices are high than when they are low. Thus over time you are likely to pay less than the average price per share and to be in position to sell at a decent profit.

Dollar-cost averaging obviously won't work if you choose an investment that falls ill and never recovers. To reduce this risk, pick a diversified mutual fund rather than a single stock. If you do buy a stock, consider one of the many blue-chip companies that let you buy shares at no fee through a dividend-reinvestment plan.

Buying stocks this way is a drag when prices are rising steadily but pays off when the market is volatile. "Cost averaging works best over a five-to-ten-year period," says Alexandra Armstrong.

12.   Keep your family informed

Take the time to call the adults in your family to annual meetings, at which all the crucial facts about your household's finances are put on the table. If those facts reside in only one person's head, they are in an unsafe place.

As often as not, members of the family are unprepared when a breadwinner falls ill or dies, leaving others to guess at what assets there are, where to find them, how to manage income and expenses, whom to trust for advice, even where to find financial records. Sharing your knowledge will prevent the problems faced by Deborah Bain, 36, a recently widowed Alaskan. "I am sorry to say that I never took my husband's advice to get a handle on our investment and financial situation," she said in a letter to *MONEY*. "I assumed there would be time in the future to do that. Now I find myself with a substantial amount of money but without the savvy to know what to do with it."

Keeping yourself and your family current on the household's financial position involves more than just preparing for the worst.

"The state of your finances will change as you parade through life, not only because of the economy and stock market but also because of life events such as a newborn child or a job promotion," says George Barbee, executive director of the Consumer Financial Institute in Waltham, Massachusetts, a division of Price Waterhouse. No sensible chairman of the board keeps company finances a secret. Neither should the chairman of the kitchen table.

1. HP Books, $9.95.
2. Published by and available from the National Insurance Consumer Organization, 121 N. Payne Street, Alexandria, VA 22314. $2 plus a stamped, self-addressed envelope.

13

SOCIAL SECURITY: SPECIAL REPORT

American Association of Retired Persons

Social Security: Myths

Having weathered a severe financial crisis in 1983, Social Security today is strong and growing stronger. But, as always, the program is subject to political pressures that give rise to misunderstandings about its health and status. Facts can help deflate the myths.

Myth Social Security once again is moving toward bankruptcy.

Fact Social Security is *not* going bankrupt. Social Security should not be viewed on just a year-to-year basis. Its financial commitments are based on lifetimes—the lifetimes of workers and beneficiaries. According to the Social Security actuaries, the program will be able to pay benefits at least through the middle of the next century.

One indication of the program's health is that it's starting to amass sizable reserves to help pay for the benefits of baby boomers who will start retiring in the next century. The reserves are projected to be enormous by 2020, at which time they are expected to start decreasing. If the reserves begin to decline more rapidly than expected, we would be able to identify this or, for that matter, any other potential problem *and* its impact through the 75-year projections that are made each year by program actuaries. In short, we will have plenty of time to fix any difficulties that may arise.

Reprinted with permission from the *AARP News Bulletin*, Vol. 29, No. 5, May 1988. Copyright 1988 by the American Association of Retired Persons.

Myth   Social Security contributes to the deficit.

Fact   With Social Security currently taking in more revenue than it's paying out in benefits, the program certainly is *not* contributing to the deficit. In fact, Social Security currently is building a huge long-term reserve.

The buildup is an outgrowth of the 1983 Social Security amendments enacted by Congress to put the system on a sound financial basis and help provide for the needs of future retirees. The amendments called for separating the three Social Security trust funds from the rest of the federal budget. Nevertheless, under the Gramm-Rudman-Hollings (GRH) budget-balancing law, passed in 1985, the annual Social Security surplus is counted each year in the calculation of the federal deficit. This inclusion of Social Security annual surpluses masks the real deficit by making it appear smaller than it actually is.

In fiscal 1988 Social Security's receipts will exceed benefits by approximately *$37 billion*, and thus Social Security will make the 1988 federal deficit appear to be $37 billion smaller than it actually is. Yet, there has been no change in the law to use these reserves for meeting the government's imbalance in other areas. Thus the contribution of the reserves to the deficit is only a hypothetical one.

Myth   COLAs exacerbate the deficit.

Fact   The annual cost-of-living adjustments (COLAs) are paid out of revenues raised for the trust funds, not general revenues, and thus money saved by a COLA cut only increases the size of the trust funds. Larger trust funds simply mask more of the federal deficit.

Myth   COLAs could be frozen without hurting the elderly.

Fact   COLAs are the only protection most older and disabled individuals have against inflation. A COLA freeze would erode the purchasing power of these persons and push thousands of those heavily dependent on Social Security into poverty and keep them there, by permanently reducing the base on which future increases are made.

The basic facts

The concept hasn't changed since 1935, but Social Security is not a static program. Provisions change periodically, however, in response to both political and economic pressures. Here are some basic facts about Social Security as it is today:

- Beginning on January 1, 1988, the *average monthly benefit* for a single retired worker rose to $513. For a worker and spouse, the average benefit is $876. An elderly widow living alone on average draws about $468 a month; a young widow with children averages $1,077. Since 1975, benefits have been indexed automatically for inflation.

- Social Security, because of its social insurance nature, has a weighted benefit formula. That means individuals at the lower end of the income scale receive a higher percentage of their contributions back in benefits than do high income earners. Social Security's *replacement rates*—i.e., the percentage of preretirement income that benefits replace—will hold relatively steady. An average-income worker who retires at age 65 in 1988 can expect to get 41.8 percent of his or her 1987 wages. A high-income worker will receive only 23 percent of his or her 1987 wages, but a worker at the minimum wage will receive 71 percent. Generally speaking, the lower one's lifetime wage history, the higher the replacement rate.

- Amendments approved by Congress in 1983 will raise the *retirement age* gradually for those retiring in the next century. The increase will come in two-month increments, beginning with people born in 1938. For those born between 1943 and 1954, the retirement age will be 66. It then goes up gradually again; those born in 1960 and after will get full benefits at age 67. When the changes are fully phased in, workers will still be eligible for benefits at age 62 but at a lower rate (70 percent vs. 80 percent) than today.

How Social Security works

From the beginning, Social Security has been a system of social insurance—so named because it seeks to achieve a number of social goals as well as to protect individuals against certain risks. Eligibility is earned through payment of a payroll tax on employees called FICA (for federal insurance contributions act). Employers contribute equal amounts.

Workers who pay their FICA tax (and at least nine out of ten of all workers pay it) earn more than eligibility for a single program. Social Security is, in fact, three separate programs, each financed by a separate trust fund. Revenues for the trust funds stem primarily from those FICA taxes.

In 1988, employees and employers each will pay 7.51 percent of the worker's wages up to $45,000 of earnings. The tax breaks down this way: 5.53 percent for old age and survivors insurance (OASI), 0.53 percent for disability insurance (DI), and 1.45 percent for hospital insurance, better known as Medicare Part A. (Medicare Part B, primarily for physician's insurance, is voluntary and is financed out of general revenues and premiums paid by beneficiaries.)

The payroll tax is by no means the only source of revenues for the trust funds. Other sources include payments from the self-employed (who pay a higher rate that covers both the employee and employer contributions); interest earned on invested Social Security reserves; and, since 1983, taxes on benefits received by higher-income retirees (starting at income levels of $25,000 for individuals, $32,000 for couples).

Thanks largely to changes enacted by Congress in 1983, the old age and disability trust funds are on solid financial ground. (Medicare's position is somewhat shakier, in large part because of the increases in health costs.)

Currently the balance in the OASDI trust funds is in excess of $67 billion; by the beginning of the year 2000, reserves are scheduled to increase to more than $1 trillion, to help meet the needs of the large influx of baby boomers who will begin retiring around 2010. One more payroll tax hike is scheduled, to 7.65 percent in 1990, to build the trust funds to the levels projected in 1983. Although some further adjustments may be necessary later, the funds are secure for many years.

Social Security now serves two purposes: Most revenues go to current beneficiaries, while the remainder are held in reserve for the huge baby boom population expected to retire in the next century. By law, the funds in reserve must be invested in interest-bearing government securities. The government has use of those borrowed funds but is obligated to repay them, just as it is for treasury notes or bonds bought by private citizens.

And because the trust funds are earmarked exclusively to pay benefits to current and future retirees and disabled workers, they are technically "off budget"—except for purposes of calculating the U.S. deficit. In reality, they neither contribute to the deficit nor offer an avenue for easing it.

Yet, a paradox remains: By law, not a penny of the trust funds can be used directly to pay for expenditures elsewhere in the budget. Despite that reality, the budget-cutters will keep their eyes on the program, and especially on the COLA and on further taxing of benefits. Should they prevail, they would do no more than generate more revenues for the trust funds. More money in the trust funds makes the federal deficit seem smaller than it really is but does nothing to resolve the deficit crisis facing the nation.

System protects entire family   Much has been made of the "intergenerational conflict" surrounding Social Security. The gains made by older Americans, this theory goes, have been at the expense of today's youth. But the plain truth is that Social Security is a "social insurance" program that provides a package of protections to workers and their families, bridging the gap between generations.

Consider these facts: Of the 38 million people who receive monthly benefits, 61 percent are retired workers. Of the rest, 7 percent are disabled workers—many of them not yet in their 60s—and 32 percent are the families of retired, disabled, or deceased workers—including 3.3 million children—who draw monthly benefits when their regular source of income stops.

Measured another way, $80 billion of the $220 billion in benefits paid out by Social Security last year went to other than retirees.

Among those eligible for survivors or disability benefits are:

- The widows and widowers of deceased workers, and the spouses of disabled workers of any age who are caring for a child age 16 or younger or for a disabled child who is also receiving benefits
- Widows and widowers age 65 for full benefits, age 60 for reduced benefits; for the disabled in this category, benefits are payable at age 50. Survivors are also eligible for a one-time lump-sum death benefit.
- Unmarried children up to age 18 (or up to age 19 if they are still full-time high school students)
- Adult children age 18 or older who were severely disabled before they turned 22 and who remain disabled.

Under certain circumstances, children may also qualify for Social Security benefits based on the earnings of a grandparent or greatgrandparent.

In addition, workers who become disabled and have enough credits (quarters of coverage)—the number needed depends on the age at which the disability occurred—can quality for monthly benefits. Families of disabled workers who qualify need no credits of their own.

Resources

One of the best sources of information about Social Security is the Social Security Administration (SSA) itself. The agency publishes a variety of booklets and brochures. To order a publications list, write to SSA's Office of Public Inquiries, 6401 Security Blvd., Rm. 4100 Annex Bldg., Health and Human Services Department, Baltimore, MD 21235.

The Employee Benefit Research Institute (EBRI) also has a variety of publications on health and retirement issues. One in particular that devotes several chapters to Social Security and planning for retirement is *Fundamentals of Employee Benefit Programs* (EBRI-ERE, 1987; $15.00 paperback, $28 hardbound.) Orders must be prepaid and sent to EBRI, 2121 K St., NW, Washington, DC 20037-2121.

A pamphlet on Social Security and the budget is available for $1.00, with a stamped, self-addressed envelope, from Save Our Security (SOS), 1201 16th St., NW, Suite 222, Washington, DC 20036.

For a more in-depth discussion of the system, consider *Social Security: The System That Works*, by Merton C. Bernstein and Joan Brodshaug Bernstein (Basic Books Inc., 1988; $21.95). Another good book: *What You Must Know About Social Security & Medicare* by Eric R. Kingson (Pharos Books, 1988; $4.95).

Address questions about pending bills to Subcommittee on Social Security, House Ways and Means Committee, Room B-316, Rayburn Bldg., Washington, DC 20515-6353 or Senate Finance Committee, Room 205, Dirksen Bldg., Washington, DC 20510-6200.

Also, by making the elderly more economically independent, Social Security removes an enormous burden from children who might otherwise have to take more care of their parents. "By so doing," says one economist, "it helps create a broader sense of the country as a community."

A disincentive to stay on the job   Workers past traditional retirement age pay a price. Under the rules, they are subject to an "earnings limit," and their monthly benefits are reduced—$1 for every $2 earned—if their income from a job or self-employment exceeds the limits prescribed by law. Currently the limits are $8,400 for those 65 through 69 and $6,120 for those under 65. People 70 or older are exempt.

Those who support the earnings limit say that doing away with it would amount to a windfall for upper-income professionals who have chosen to keep working. Opponents argue that the test is a disincentive to work and that it adversely affects middle-income workers—especially women. They are seeking its repeal or substantial change.

Congress has already acted to increase incentives to work.

First, it changed the law so that starting in 1990, benefits reduction will drop to $1 for every $3 earned. Congress also approved a more generous formula for computing "delayed retirement credits," so that over a lifetime, beneficiaries between age 65 and 69 will get the same dollar value regardless of the age at which they retire. This more generous formula, scheduled to be phased in between 1990 and 2009, will remove a disincentive to remaining in the work force for those 65 through 69.

How to use Social Security

Although most workers are eligible to receive Social Security benefits, there are certain steps that must be taken to get the process started.

The Social Security Administration (SSA) advises getting in touch with one of its offices if (1) you are 62 or older and plan to retire or are within three months of turning 65, even if you don't plan to retire; (2) you are unable to work because of an injury or illness expected to last a year or longer; or (3) a worker in your family dies.

Visit or write before you reach 65, not only to find out about retirement benefits but also about Medicare, which is available whether you retire or not. People who plan to retire before 65 should apply no later than the last day of the month they want benefits to begin, although it's advisable to apply at least three to six months before you want benefits to start. If you apply after you turn 65, you can get back payments for up to six months before the month you apply for retirement or survivor's benefits.

You will need (1) your Social Security card or record of the number; (2) proof of age; (3) a marriage certificate if applying for spouse's or widow/widower benefits; (4) your W-2 form for last year's federal income tax return. If you are applying for disability, also have the names, addresses, and phone numbers of the doctors and hospitals that treated you. To receive widow/widower benefits, you will need certification of your spouse's death.

To make sure your wages have been properly credited, check your earnings record. Call or visit your local Social Security office and fill out the form SSA personnel specify; in return, SSA will send you a copy of your earnings record. It will not, however, give you a breakdown of wages from particular employers. To get that, you will have to pay for an itemized listing.

You earn one credit (quarter of coverage) for every three months worked per year. People who turn 62 in 1988 will need 9¼ years, or 37 quarters to qualify for benefits; in 1991, the requirement will be 10 years, or 40 quarters.

If you stopped working before you earned enough quarters, you are not eligible for benefits. But the credits stay on your record; you can add to them by resuming work. Having enough credits means only that you are eligible to get checks.

Anyone who is not satisfied with a decision made on a claim has the right to appeal. The first step is through the SSA itself. Next is a hearing before an administrative law judge; then, a review by the Appeals Council; and finally, review by the federal court system. There is no charge for any of the appeals before SSA, although people who engage legal advice may have to pay the attorneys' fees. AARP experts advise anyone who appeals to maintain a record of all correspondence with the SSA, since deadlines are tight and missing one may jeopardize the case.

Since the minimum Social Security benefit payment was eliminated in 1981, older persons with extremely low income need to rely on assistance that is provided through the Supplemental Security Income (SSI) program. SSI is an income assistance program for poor persons who are aged, blind, or disabled and who meet strict income and asset criteria. Many poor older persons receive both SSI and Social Security benefits. Your local SSI office can tell you what documents are needed to determine eligibility for SSI.

There are more than 1,300 SSA offices across the country. For more information about the rules and your rights, contact any SSA office. To find the address of the nearest office, look in the phone directory under "Social Security Administration" or "U.S. Government."

Will there be Social Security for baby boomers?

Baby boomers are going to be in for a pleasant surprise. Despite predictions of doom, Social Security is on a sound financial footing through the middle of the next century, and it will still buy more comprehensive coverage than anything today's workers could afford on their own.

The big worry among the younger generation of workers since the 1983 Social Security "crisis" was that the program would not "be there" when the influx of 76.4 million boomers—the generation that began in 1946 and ended in 1964—began to reach retirement age.

In the 1983 reform package, Congress essentially fixed the

program, guaranteeing huge reserves that are projected to swell to $12 trillion by 2020, (about $2 trillion in today's dollars). They are expected to help ease the benefit burden at least through 2030, when the first wave of boomers is well into the system. Economic vagaries prevent precise predictions much beyond that, but it is a virtual certainty that lawmakers will step in once again if it seems that the system is running into trouble.

The other big baby boomer concern was getting one's "money's worth." It's true that today's workers are paying a historically high 7.51 percent of their earnings into Social Security—considerably more than the 1 percent their parents were putting in in the 1940s—and on a higher base of earnings ($3,000 in 1947 vs. $45,000).

It's also true that on a strict dollar-for-dollar basis, younger workers will get less back than their forebearers. According to Social Security scholars Merton and Joan Bernstein, a married couple retiring at age 65 in 1985, for example, could expect cash benefits worth about 3.5 times the amount they and their employer put in (plus interest); the same couple retiring in 2025 would get only about 1.75 times the original investment. To a large degree, the change simply reflects the maturing of the Social Security system.

But, advocates of the system say, younger workers will still get a good deal. As AARP Executive Director Horace Deets observes, Social Security is more than a retirement package. It is also insurance against a disabling illness or injury that can strike workers of any age, a life insurance plan for widows and children, and insurance against burdensome hospital costs. Plus, with the automatic COLA, there is built-in protection against inflation. As a package, such insurance simply isn't available in the private sector, authorities point out.

Some critics, however, insist that even average-income younger workers could buy comparable retirement coverage (IRAs or other type of pension) in the private sector for less than the maximum combined employee-employer tax (currently, more than $6,700 a year) and get better returns over their lifetimes, even with a real rate of return as low as 4 percent.

But, says AARP's John Rother, only the very wealthy could do that, and, human nature being what it is, many of them would not. People who did not invest so wisely or were not so lucky would not do well and would eventually become a pubic responsibility, supported by higher taxes. "Social Security is the best expression of community that we have as a country," he says.

14

MAKING THE MOST OF YOUR PENSION PLAN

Gene Swearingen and
Margot L. Tripi

Rarely these days do people begin planning early for retirement. Life is different now—many of us live far from our extended families, our mortgages spread to huge portions of our take-home pay, grocery bills soar. We're on our own more. There are more pressures on our spendable income, and retirement planning isn't always a priority.

Besides, we have our pension plans to take care of us. Pension benefits can and often do form the core of our retirement income. However, these benefits alone are not always enough for us to live on comfortably and do all the things we dream of doing when we retire, when we finally have the leisure time we have worked for all our lives. These benefits must be supplemented.

But how do we begin retirement savings early enough when there are so many other demands on our income? Many of us have pension plans in which opportunities abound for saving additional money. Local government employees are fortunate to have several types of tax-deferred plans at their disposal, which allow the opportunity to save money and build retirement income in relatively painless ways.

The fact is that many public employees, when given a choice, choose not to invest the salary contribution required to activate their employer's matching contribution to their pension plan; they work for many years without building pension benefits. Furthermore, all state and local government employees are eligible for special supplemental plans such as Section 457 deferred compensation plans but often do not investigate whether such a plan is available under their current employer. Even when these plans are available, most employees do not take advantage of them. Only about 15 percent of eligible employees participate in deferred compensation plans.

The reason for such low participation is that most of us do not begin saving for retirement until late in our careers. Many of us balk at tying up portions of our income in retirement accounts when retirement is far off on the horizon. Many of us simply do not realize the growth potential of small contributions to a voluntary, tax-deferred plan if those contributions are made early and have years to grow.

This article explores the many reasons for taking full advantage of your public employer's pension plan and describes two of the most popular plans available to local governments.

Tax deferral: How it works

Taking full advantage of your pension plan package, even with small payroll contributions, can significantly increase your retirement income. Suppose you decide to save $10.00 a week toward retirement. You have the option of placing the money in a regular savings account or in a deferred compensation plan. If we assume you are in a 25 percent tax bracket, you will have to pay $2.50 in taxes on that weekly savings, essentially leaving you only $7.50 to invest in a savings account. If you place that money in a deferred compensation account, you invest the full $10.00 now.

Now suppose that in both accounts you can earn an annual interest rate of 8 percent. In the savings account, you must pay taxes on the earnings, so that your net interest rate is reduced to 6 percent (still assuming you are in a 25 percent tax bracket). In the deferred compensation account, earnings are also tax deferred, so you earn the full 8 percent. Over time, your accounts look like this:

	Savings account	Deferred compensation account
Weekly savings allowance	$10.00	$10.00
Taxes	2.50	—
Net investment	7.50	10.00

Interest rate	8%	8%
Tax rate	25%	—
Net interest rate	6%	8%
Account value after 10 years	7,123.27	7,960.16
Account value after 20 years	20,083.34	25,628.83
Account value after 30 years	43,662.83	64,846.92

If you translate your account value after 30 years to monthly benefits over the ensuing 15 years and pay taxes on the deferred benefits at the time you receive them, you still come out ahead with the deferred compensation account:

	Savings account	Deferred compensation account
Account value after 30 years	$43,662.83	$64,846.92
Monthly benefit, 15 years	366.62	615.61
Taxes (25% tax bracket)	—	−153.90
Net monthly benefit	366.62	461.71

These tables illustrate two things. First, in this example your monthly benefit, after all taxes are paid, is 25.9 percent higher in the deferred compensation account than in a regular savings account. The example assumes that you are in the same tax bracket before and after retirement, but most likely you will be in a lower tax bracket after retirement and therefore would receive an even higher net monthly benefit under the deferred compensation plan.

Start early   The second point demonstrated by the tables is that it pays to get an early start in taking advantage of a tax-deferred plan, even if you start small. The tables show that an investment of only $10.00 a week (approximately $43.00 a month) deposited for 30 years will grow to a benefit almost eleven times its size if invested in a deferred compensation account. This is significantly higher than if the investment is made for 10 or 20 years:

	30 years	20 years	10 years
Account value	$64,846.92	$25,628.83	$7,960.16
Monthly benefit, 15 years	615.61	243.30	75.57
Net monthly benefit after taxes	461.71	182.48	56.68
Growth of monthly investment	1,066%	421%	131%

The example shows that, even if you contribute only $10.00 a week throughout your career, your benefit after 30 years will make a significant difference in your retirement income. Realistically, however, if you start small, you will probably increase the periodic amount you save, which will greatly increase your benefit. For example, a $50.00 weekly contribution would yield a benefit five times the size of those shown above. And if your employer offers a matching contribution, your benefits are even greater.

Investment opportunities   Most employers' tax-deferred plans are handled by outside administrators and offer a wide range of investment options. During early career years when you may not otherwise have expendable income to invest in stocks, you have this opportunity, usually in supplemental plans such as the 457 plan to be described in a later section. The investment options typically include stock, bond, and fixed-rate funds, carefully designed to yield higher returns over the long term.

Again, the longer you have to invest, the more you can take advantage of the typically higher returns stock investments offer over longer periods of time. In addition, you usually have flexibility in choosing your investments and designing an investment mix that suits your needs.

Two types of plans available to public employees

There are a multitude of retirement or savings plans, but only two will be described here. The first, known as a 401(a) money purchase plan, is a primary pension plan available in both the private and the public sectors. The second, the Section 457 deferred compensation plan, is available *exclusively* to state and local government employees. These two plans, as offered by state and local government employers, take advantage of the employer's tax-exempt status. Employer and employee contributions under both plans may be fully tax deferred.

The following discussion is limited to the 401(a) and Section 457 plans because these two plans are the most useful and readily available to the great majority of local government employees.

The 401(a) money purchase plan   Used as an employer's primary pension plan, the money purchase plan requires an employer contribution on the employee's behalf. The employer may require you to make a contribution in order to receive the employer's match. The match may be any proportion of your contribution, up to and including 100 percent.

Both employer and employee contributions may be fully tax deferred. Some employer plans have a "voluntary" feature that allows you to invest after-tax dollars in the plan and still receive the advantage of tax-deferred earnings.

Some employers require that contributions be invested only at guaranteed rates. More commonly, only employer contributions are restricted, but employee contributions may be invested in other options offered through the plan.

Since the money purchase plan is considered a primary pension plan, participation in an Individual Retirement Account (IRA) may be curtailed if you (or your spouse) participate in a money purchase plan and your salary is above a certain level. You may still contribute to an IRA, but contributions may not be fully tax deductible.

Employer contributions may be subject to a vesting schedule; that is, you have full rights to them only after you have worked a specific number of years for that employer. Withdrawals are allowed upon termination of employment but may be subject to a 10 percent tax penalty if taken before age 59½. Or you can postpone benefits to a later date. You may also roll funds to another employer's qualified plan or to an IRA.

The 457 deferred compensation plan   The 457 plan is used most commonly as a supplement to the employer's primary pension plan. Participation is voluntary, and contributions can be started, stopped, and restarted at any time, usually without penalty. The contribution maximum is set by the Internal Revenue Code as 25 percent of salary, not to exceed $7,500 per year. Many plans have no minimum contribution. Some employers elect to make a contribution on behalf of employees. If there is a vesting schedule, it applies only to employer-made contributions.

Withdrawals may be made when you leave employment, or you may postpone receiving benefits until a later age (up to age 70). You have a great deal of flexibility in setting up a payment schedule. There is also a strictly defined unforeseeable-emergency withdrawal provision. Funds are portable but may be transferred only to another public employer's Section 457 plan.

The 457 plan is available only to state and local governments. It can be used in conjunction with a 401(a) money purchase plan or other primary pension plans. In addition, there are no contribution reductions if you also have an IRA.

Advantages of the 401(a) and 457 plans

One of the biggest advantages of the 401(a) and 457 plans is their portability. It is less likely nowadays for someone to spend an entire career with one employer. If pension benefits cannot be transferred from employer to employer, you run the risk of losing the growth potential of retirement benefits.

Both plans have provisions that allow you to carry your pension account with you to other public employers. The accounts can be combined with your new employer's plan, and you can continue contributing. The money purchase plan, in addition, can be rolled tax free into an IRA when you leave or change employers.

No pain, but still a gain   Another advantage of these retirement plans is the convenience of payroll deduction. You don't have to worry about physically depositing the money. You can ask your employer to deduct a percentage of your gross salary to a deferred compensation plan, so that the amount deducted increases automatically every time you receive a salary increase. Or you can elect to defer a portion of a salary increase.

In addition, the amount you defer may put you into a lower tax bracket. Because of this you will see immediate benefits in that your take-home pay is reduced by less than the amount you elect to save.

Defined contribution versus defined benefit Both of the plans just described are defined contribution plans. That is, the amount contributed by both employer and employee is defined contractually. You know at any given time how much your employer is investing on your behalf, and you know exactly how much you are contributing from your paycheck. Your monthly benefit at the time you begin withdrawing depends on what you've contributed to the account and how it has been invested.

There are other types of plans that have defined benefits rather than defined contributions. A formula, using the number of years of service and your average salary for the last years you worked for that employer, determines the benefit, but you cannot receive that benefit until retirement.

Defined benefit plans have the advantage of guaranteeing a certain level of income at retirement, but because defined contribution plans offer portability, they are more suited to mobile employees who do not spend their entire career with one employer. Moreover, with prudent investment planning, defined contribution plans often yield higher benefits at retirement than do defined benefit plans because of the potential for investment growth.

Other plans

Other plans available to local government employees include Individual Retirement Accounts (IRAs) and tax-sheltered annuities (TSAs). As noted earlier, IRAs may not be fully deductible if you or your spouse is covered by any primary pension plan and your income exceeds a certain level. Tax-sheltered annuities, or Section 403(b) plans, are generally available to employees of public schools and hospitals. They carry penalties similar to IRAs if money is withdrawn before age 59½. Another plan, the 401(k) plan, is no longer available as a new plan for local government employees. You may take advantage of a 401(k) plan only if you work for a municipality that has an established plan.

Watch out for fees

Although almost any tax-deferred savings plan has much to offer, the small investor should be aware of the fees charged to handle the plan. Most plans carry a percentage fee applied to the account balance. That fee can vary from 1 percent to 3 percent. In addition, there are often account-maintenance fees, set-up charges, transfer charges, or withdrawal penalties. These fees are sometimes difficult to determine without a careful reading of the plan information. These fees can have a significant impact on total return and should be considered when making an investment decision.

Conclusion

The 401(a) and Section 457 plans offer an unparalleled opportunity to increase your accessible income—through tax deferral—during your peak earning years. Those are also the years when your financial needs are likely to be the greatest for the education of your children and possibly for the support of elderly parents.

The 457 and 401(a) plans can be used in combination to provide a well-rounded pension plan. They offer the best benefit to you if you begin saving for retirement early. Start early in a tax-deferred plan, even if you start small, and your contributions, including money you would have paid in taxes, will have time to grow and yield healthy retirement benefits.

15

YOUR IRA: STILL A GOOD DEAL?

Consumer Reports

Editor's note: Local government employees who participate in a 457 deferred compensation plan may have up to 25 percent of their salary or $7,500, whichever is lower, deducted annually from their paycheck to reduce their W-2 salary. The lower reported wages may permit them to claim an IRA tax reduction. For example, a single person who earned $40,000 a year and contributed $7,000 to a 457 plan would report only $33,000 in salary, thus becoming eligible for a partial IRA deduction.

If your employer has set up a 457 plan, invest all you can in it before you contribute to a nondeductible IRA. Everything in that plan [like the 401(k) and the 403(b) plans]—contributions and earnings—remains untaxed until you withdraw it.

Until this year, the Individual Retirement Account, or IRA, was the tax shelter for people who didn't have tax shelters—and for a lot of people who did. With an IRA, you could put away up to $2,000 per year toward retirement and reduce your taxable income by the amount invested. The investment, and any earnings on the investment, remained untaxed until withdrawn. By then, presumably, you'd be in a lower tax bracket than you were when you set the money aside. By the end of 1986, some 20 to 40 million Americans had pumped $260 billion into IRAs.

The tax reforms that go into effect this year, however, change the rules. You can't automatically assume, as you could last year, that an IRA is the best place to put retirement savings.

The vanishing deduction

The new tax law places sharp restrictions on who may take an IRA deduction and on how large the deduction may be. As a result, an estimated 5 million current IRA participants will not be able to deduct any contribution for 1987 or thereafter, and many others will find themselves eligible for much less than the $2,000 deduction they've taken in the past.

The IRA remains just as it was last year only for those who are not covered by an employer-sponsored pension plan.

If you or your spouse is covered by a pension plan, you may still contribute as much to an IRA as in the past. But the amount of the contribution that's deductible depends on your income. Single people who earn $25,000 or less may still deduct up to $2,000 for an IRA, even if covered by a company pension plan. Married couples with joint income of $40,000 or less can take the full IRA deduction—up to $4,000 if both work and each earns at least $2,000.

Single people with an income above $35,000 may not deduct any IRA contribution. Married couples filing jointly lose the right to claim an IRA deduction when their joint income exceeds $50,000 a year, even if only one of the two is covered by a pension plan. (Nor can one of the couple claim an IRA deduction by filing separately, if the spouse's income exceeds $10,000.) So, while high-income people may contribute to an IRA, it will be a "nondeductible" IRA.

Taxpayers who earn less than those amounts may take partial IRA deductions. Generally, you may deduct $200 worth of IRA contribution for every $1,000 in income below the $35,000 and $50,000 ceilings.

Those income ceilings apply not to gross income but to "adjusted gross income." Adjusted gross income is the income shown on your tax return after excluding certain kinds of expenses—alimony and, for those who are self-employed or who have some self-employment income, any contribution made to a Keogh plan.

Say you're a divorced man with $40,000 in income and $7,000 in alimony payments. The alimony payments reduce your adjusted gross income to $33,000, making you eligible for an IRA deduction of up to $400.

But you can't use garden-variety deductions like the interest on a mortgage to get under the ceiling. Unlike "adjustments," which reduce "gross" income to "adjusted gross" income, the deductions taken on schedule A and certain other tax forms reduce "adjusted gross" income to "taxable" income.

You may also be able to lower your income by participating in a company-sponsored 401(k) plan or, if you work for a nonprofit organization, a 403(b) plan.

These increasingly popular plans, often called salary-reduction plans, are like glorified IRAs. With a 401(k) plan, you may earmark up to $7,000 a year of your annual salary to a retirement fund; with a 403(b) plan, you may set aside up to $9,500. The money is deducted from your paycheck and doesn't even appear on your W2 form. A single person who earned $40,000 a year and contributed $7,000 to a 401(k) plan would report only $33,000 in salary, thus becoming eligible to claim a partial IRA deduction.

Tax-deferred compounding

Interest, dividends, or capital gains earned inside an IRA will continue to compound untaxed until you make a withdrawal—and this is the sole remaining reason to contribute to an IRA when you can't deduct the contribution.

That tax break, however, will become less valuable as lower tax rates are phased in this year and next. Marginal tax rates (the rate on the last dollar of taxable income) last year ranged from 0 percent to 50 percent in fifteen steps, or brackets. Next year, there will be only three tax brackets—15 percent, 28 percent, and 33 percent. This year, 1987, is a transitional year with five brackets, from 11 percent to a top of 38.5 percent.

If a family had $40,000 in taxable income last year, part of that income fell into the 33 percent federal tax bracket. Starting this year, their highest tax bracket will be 28 percent. Last year, an IRA investment yielding 8 percent was, for that family, equal to a taxable investment earning 12 percent. This year, it's equal to a taxable yield of only 11.1 percent. For those in the top federal tax bracket, 8 percent tax free equaled 16 percent taxable; next year it will equal 12 percent taxable.

When you cash it in

Just about all the old rules pertaining to IRA withdrawals still hold. You may not withdraw IRA money before age 59½ without paying a 10 percent penalty in addition to the tax due, unless you're disabled. And you must begin making withdrawals soon after you turn 70½ (to be precise, by April 1 of the next calendar year).

But a nondeductible IRA is not quite as untouchable as the deductible IRA. Should you withdraw money early, both the 10 percent penalty and the tax due apply only to the earnings, which have not been taxed. Taxes and penalty do not apply to the non-deductible contribution, which was made with money that was taxed the year it was earned.

Say you start a nondeductible IRA this year, investing $2,000 a year at 8 percent. Five years from now, having accumulated $12,670, you decide to withdraw the money early. Since you have already paid tax on $10,000 ($2,000 a year for five years), that money is yours to do with as you please; the government cares only about the $2,670 that has accumulated tax free. You'd pay taxes on that amount, plus a penalty of $267 (10 percent of $2,670) for early withdrawal.

The same principle holds true for withdrawals after age 59½. Tax is due only on money not already taxed—the total of contributions previously deducted and of tax-deferred earnings. No tax is due on nondeductible contributions you may make from now on.

If you already have an IRA and intend to stick with it, keep a record of all nondeductible contributions. Only by so doing will you be able to calculate what part of your withdrawal is taxable.

Note that the new law doesn't allow you to delay taxes by withdrawing nontaxable funds before taxable funds; rather, you must prorate any withdrawal, designating the taxable and nontaxable portions. Say you will have made $4,000 in deductible contributions and $10,000 in nondeductible contributions, and that the account has earned $8,000. You have a total of $22,000, of which $12,000 (the deductible contributions plus the earnings) is taxable. The taxable amount comes to 55 percent of the total. If you withdraw $4,000, you owe taxes on 55 percent of it, or on $2,200. If it's an early withdrawal, the 10 percent penalty will be applied against $2,200, the untaxed portion.

If you already have an IRA, there's no bookkeeping advantage in opening a new IRA account for nondeductible contributions. You must still prorate taxable and nontaxable withdrawals based on all your IRA assets, whether they're in one account or spread over two or more.

Under the new tax law, there is one way you can make early withdrawals from any pension plan, including an IRA, without paying a penalty tax. At any age, you can begin a program of penalty-free annual withdrawals from an IRA by basing the number of withdrawals on your life expectancy (or the combined life expectancy of yourself and a beneficiary) and making withdrawals of equal amounts each year of the remaining life expectancy. The trustee of your IRA fund should be able to do the calculations for you. You can continue making contributions to the IRA even after starting such a withdrawal program.

Recommendations

Should you forget about IRAs if you are no longer eligible to make tax-deductible contributions? Maybe not. Table 1 compares a set of hypothetical investments of $2,000 a year for 10 years and for 20 years, made both inside a nondeductible IRA and outside the IRA. As the table shows, the tax-deferred-earnings feature means that a nondeductible IRA would grow into a larger fund than would the same investments made outside the IRA. That's because the taxes paid annually on investment earnings outside the IRA effectively lower the annual rate of return by reducing the amount of money working for you.

At the end of the investment periods shown, however, interest and dividends earned outside an IRA are all yours, while tax remains to be paid on the earnings accumulated inside the IRA. The table illustrates the impact of taxes due on the IRA fund at two of the three marginal tax rates in effect starting next year. The 28 percent rate would be the probable consequence of withdrawing all your IRA money in a single lump sum upon retirement rather than spreading withdrawals over several years or over your remaining anticipated lifespan. The higher rate might also result if you had substantial retirement income in addition to IRA withdrawals and Social Security payments. (It's also possible that a portion would be taxed at 33 percent, if the lump-sum withdrawal or additional income was very large.)

As the table shows, a nondeductible IRA eventually results in a bigger after-tax fund than the same investment outside an IRA. But over a fairly short time, such as ten years, the difference is small enough so that it may not offset the relative inaccessibility of the money in an IRA.

Any *deductible* IRA investment, however, remains far superior to the same investment outside the IRA.

If your employer has set up a 401(k) plan or, for nonprofit organizations, a 403(b) plan, invest all you can in it before you contribute to a nondeductible IRA. Everything in those plans—contributions and earnings—remains untaxed until you withdraw it.

Table 1. Invest inside or outside the new IRA?

Table 1 compares the result over two time periods—ten years and twenty years—of hypothetical investments made inside and outside a nondeductible IRA. Earnings of an investment outside an IRA are taxed each year, thus reducing the true yield. The taxes on earnings of an investment inside an IRA are deferred until you withdraw funds from the IRA.

1. Annual investment We assume a $2,000 annual investment in each vehicle made at the start of each year. We did not subtract any sales commissions or loads. In almost all cases, you can invest for retirement without such charges, either through a bank or through a no-load mutual fund.

2. Hypothetical annual yield Yields toward the high end shown are what you might aim for with relatively risky investments, such as mutual funds invested in stocks or corporate bonds. Yields toward the low end shown have been typical of more conservative investments, such as money-market funds, certificates of deposit, and mutual funds invested in Treasury bonds and notes. The yields shown for investments outside an IRA are the net after a 28 percent tax, since you pay tax annually on the earnings.

3. Accumulation We assume reinvestment of all earnings. For investments inside the nondeductible IRA, the part of this sum that represents earnings on investment is subject to taxation on withdrawal. The remaining portion, the sum of the annual investments, represents after-tax dollars and is not subject to taxation on withdrawal.

4. After-tax value Based on 1988 rates for a married couple filing jointly. The 15 percent rate might apply to withdrawals made in installments; the 28 percent rate might apply to lump-sum withdrawals and to periodic withdrawals made in years with substantial other income. This figure does not include the effect of any state and local income taxes that may be due on withdrawal.

	1 Annual investment	2 Hypothetical annual yield (%)	3 Accumulation	4 After-tax value at 15% rate	4 After-tax value at 28% rate	3 Accumulation	4 After-tax value at 15% rate	4 After-tax value at 28% rate
Inside	$2,000	12	$39,309	$36,413	$33,902	$161,397	$143,187	$127,406
Outside	2,000	8.64 net	32,449	32,449	32,449	106,769	106,769	106,769
Inside	2,000	10	35,062	32,803	30,845	126,005	113,104	101,924
Outside	2,000	7.20 net	29,904	29,904	29,904	89,838	89,838	89,838
Inside	2,000	8	31,291	29,597	28,130	98,846	90,019	82,369
Outside	2,000	5.76 net	27,568	27,568	27,568	75,831	75,831	75,831
Inside	2,000	6	27,943	26,752	25,719	77,985	72,287	67,349
Outside	2,000	4.32 net	25,424	25,424	25,424	64,233	64,233	64,233
Inside	2,000	4	24,973	24,227	23,581	61,938	58,647	55,795
Outside	2,000	2.88 net	23,485	23,458	23,458	54,619	54,619	54,619

As with an IRA, you can withdraw funds at age 59½ or on retirement. (Early withdrawal brings on the same penalty as early withdrawal from an IRA.)

The new tax law gives all 401(k) participants two withdrawal

The municipal-bond alternative

One potential alternative to a nondeductible IRA is an investment in a no-load mutual fund that specializes in municipal bonds. After a minimum initial investment, typically $1,000, you can invest as much or as little as you like, each year. Most of the fund's earnings are tax free both as they accumulate and when they're withdrawn.

Although the price of shares fluctuates, you can sell your shares in the fund anytime without incurring a tax penalty or a penalty imposed by the fund.

However, the yield on tax-free municipal bonds is almost always lower than the yield of conservative taxable investments, such as a fund invested in Treasury bonds. In the past, low yields made municipals attractive mainly to those in a high tax bracket. For someone in the 50 percent federal bracket, a municipal-bond fund paying 6 percent equaled a taxable investment yielding 12 percent.

According to Lipper Analytical Services, municipal-bond funds yielded an average of 7.3 percent during the twelve-month period ending last October 31 [1987]. You'd have to find an investment yielding about 10.1 percent to equal that after a 28 percent tax on the yield. During the same period, funds that invested in Treasury securities yielded an average of 8.1 percent.

Do note, however, that the effect of compounding reduces the apparent advantage of municipal bonds. Over a twenty-year period, and assuming eventual tax at 28 percent, 7.3 percent tax-free equals about 8.7 percent tax-deferred. Note, too, that yields on both municipal bonds and Treasury bonds fluctuate with changes in interest rates generally, as does the relationship between yields. Small changes in that relationship can tip the balance one way or another. The workings of the marketplace generally impose a rough parity between tax-free and taxable government securities.

At recent yields, though, investments in tax-free municipal-bond funds looked better than many conservative taxable investments whose earnings were sheltered in an IRA.

State taxes might also weigh in favor of a municipal-bond investment. In high-tax states, some municipal-bond funds advertise themselves as free from state and local taxes as well as from federal taxes. Such taxes can add as much as 10 percentage points to the eventual tax burden of an IRA investment, even an IRA investment based on Treasury bonds. (While the yield of *individual* Treasury bonds is free of state and local taxes, dividends paid by a mutual fund that invests in Treasury bonds are subject to tax in many states, including New York.)

The annuity alternative

Some financial advice givers are touting annuities sold by life insurance companies as an alternative tax-sheltered investment for those who can no longer deduct their contributions to an IRA.

Annuities enjoy the same tax benefit as a nondeductible IRA. Earnings are not taxed as they're earned; instead, they are taxed when the money is withdrawn.

You may invest as much as you wish in the annuity each year—you are not limited to $2,000. But while you can usually find IRA investments that require no sales fees (no-load mutual funds, money-market accounts, certificates of deposit), insurance companies typically charge a 4 to 5 percent sales commission on all payments to an annuity. If you invest $2,000 in an annuity with a 5 percent commission, only $1,900 goes to work for you.

For early withdrawals—made before age 59½—the Internal Revenue Service levies a 10 percent penalty on annuities, just as on IRAs. And insurance companies also often extract so-called back-end surrender charges on withdrawals made before the annuity is six years old. These can run as high as 7 percent of the withdrawal. From that point, surrender charges tend to decline each year until they disappear completely after you've had the annuity for ten to twelve years.

You can direct the insurance company to invest your annuity in one or more of a variety of vehicles. Fixed-dollar-account annuities, in which the insurance company guarantees you a certain interest rate for one to five years, are usually invested in certificates of deposit and Treasury bills and bonds. Consequently, yields tend to follow money-market interest rates. But changes in interest rates tend to hit annuities later than they hit the underlying investments. Last August, when interest rates were falling and money-market funds were paying an average 6 percent annual yield, annuities were still paying an average 8.5 percent. When interest rates rise, however, money-market funds would probably provide a higher yield than annuities.

Annuities can also be invested in stocks and bonds. The insurance company does not guarantee the return of such investments. You may withdraw the money in your annuity in one lump sum or in installments, with a variety of withdrawal options.

In Consumers Union's view, an annuity is not an attractive alternative to a nondeductible IRA. Early withdrawals incur the same tax penalties as early IRA withdrawals, as well as potential surrender charges. Thus, annuity funds are even less accessible than money invested in an IRA. And the sales charge imposed by the insurance company means that less of your investment goes to work for you. While the guaranteed interest rate on some types of annuity investment may look attractive now when compared with interest rates generally, they may not compare favorably in the future.

options. They can take their distribution in a lump sum and pay taxes as if they had withdrawn the fund in equal installments over a five-year period, using the new tax rates. (Such "five-year forward averaging" reduces the number of dollars taxed at the highest rate.) Or they can roll over the fund into an IRA; the fund then comes under the IRA's withdrawal rules, which could be more advantageous.

People who were 50 or older at the beginning of 1986 have one additional option for lump-sum distributions of pension funds. They may use 10-year forward averaging rather than five-year forward averaging. But if they choose ten-year averaging, they must base tax payments on the rates in effect in 1986, not on the new rates.

If you have self-employment income, set up a Keogh plan. It has the same advantages as a deductible IRA and similar withdrawal rules. With some Keogh plans, you can invest up to 20 percent of your self-employment income or $30,000, whichever is less.

Some investment advisers have recently been suggesting annuities and municipal-bond funds as good alternatives to a nondeductible IRA, since the earnings of those investments are either tax deferred or tax free.

At recent rates, tax-free municipal-bond funds would provide a better return for people in high brackets than would similarly conservative taxable investments sheltered inside an IRA (see sidebar on municipal bonds). But annuities involve undesirable sales charges, tax penalties, and, often, redemption fees for early withdrawal.

16

LIFE INSURANCE—
SHOULD YOUR PROTECTION
DOUBLE AS AN INVESTMENT?

Diane Harris

Editor's note: Also see Chapter 18, "Insurance: Know What You Need Before the Agent Calls."

The next big investment your broker raves to you about may not be traded in the stock market. No, it isn't Ginnie Maes or zero coupons or even, exactly, mutual funds. Your broker's hot tip may be life insurance.

Yes, life insurance. Not since federal revenues torched the 3-for-1 write-off has any type of security been marketed this zestfully. Yes, security. Some of the new permutations of policies so closely resemble an account for trading stocks and bonds that you need a broker's license to sell them.

No longer is life insurance just a moral obligation, a staid old contract that provides your dependents with financial protection against your untimely death. Inspired by the crackdown on abusive limited partnerships and inflamed by tax reform, it is becoming an all-purpose financial instrument—a death benefit, a high-yield or even go-go investment, and a source of instant cash.

Packaged this way, life insurance looks almost irresistible, especially to the average Joe who never understood what even simpler policies were all about. Who among us cannot complain, along with Garry Houston-Garner, a Kansas City, Missouri, father of three, "Life insurance is like a foreign language to me." Houston-Garner is, of course, utterly conversant in his own field, real estate, and it's an unfortunate fact that too many equally sophisticated U.S. business people are paying too much for the wrong type of coverage.

No, the industry doesn't necessarily make it easy. Insurance that doubles as an investment comes under such generic names as whole life, variable life, universal life, flexible-premium variable life and single-premium life. The policy most heavily promoted by brokers is single premium, but in all forms the new insurance is getting a tremendous lift this year from the twin forces of a rousing stock market and a confusing tax code. Now that most other shelters have been either eliminated or sharply restricted, the multi-million-dollar insurance lobby's successful campaign to preserve the top breaks on insurance policies has made investing in them one of the few ways left to protect your stock market gains from immediate taxation.

To exploit the advantage, insurers and investment houses are joining forces. While in the past you might have found it odd to invest in mutual funds by buying a life insurance policy and odder still to buy that policy from your stockbroker, in the future such transactions are going to seem commonplace.

As you contend with the various insurance agents, new- and old-line, you will be the target of a barrage of persuasive but not always straight sales talk. You will hear, correctly, that current policies give you tremendous flexibility in the price you pay and the benefits you receive. But do not let the bells and whistles distract you from the risks of mixing family protection with the vagaries of the stock and bond markets. Heady advertising claims of high tax-free returns can lull you into buying a policy that leaves your dependents underinsured. Despite the investment wrapping in which policies are now advertised, you should not forget that making certain your survivors will not suffer financially after your death still remains the most compelling reason to buy life insurance.

Buying it unhitched from investments is still one of your options. You can get pure protection in a term policy, which pays off if you die but not if you live. Because you buy only protection against death, term insurance generally takes far less of a cash outlay than any policy that builds cash value. So term is still the coverage of choice for upwardly mobile young families.

Nevertheless, term policies have been losing sales in recent years to sexier plans, mainly universal life. In 1985, term policies accounted for 38 percent of all individual life insurance coverage sold, down from a peak of 60 percent just three years before, according to the Life Insurance Marketing and Research Association, a trade group.

Today the insurance industry is putting its marketing muscle and advertising dollars firmly behind policies that emphasize tax-sheltered investing first, high returns second, and insurance protection last. Consider this year's hottest insurance product: single-premium variable life. Single premium refers to the way you buy it —by paying one lump sum ranging from $5,000 to $1 million rather than smaller annual premiums. Variable is the name given to insurance that allows policyholders to dictate where their money will be invested among the several mutual funds managed exclusively for life insurance customers.

The most serious problem you face with investment-oriented insurance policies—and with single-premium life in particular—is that they could go swiftly the way of the limited-partnership tax shelter. Brokers and agents may not talk about it, but their Washington envoys are already on the defensive. Says Irwin Goldberg, an official of the Life Insurance Marketing and Research Association: "The industry is paranoid that Congress is readying an attack."

The move most feared is that Congress will take a machete to the basic idea that investment earnings should be allowed to pile up untaxed inside a life insurance policy—the very feature that gives insurance its new cachet as one of the last surviving sheltered investments. But most old Washington hands expect the industry to beat back any assault on this nearly sacred sanctuary of family security. "Never underestimate the power of the insurance lobby," advises James Hunt, a director of the National Insurance Consumer Organization, a public-interest group.

The more likely target, however, is policy loans on single-premium life. Under current law, this type of contract lets you borrow your investments earnings essentially tax free yet at little or no net cost. Instead, you are credited with enough earnings on the borrowed money to offset most and sometimes all of the interest on the loan. Specialists such as Chris Seaman, senior manager in the tax department of the Los Angeles office of Ernst & Whinney, believe that in the next two years or so Congress is likely to change the rules to treat such loans as taxable distributions, much the way early withdrawals on annuities are now taxed. If such a change occurs, unsuspecting policyholders could find themselves in the position that limited-partnership shareowners are in today—with their write-offs phasing out. A likely possibility is that outstanding loans on existing policies would remain exempt from taxation but that future loans would be taxed. Says Seaman: "The insurance industry has shown that it is adept at squeezing favorable transition rules out of Congress."

Assuming the industry successfully defends the tax-deferred growth of cash values, look for further proliferation of investment-oriented policies. To date, about forty of the nation's one hundred largest life insurance companies offer some kind of variable contract. By the end of the decade [1980s], however, insurance marketers predict that armies of variable life agents from major companies as well as upstarts will be ringing your doorbell and telephone, and that 50 percent of all the insurance sold will be the variable kind.

According to this not-so-futuristic view, you will hardly be able to tell an insurance agent from a mutual fund salesman. Already fund managers at Scudder Stevens & Clark tend portfolios for Charter National Life and Security Mutual Life, Value Life does so for Guardian Life, and Neuberger & Berman for Sentry Life. Moreover, Fidelity Investments, the colossus of the industry, has developed a fund for a single-premium variable life policy to be called Fidelity Future Reserves. The policy will be issued by Monarch Resources, the leading underwriter of single-premium contracts, and marketed by Fidelity. Other insurers, including National Home Life and Bankers Life of Nebraska, have expressed interest in using Fidelity funds for their variable life policies.

The primary sellers of single-premium variable life thus far have been stockbrokers, not insurance agents. This is a mixed blessing for buyers. Brokers, being more familiar with the investment aspect than with the insurance side of the deal, may be ill equipped to advise you whether the policy will adequately fill your family's highly personal insurance needs. Worse, they may not warn you that the policy loans being ballyhooed as a benefit will come out of your survivors' pockets if you die with a big balance due. In either case, that could aggravate the most common life insurance problem facing families: insufficient coverage.

The big push on investment-oriented insurance comes at a time when U.S. households would benefit most from professional guidance in buying policies primarily, if not exclusively, for survivor benefits. As the number of two-income and female-headed households grows, women are increasingly buying separate coverage. In 1975, men purchased twice as many life insurance policies as women. By 1985 the ratio had narrowed to 1.6 to 1. But the most pertinent demographic force in life insurance is the baby boomlet. The populous generation born between 1946 and 1964 has entered its prime child-rearing years, when insurance is most important. This generation now accounts for about half of all life insurance purchases, a percentage that will inevitably rise over the next decade. Variable-life marketers are especially eager to exploit the awesome buying power of this new contingent of two-career parents.

It adds up to this: Planning your insurance program, never a simple task, has become even more daunting. If you are tempted by the new insurance, listen to its main man, Jerome Golden, president of Monarch Resources. "A policy can no longer be viewed as a passive purchase that you put away in a drawer and forget about," he says. "You should look at it instead as a living, breathing document that requires periodic review, much as you would monitor your IRA, to make sure you are always getting the most for your money."

17

How to Retire on the House

Clint Willis

Editor's note: No matter what your income level, this article offers ways for you to tap the equity in your home to help finance your retirement.

Tom and Mary Stott are getting ready to sell their ten-room Cape Cod–style home of ten years and move into a six-room condominium. Their trade-down is not a reluctant retreat but part of a well-thought-out plan for a comfortable retirement. The Stotts, who both turn 65 this year, are asking $385,000 for their house in the Cape Cod community of Cummaquid. Of the proceeds, they will spend $190,000 on the condo, which overlooks a golf course in nearby Yarmouth Port. Another $35,000 will go for improvements to the condo, leaving them about $160,000 to invest in tax-exempt bonds.

   The housing swap, in fact, is what makes the difference between a tight retirement budget and the more easeful one the Stotts have mapped out. Tom, who called it quits four years ago as president of a Swedish shipbuilding firm's American subsidiary, estimates that lower property taxes, insurance premiums, and maintenance costs on the condo will help reduce the couple's annual expenses to about $40,000; they would be $47,000 or so if the

Stotts kept the house. His $300,000 Keogh account, which is invested in certificates of deposit, will supply income of about $18,000 a year, while Social Security payments will come to $14,000. The bonds will add about $12,800. "Our five kids will inherit the condo when we're gone," says Tom. "Meanwhile, we can entertain them in pleasant surroundings—just as we did in our old house."

Jimmy and Jacki Whitney also used their seven-room traditional brick house in Dallas as a centerpiece of their retirement plan. The couple sold the house last year for $148,000. They used part of the proceeds to pay off their $76,000 mortgage, put down $5,000 on a new Lincoln Town Car, and moved to Oklahoma City.

The couple chose Oklahoma City because they had lived there until 1971, and so that Jacki, 57, could be near her 83-year-old mother. Unwilling to buy a home that might prove difficult to sell if they move later, the couple instead rent a seven-room ranch-style house for $650 a month.

Jimmy, 59, a retired sales executive, plans to invest the $67,000 remaining from the sale of the house in a balanced portfolio of mutual funds that he estimates will earn 8 percent to 10 percent. He figures that the fund payouts, plus his $23,000 pension and income from other investments, will be more than enough to meet expenses. "Paying off the old mortgage freed up $1,165 a month," says Jimmy. "On that money we can go to Europe twice a year."

Like the Stotts and the Whitneys, more and more people are turning to the family residence, its value fattened by inflation, for retirement income. About 75 percent of Americans over 65 own their own homes, with an average of more than $50,000 in equity waiting to be tapped. Most retirees living on fixed incomes, however, don't earn enough to qualify for conventional home-equity loans, the simplest way to exploit this burgeoning asset. But selling out and buying or renting a smaller place is usually the smartest move anyway. On balance, it also out-performs such alternatives as taking a reverse mortgage, which is a loan against home equity that allows the borrower to defer repayment, or just staying put. Tables 1–3 show these three alternatives for a 65-year-old couple with a mortgage-free house worth $250,000.

What's best for you depends greatly on whether you need to raise money from your home—and how much. Your retirement costs probably will come to about 70 percent of your pre-retirement expenses. If your expected income from investments, Social Security, pensions, and other sources falls well short of your requirements, you may have little option but to tap your prime asset.

Table 1. Trade-down.

Year	Additional income	Annual housing costs	Home equity and principal	How it works
1	$13,500	$3,200	$254,000	The couple get the biggest
5	13,500	3,744	271,665	payoff if they sell the house
10	13,500	4,555	298,024	and buy a smaller one for
15	13,500	5,541	330,094	$100,000. Then they can in-
20	13,500	6,742	369,112	vest their $150,000 gain in a
25	13,500	8,203	416,584	diversified portfolio of invest-
				ments, in this case yielding 9
				percent. The income will
				more than cover their hous-
				ing costs.

Sources: Houston Asset Management; American Homestead.

Even if you can afford to stay in your home, you will have to pay a price. "People wrongly think that if their home is paid for, it doesn't cost them anything to stay in it," says Robert Frater, a certified financial planner with Houston Asset Management Inc. "They don't realize that trading down is the best way to raise your income, lower your living costs, and preserve the value of your estate."

Trade-downs

Executing a trade-down calls for careful planning. Financial planners and housing specialists give the following advice:

Estimate your profit in advance Before you sell your old house, try to find out what you will need to spend for a suitable replacement. If your potential profit is small, trading down might not be worth the trouble and expense. But be sure to take into account any savings you will realize from reduced maintenance and property taxes on a smaller home. "Lower costs might make it worthwhile to move even if your profit from the trade-down is only $50,000," says Laura Adams, a certified financial planner in Princeton, New Jersey.

Time your sale to take advantage of tax benefits If you or your spouse is 55 or older, you may be able to exclude from taxes up to $125,000 of the capital gain on the sale of your home. Should your gain exceed $125,000, you can defer tax on the excess by reinvest-

Table 2. Reverse mortgage.

Year	Additional income	Annual housing costs	Home equity	How it works
1	$5,676	$8,000	$223,312	The couple can take out an
5	5,676	9,359	185,293	Individual Reverse Mortgage
10	5,676	11,386	106,979	Account, which provides pay-
15	5,676	13,853	0	ments of $5,676 a year for
20	5,676	16,855	0	life. If they live for at least 15
25	5,676	20,506	0	years, their estate will owe
				the lender an amount equal
				to the home's value. (For de-
				tails, see the accompanying
				story.)

Sources: Houston Asset Management; American Homestead.

ing the money in a new residence. If you have lived in your home for less than three of the five years preceding the sale, however, you do not qualify for the exclusion. In that case, it's probably worth delaying the sale until you can take the tax break.

Consider lending the buyer part of the purchase price   Interest payments on the loan will provide more income than you would receive if you sold for cash and invested the proceeds conservatively, such as in five-year Treasury notes, recently paying 8.3 percent. Reason: mortgage rates are currently almost two percentage points higher. Insist on a down payment of at least 20 percent. That will protect your principal if the buyer defaults on the loan and, in fact, is an incentive for him *not* to default.

Pay cash for your new home   You could take out a mortgage and invest your money elsewhere, but the returns on conservative investments would not cover the loan payments. Just be sure that you leave yourself enough cash to meet emergencies and that you have other investments to offset the risk that your house might lose value. "When you tie up all of your cash in a house, you lose the protection of a diversified portfolio," points out Harold Evensky, president of Evensky & Brown, a financial planning firm in Miami.

Avoid variable-rate mortgages   If you must borrow to pay for your new home, get a mortgage with a fixed rate so that you will never have to worry about payments rising sharply.

One alternative to trading down is selling and renting permanently. In the long run, selling your house and becoming a tenant

Table 3. Do nothing.

Year	Additional income	Annual housing costs	Home equity	How it works
1	0	$8,000	$260,000	If they stay put and leave
5	0	9,359	304,164	their equity intact, the cou-
10	0	11,386	370,061	ple will retain the full value
15	0	13,853	450,236	of their property, which in-
20	0	16,855	547,781	creases by 4 percent a year
25	0	20,506	666,459	in our example. But they will need income from other sources to meet rising costs, including maintenance, in- surance, and property taxes.

Sources: Houston Asset Management; American Homestead.

might be less financially rewarding than trading down. But it might well provide enough cash to defray your housing costs and free considerable cash. And if you decide to move again, you won't be pinned down by the task of selling a home, which could prove difficult if the real estate market in your area goes soft.

Of course, you may be among the homeowners who, like impoverished nobility in an English novel, wouldn't think of abandoning their castle even if they have to sell all the silver to pay the upkeep. In that case, you may want to consider one of the following techniques to hold on to the old place. Some of them are limited to certain regions, and others require the cooperation of relatives or outside investors.

Reverse mortgages

Dora Lissemore, 89, of Tenafly, New Jersey, has lived since 1944 in a two-story house set among hundreds of rosebushes, many of them planted by her late husband Jack. When he died in 1981, Lissemore's widow's income consisted of Social Security, a small annuity, a teacher's union insurance policy, and royalties from a rose that the couple hybridized seventeen years ago. The money wasn't enough to meet her expenses. "I had begun to wonder how I could carry the house by myself," she says. "But I didn't want to leave my garden and my friends and start all over." In 1982, Lissemore responded to an advertisement by American Homestead, a Mount Laurel, New Jersey, mortgage bank, and took out a reverse mortgage that pays her $700 a month. The extra money helps cover her property taxes, utility costs, medical bills, and dues

---

Questions to ask about an IRMA

Before deciding whether an Individual Reverse Mortgage Account is for you, consider:

What are the monthly payments? Will they adequately add to your income? Remember that, over time, your expenses will increase but your payments will not. Can you rely on other assets to take up the slack? If not, look to a more lucrative strategy, such as trading down.

How long do you intend to live in the house? If you plan to move within five years, the costs of an IRMA will be exorbitant.

Are you likely to outlive your actuarial life expectancy? If so, an IRMA might be a bargain. But if you are in poor health, there is considerable risk that the loan's cost to your estate will outweigh the benefits it provides to you during your lifetime.

Do you have children or other heirs to consider? Discuss your plans with them, since any repayment of your loan, as detailed in the accompanying story, will come out of your estate. You can ensure that you and your heirs always retain some equity in your house by exempting a percentage of its value from the transaction. But then you must settle for lower monthly payments from the lender.

How much is your house likely to appreciate? If the prospects for appreciation are poor, an IRMA may prove to be relatively inexpensive. But if you are in a hot housing market, remember that you will give up part or all of the profits to the lender. In that case, consider whether you can afford to accept lower monthly payments and retain a greater share in the potential appreciation.

Do you plan to make major improvements to the house? They will increase its value, all or part of which will go to the lender.

---

to half a dozen clubs and other organizations, such as the American Rose Society. It also covers her subscription to *Baseball Digest*, in which she follows the fortunes of the New York Mets.

Reverse mortgages—complete with typical closing costs of 2.5 percent of the total loan—pay the borrower a fixed monthly amount and defer repayment. They come in several forms, the most attractive being the Individual Reverse Mortgage Account (IRMA) that Lissemore opened, whereby the lender receives part or all of the value of your home, including its appreciation during the term of the loan, in return for deferring repayment until you either move or die. (In the latter case, your estate pays off the loan.) American Homestead offers IRMAs in Connecticut, Delaware, Maryland, Massachusetts, New Jersey, Ohio, Pennsylvania, and Virginia; in addition, the mortgage bank plans to introduce them in California and New York this year.

Your income from an IRMA depends on the size of the mortgage and the life expectancies of you and your spouse. (A detailed example appears in Table 2.) If you live beyond your life expectancy at the time you signed the mortgage agreement, your lifetime payments from an IRMA may exceed the value of your home. But if you die soon after you enter the program, your estate must repay the lender all of the monthly checks you received, with interest, plus all or part of the appreciation in the value of the house since the mortgage was signed.

One variant on this type of loan, called a term reverse mortgage, is downright dangerous for most homeowners. With a term reverse mortgage, the lender makes monthly payments to a homeowner for a given period of time, typically seven years. At the end of that term, the homeowner must repay the loan, which often means selling the house. But, occasionally, the loans do make sense. For example, an elderly person who is on a waiting list for a place in a nursing home might take out a term reverse mortgage to meet expenses in the interim.

Sale-leasebacks

Helen Jordan, 79, sold her Marin County, California, home in 1984 to an investor for $92,400. She received a down payment of $25,000 and granted the investor a 13-year mortgage that pays her $825 a month. Just over $400 goes for the rent she pays to the investor, who qualifies for tax benefits because the house's status as a rental property. The rest supplements her income from Social Security and the violin lessons she gives to local children. The mortgage payments will stop in 1997, when Jordan is 89. To ensure that her income continues indefinitely, she took the precaution of investing $6,800 from the down payment in a single-premium deferred annuity, which will begin paying her $825 a month when the mortgage payments stop. Meanwhile, the lease limits her annual rent increases to 2 percent, and she has managed to set aside some money for her heirs. "I live here just as if it were my own home," she says. "It's still my place."

With a sale-leaseback, the buyer generally agrees to a 10 percent to 20 percent down payment and a 15-year mortgage, and the buyer also covers the cost of property taxes, insurance, and maintenance. A sale-leaseback arrangement with a 10 percent down payment and a 15-year mortgage on a $250,000 house might, during the first year, generate $32,000 in income to the seller, who would pay about $21,000 in rent during the first year. The income would remain constant, but the rent might climb to about $36,000 by the end of the mortgage term. Like Helen Jordan, you probably should invest part of the down payment in a deferred annuity so that you will continue to receive income should you outlive the mortgage.

Finding an investor to take part in a sale-leaseback may be difficult, unless your children or other family members can afford to make the investment. Either way, enlist the help of an experienced attorney. Local bar associations and real estate boards might recommend professionals who can help you structure a typical deal for $1,500 to $2,000. For $35, the National Center for Home Equity Conversion (110 E. Main St., Madison, Wisconsin 53703) will send you its brochure, *Sale Leaseback Guide and Model Documents.*

Charitable donations

If you can't find an investor to do a sale-leaseback and you have no children, you might try a school, hospital, or charity. They will sometimes grant you a lifetime annuity in exchange for a remainder interest in your property. You continue to own it, but when you die it's all theirs.

Accessory apartments

If you have rooms to spare in your home, you might consider turning them into an apartment that you can rent out. Before you do anything, find out if the zoning regulations in your community permit such an arrangement. If so, ask a contractor to estimate the cost of renovation and ask real estate agents how much rent you will be able to charge. Ask your local agency on aging if there is a household matching service, which helps bring people with extra rooms together with prospective tenants, in your area. The service might help you find a suitable tenant; otherwise, try real estate agents. The book, *Creating an Accessory Apartment* (McGraw-Hill, $16.95) by Patrick H. Hare and Jolene N. Ostler, includes a sample lease and other useful information.

While you are weighing these options, give careful consideration to the emotional factors as well. Anything that makes you uncomfortable is not worth doing, no matter how smart it is in dollars and cents.

PART THREE

Protecting What You've Worked For

The assets you've accumulated over your lifetime—your home, pensions, investments, and other possessions—must be protected. This section discusses several strategies for doing just that: having the right amounts and kinds of insurance, developing a well-organized record-keeping system, knowing when and how to obtain expert advice, and detailed estate planning, especially preparing and periodically updating your will.

Life and disability insurance—who needs it, how much, and for how long—are addressed in Chapter 18.

Another area of vital concern to people planning for a successful and secure retirement is finding high-quality health care and appropriate health care insurance. The myth that Medicare pays for most health care costs persists. While the June 1988 Medicare Catastrophic Coverage Act increased Medicare coverage, sizable out-of-pocket costs remain, and there is no coverage for long-term nursing home care. Chapters 19 and 20 look at options for health care, health care insurance, and long-term care insurance.

Are your personal and financial documents scattered about the house—in shoe boxes, desk drawers, and various other places? Chapter 21 suggests a basic system for organizing that information so that you'll have it at your fingertips when important decisions must be made.

People retiring today and in the future will be expected to take a greater personal responsibility than previous generations for their financial security. At the same time, the financial arena is becoming increasingly complex. This fact of life has led to rapid growth in the as yet unlicensed field of financial planning. Chapter 22 explains what a financial planner can and cannot do for you and how to evaluate a planner's services.

Your estate, small or large, needs to be protected now and distributed as you wish after your death. Chapters 23 and 24 explain how to value your estate (it is probably larger than you think), how estates are taxed, and how the will and other tools protect and distribute your wealth according to your wishes.

Finally, to help put basic ideas together, turn to the Conclusion, "Retirement Planning for Life Fulfillment."

18

INSURANCE: KNOW WHAT YOU NEED BEFORE THE AGENT CALLS

Medical Economics

Editor's note: No matter what your profession or income level, this article offers ways for you to plan your insurance coverage.

Insurance agents are out in force telling you that there are gaps in your coverage, or that your coverage hasn't kept pace with your needs, or that there's a host of newer policies that will work better for you than what you have. They may be right. But before you can tell, you'll have to review your current coverage and compare what you're paying now with what it would cost you to "improve" it. Coverage by coverage, here's how to get what you need without paying more than you should.

Life insurance: What you really need

If you're diligent over the years about your savings, investments, and retirement funding, your death at 65 isn't the cataclysmic financial blow to your family that it would have been when you were 35. Which means, of course, that you need substantial life insurance when you're young, much less as you get older.

In reassessing your current needs, keep in mind the two purposes of life insurance: to preserve your family's standard of living if you die before you've built up an adequate estate and to provide ready cash to pay various estate costs. It's easy to lose sight of those needs when you face the insurance industry's bewildering array of options and jargon. There's not only traditional whole life but also universal life, variable life, and an assortment of hybrid policies that combine features of both. But the basic choice you've always faced remains the same: whether to buy term or whole life.

Term—pure death protection with no frills—has long been regarded by many financial advisers as a better buy than the higher-premium whole life. And term has never been cheaper. A term policy can run a 35-year-old male nonsmoker as little as 60 cents per thousand of coverage. So $500,000 worth of protection can cost him as little as $300 a year for the first few years of the policy. The same amount of whole life might run that same person $8,000 a year.

Agents will try to counter that argument by pointing out that the term policy will probably not be renewable beyond age 65 or 70. Remember, though, how your need for life insurance diminishes as you get older.

Agents will also stress that your annual term premium will increase as you get older, whereas the premium for whole life remains steady (and, if fact, will get lower if there are policy dividends to reduce the premium). But you pay so much less for term in the early years that you're likely to end up paying less over the full period you keep the policy, even if that's to age 65 or 70— provided you assiduously invest the difference between the term and whole-life premiums.

What can you do with the premium difference you save each year? Assume the term policy costs you $300 for each of the first five years before it goes up. If you invest the $7,700 you're saving each year at 10 percent annually, you'll have a fund worth $51,710, before taxes, after five years. Even though your term premium goes up in the sixth year, and periodically thereafter, you'll still be able to squirrel away some savings. More savings than the whole-life policy's cash value? Probably. But even if it isn't larger, the fund you set aside from premium savings is always yours. The cash-value fund the life insurance company sets aside for you is buried in the policy. When you die, your beneficiary gets the face amount, but the insurance company pockets the cash value.

Ah, yes, counters the agent, but the whole-life policy's cash value builds tax-deferred—and you can borrow against it anytime. True. But if you put the difference between term and whole-life premiums into your retirement fund, you'll get the same tax-deferral benefits. Compounding tax-free, even at the most conservative rates, this investment will almost certainly grow faster than a traditional policy's cash value.

As for the borrowing provisions, insurance regulations now permit insurers to charge whatever they want on policy loans. While some companies still charge the old ceiling of 8 percent, many charge more. And the interest rate on new policies often varies with market rates.

So whereas you once could borrow the cash value at 8 percent annual interest—or less, depending on how old the policy was—and invest it on the outside at 10 percent or even more, now you may not be able to take advantage of that attractive spread.

Many agents will try to disarm these arguments with a pitch for variable or universal-life insurance. They'll point out that universal life offers a much higher return than traditional whole life (lately as high as 10 percent, compared with the traditional policy's 4 or 5 percent). What they aren't likely to tell you if you don't ask is that universal life may soon become less attractive. The tax law passed in 1986 places a new limit on the cash-value buildup for policies issued after this year. If, for example, that buildup exceeds 40 percent of the policy's face amount while the policyholder is 40 years old or younger, the entire cash value becomes taxable income to him.

Let's assume he has bought a universal-life policy with a death benefit of $100,000. Under the new law, if the cash-value fund reaches $40,000 before he turns 40, every dollar in that fund becomes taxable as ordinary income.

No problem, says the insurer, promptly raising his death benefit to, say, $150,000. But there *is* a problem. Now the policyholder's paying for a $150,000 policy instead of a $100,000 one, which means more of his premium is rerouted to pay for the death benefit and less goes into the cash fund. So the cash fund grows more slowly, and the effective return on his investment shrinks.

Though the law will have little impact on variable life insurance, there are reasons to be wary of this type of coverage, too. To be sure, variable life lets you direct the investment portion of your premium to one or more investment funds—typically, in stocks, bonds, or money-market instruments—and switch from one to another a specified number of times a year. Both the policy's death benefit and its cash value rise with the investment return. And giving you the responsibility for how your premium is invested counters the long-standing complaint that insurance companies pay paltry returns on whole-life policies.

Of course, with the investment responsibility comes the risk: What happens if your bets are wrong? Not only could the cash value fall, but the death benefit could also drop all the way to its original face amount. And with both these types of insurance policies, even healthy returns will look less robust once the fees for administration, sales load, investment management, and state premium tax are deducted.

Bear in mind, too, that the quality of life insurance policies varies widely from company to company. That makes it important to shop around. You may find, for example, that some cash-value policies pay a high enough return to make them a better deal than term coverage.

Still, the type of policy you need is only half the dilemma. The other half is: How much insurance do you need now? And how much will you need in the future? To see how insurance needs change with age, turn to Figure 1. To find out what your current needs are, fill out the worksheet.

Disability insurance: Review it before it's too late

If it's been a while since you reviewed your individual disability insurance coverage, don't wail a moment longer. According to the actuaries, a 35-year-old runs a greater risk of being seriously disabled before he's 65 than he does of dying. And if he's disabled, he must have sufficient assets to provide not only for his family but also for himself. His needs remain the same—in fact, with his medical bills, they increase—but his income slows to a trickle.

In reviewing your existing coverage, you face four questions: How much? How soon? How long? What kind?

How much? Insurance companies will let you buy only a limited amount of individual disability insurance, equal to perhaps 50 or 60 percent of your income. You can't exceed that, even by going to several different carriers for additional individual policies.

You may be able to supplement your protection by buying into group policies, such as those available through your state or county medical association. But make sure the bulk of your coverage is from individual policies. Group policies are usually loaded with loopholes. For instance, they generally aren't noncancelable or guaranteed renewable, so the insurance company can raise your premium or even cancel your coverage when it chooses. Most of the better individual policies state that the insurer can't cancel your coverage as long as your premiums are paid up, and they severely restrict how the company can raise your premiums.

For a 40-year-old earning $100,000, a good $60,000 individual policy will cost only about $2,000 to $3,000 a year. At that price, you probably should buy full coverage. As you grow older and your need for protection diminishes, you can cut back.

How soon?   Few policies begin paying you for the first day you're disabled. Most have a waiting period—sort of like a deductible clause. If you wait 90 days before your benefits begin, your premiums will be about 20 percent less than if you wait only 30 days. If you can wait 180 days, you'll save another 15 percent. When you're trying to determine how long you can wait, however, be aware that

Expenses, assets, and insurance needs	Age 40	Age 60	You
1. Survivor's annual living expenses (50% of your present earnings for your family; 33⅓% for a widow alone)	$ 37,500	$ 40,000	$
2. Annual Social Security benefits (for wife and two minor children; or for a widow 60 or over)	16,080	5,280	
3. Net living expenses for survivors (line 1 minus line 2)	21,420	34,720	
4. Capital needed to produce amount on line 3 (for the 9% return assumed in the examples, divide line 3 by .09)	238,000	385,778	
5. Special needs (college tuition, home mortgage, debts)	185,000	60,000	
6. Sum of lines 4 and 5	423,000	445,778	
7. Final expenses and estate costs (about 10% of line 9)	10,000	50,000	
8. Total funding needed (add line 6 and line 7)	433,000	495,778	
9. Present funds available[1]	100,000	500,000	
10. Present value of retirement fund	50,000	250,000	
11. Present assets (add line 9 and line 10)	150,000	750,000	
12. Life insurance needs (line 8 minus line 11)	283,000	—	
13. Present insurance coverage	100,000	200,000	
14. Insurance to be added or dropped (difference between line 12 and line 13)	$183,000	$(200,000)	$

[1] Value of personal investment portfolio, savings, real estate equity, etc.

Figure 1.   How much life insurance do you need? The examples here are estimates of what two doctors would need to enable their families to maintain their current standard of living. In the blank column, you can roughly determine your own needs. Use exact figures when you have them; otherwise, estimates will do.

payments don't begin immediately upon completion of the waiting period. With a 30-day wait, you're not likely to see a check from the insurer until the 60th day or so.

How long?   You can buy a policy to pay you disability benefits for a year, two years, five years, to age 65, or for life. the longer it pays, the better, right? Not necessarily. Unless you're just starting out, you probably shouldn't buy coverage that pays benefits beyond age 65. By the time you're 65, your savings, investments, and pension plans should be ready to take over.

And if you *are* just starting out? Chances are you don't have much in savings, investments, and pension plans. Then buy a policy that will provide lifetime benefits. It will cost you more, but you can drop to a shorter term as you get older and your nest egg grows.

"As a general rule," says John Hamner, a disability-insurance agent based in Denver, "I tell my clients to buy all the short-term coverage they need and all the long-term coverage they can afford."

What kind?   This is the most important question to answer, and the hardest. How much coverage you carry may become incidental if you don't have the right kind of policy. The major consideration is the policy's definition of disability. Most policies define disability in one of two basic ways:

Ability to work   Some policies regard you as disabled only if you can do no work at all. At the other end of the spectrum are policies that consider you disabled if you can't go back to your regular occupation, no matter how fit you are to earn a living in some other work. The latter type of policy is likely to cost 40 to 50 percent more than the former.

Most people try to go back to their own occupations after a disability, even if just part time. So your policy should also cover a partial disability with reduced benefits. The better policies have partial disability benefits built in, at little extra cost.

How do these "residual benefits" policies work? Say you've been earning $150,000 and have coverage worth $90,000 a year. After a period of total disability, you return to earn $100,000, or two-thirds your per-disability income. The policy will pay you one-third of your full benefit—or $30,000 a year. If you didn't have a residual-benefits policy, the first dollar you earned in your profession would wipe out all benefits.

Loss of income   There are also disability policies that simply measure your loss of income from sickness or injury, rather than attempting to define your ability to work. Some experts feel this type of policy makes the most sense. One reason is that the policy can start paying benefits based on the first day of lost income, whereas most own-occupation policies require you to be totally disabled for a substantial period—often as long as a year—before you can work part time and collect partial benefits. (Of course, loss-of-income policies are also available with waiting periods of 30, 60, 90 days or longer, keeping the premium down.)

Loss-of-income coverage will also pay proportionate benefits until your income recovers to 80 percent of its pre-disability level. Own-occupation policies will pay partial benefits for only a limited period of time.

The advantages of loss-of-income coverage come at a price: A 45-year-old ordinarily will pay nearly 30 percent more for a loss-of-income policy with a 30-day waiting period than for an own-occupation disability policy with comparable benefits. However, differences among insurers' rates are so great that a persistent shopper can find loss-of-income policies at lower premiums than other companies' own-occupation policies. Clearly, it pays to shop.

19

A COMMON-SENSE GUIDE TO HEALTH INSURANCE

Morton Hunt

Editor's note: Since this article was written, the Medicare Part B monthly premium paid by program enrollees has increased by 38.5 percent, from $17.90 in 1987 to $24.80 in 1988.

In June 1988, Congress passed the Medicare Catastrophic Coverage Act (H.R. 2470). Among its provisions to improve health care coverage, the Act limits out-of-pocket payments that Medicare beneficiaries must make for certain Medicare-covered services, expands coverage for outpatient prescription drugs, provides greater access to Medicare-covered skilled nursing facility care and home health care, and institutes protections from impoverishment for spouses of Medicare-funded nursing home residents.

To judge by the junk mail, television commercials, and print advertisements, a great many people are worried that you, whoever you are—corporate employee or self-employed, old or young, white collar or blue collar—do not have the right kind of health insurance.

They may be right. Hospital rates and doctors' bills continue to rise far faster than the cost-of-living index. Innovative high-tech medical treatments—organ transplants, for instance—can run to hundreds of thousands of dollars. Long-term illnesses of the elderly often use up life savings and home equities. President Reagan's recent proposal to expand Medicare to include "catastrophic illness" coverage, even if it isn't beaten back by conservatives and the insurance industry, will safeguard only the elderly from disastrous medical bills.

No wonder private insurance companies, Blue Cross and Blue Shield plans, and others are pelting us with advertisements touting all sorts of new health insurance plans. No wonder many large employers now offer a wide range of policies and options at varying costs to their employees. No wonder fraternal organizations and business associations keep urging their members to buy the health plans they have available.

This unprecedented plethora of choices has created a baffling problem: how to choose the right—and the right amount of— health insurance. Today's "medical consumers" are confronted not by a mere dilemma but by a polylemma: a vast number of possibilities, each with advantages and assurances, disadvantages and dangers. As Dr. William L. Kissick of the University of Pennsylvania School of Medicine told an audience of physicians a year ago: "Financing of health care . . . has evolved into a maze of inconsistencies, exceptions, adaptations, and almost uncomprehensible regulations."

Many people, including the knowledgeable and sophisticated, do little more than mentally toss a coin to choose their health insurance. But an uninformed choice may be a poor one. The penalty can be anything from long delays in seeing the doctor to refusal of hospital admission, from going untreated to bankruptcy. In an era when a ten-minute visit to a dermatologist for the removal and biopsy of a tiny skin lesion can cost $400 and a ten-day hospitalization for surgery can run $7,500 plus doctors' fees, making the right health insurance choice can mean the difference between security and ruin.

But what is the right choice? Is it better to select an indemnity plan that returns a fixed sum for each medical procedure, or a prepayment plan that provides virtually unlimited care for a flat monthly sum? Are the new "dread disease" policies, covering specific disorders such as cancer or leukemia, a good buy? What is an "HMO," and how does it compare with conventional insurance? How important is disability income insurance that will pay you cash if an illness keeps you out of work for months? A rehabilitation policy in case you have a crippling accident? If you're 65 or over, will Medicare cover all your medical expenses?

The choices are many and confusing. Nevertheless, they constitute what Glenn M. Hackbarth, Deputy Administrator of the

Health Care Financing Administration, the agency in charge of Medicare and Medicaid, calls "a rich portfolio of options."

Understanding the menu

Before you can choose wisely, you must be able to decode the menu. Here is a brief rundown of the main items:

Private insurance refers to health policies purchased either from a traditional for-profit insurance company or from a Blue Cross and Blue Shield plan. (The "Blues" are a network of non-profit organizations that sell insurance against hospital costs and doctors' bills.) The for-profit companies reimburse policy-holders by fixed amounts or percentages for either kind of care; if the hospital or doctor charges more than those amounts, policyholders are responsible for the difference. The Blues pay hospitals directly—in most cases, the patient pays nothing—and negotiate discounted fee schedules with doctors.

Most private health insurance is now sold in the form of *group insurance.* A generation or so ago, private health insurance consisted largely of policies bought by individuals. Insurers, however, seeking a competitive advantage, gravitated toward lower-cost group insurance; they could calculate the average risk within any known group and so eliminate the physical examinations to ferret out the bad risks. Group coverage, accordingly, is 15 percent to 40 percent cheaper than comparable individual coverage.

Employer-provided plans are group insurance programs supplied as part of employee benefits packages; currently, 90 percent of all group health insurance is employer provided. Nearly all medium to large corporations furnish health plans to their employees. Such health insurance is not totally free: employees generally pay a small part of the premium; a deductible of $100 to $500; copayments, or fixed sums, toward each office visit or prescription; or coinsurance—a share often 20 percent, of every bill.

Many workers are offered a "flexible plan" or "cafeteria package" of benefits and must annually choose from an assortment of possibilities. Chrysler Motors Corporation employees, for example, must pick from among three plans, each with numerous variations. Federal employees in Washington face a mind-boggling selection of at least twenty-five plans.

People who are not covered through employment often obtain insurance through group plans offered by social and professional organizations. Although these individuals pay the whole cost of their insurance, premiums are considerably lower than for individual health insurance.

Prepaid plans are the most significant recent development on the national health insurance scene. Historically, doctors and hospitals have been reimbursed by insurers on a "fee-for-service" basis—a specific sum for each function performed. Prepaid insurers, generally called health maintenance organizations (HMOs), take a different approach. Subscribers are charged a fixed annual sum, usually paid in monthly installments, and in return are provided with practically all the office care, hospitalization, and surgery they may need. There are some exceptions; psychotherapy, for one, can be limited.

Government-provided health insurance consists chiefly of Medicare and Medicaid. As medical costs soared during the 1960s, Congress realized that many elderly people and the poor could afford neither full medical care nor private health insurance, and in 1965 it created Medicare for people 65 and over and for certain disabled people, and Medicaid for certain categories of the poor.

Medicare pays part of elderly persons' doctor bills and much of their hospital bills. But because health care costs soared at an alarming rate during the last two decades, Medicare patients now generally pay substantially more than before out-of-pocket toward their medical bills.

Weighing your options

Most health insurance officials, actuaries, and consumer-affairs experts cite certain guidelines to use in choosing among insurance options.

Cost is obviously a major criterion. Within employer packages, association plans, and individual plans, there is a spectrum of protections at varying costs. In the Chicago area, for example, an employee of a large corporation might pay through a salary deduction the equivalent of $25 per person per month (for a family of four) for standard Blue Cross/Blue Shield insurance. But a Blues HMO might cost the employee only $15 per person per month.

Often, extra options are available within any one plan an extra cost: employees might select an HMO plan costing nothing monthly but charging them $3 per office visit and $2 per prescription. Alternatively, they could pay a flat monthly sum of $15 to $25 per family member for fully prepaid care. Many non-Blues plans likewise offer differing kinds of coverage at varying costs to the employee.

An HMO, of course, might be farther away than many private doctors' offices, and delays in getting appointments might be longer. In addition to the inconvenience of HMO care, *freedom of choice* is a critical consideration in choosing between prepaid plans and traditional insurance. Many people, understandably, find the ability to go to the doctors they prefer extremely important, although the cost of "high-option" health insurance allowing that freedom can be burdensome.

A recent innovation provides partial respite from the stark choice between freedom and prepayment. The preferred provider organization (PPO) is a hybrid of an HMO and traditional fee-for-service care, a group of private practitioners who collectively sell their services at discounted rates to insurance companies, HMOs, and employers. Over 350 PPOs already exist, 50 of them under contract to Blue Cross and Blue Shield plans. As with HMOs, most PPO subscribers have all their medical needs taken care of for a fixed monthly amount. Employees or others who choose a PPO aren't restricted to its doctors or hospitals, but if they go to others, they must pay, on the average, 20 percent of the doctors' or hospitals' charges, in addition to their annual premium.

"Basic" medical insurance often pays only up to $2,000 or $3,000 per illness for doctors' fees and hospitalization. That's good enough for most common illnesses, but not for serious or prolonged ones. For that reason, *major medical protection* is essential these days. A major medical policy can have a high deductible and starts paying when the basic policy runs out. It can cover the next $250,000, or even more, of expenses per illness, although some have a lifetime cap. Most employer packages either include major medical protection or offer it as an extra-cost option. If not, employees can buy it on the outside. An HMO, if one is available, is another way of getting affordable major medical protection.

Comprehensiveness is a fundamental criterion in choosing a health-insurance program. "*Always* think comprehensive," says J. Robert Hunter, president of the National Insurance Consumer Organization. Some plans exclude from coverage or put strict limits on certain illnesses—such as mental disorders and pre-existing conditions. Choose one with as few exclusions or limitations as possible.

In many new policies, acquired immune deficiency syndrome (AIDS) is specifically excluded from coverage; in some cases, an applicant must take a blood test for the AIDS virus before coverage is granted. However, an AIDS exclusion cannot be applied retroactively in existing policies. And last month, New York ruled that insurance companies cannot require health insurance applicants to take an AIDS blood test.

It is also a good idea to avoid so-called "dread disease" policies that cover single ailments. The sales pitch for such policies is powerful: they are cheap, and a disease like cancer can destroy a family financially. "Not everyone can afford a comprehensive major medical policy," says a spokesman for Mutual of Omaha, which offers dread disease coverage. "This is an economical way to fill in some of the gaps." But even the Health Insurance Association of America, which represents 85 percent of the commercial health insurance companies, says of dread disease insurance: "You should have full, major medical coverage before you consider it. Otherwise it's a gamble." Robert Hunter is more outspoken: "It's a terrible rip-off."

To assure employees of comprehensiveness, many states have laws specifying the services employer plans must offer. But if a company "self-insures"—sets up its own trust fund to pay for medical benefits instead of buying plans from insurance companies— it is not bound by these laws. It is your responsibility to assure yourself of comprehensiveness if you buy health insurance through an association or individually. Compare the lists of covered diseases and conditions, or contrast the services offered and the number of hospitalization days allowed, in the plans for which you are eligible and pick the most comprehensive.

Foreseeable medical needs are another useful criterion. Sometimes medical costs are predictable by the consumer but not the insurer; when that's the case, the consumer can place a winning bet.

A planned pregnancy is a case in point. Warren Greenberg, an economist for the Department of Health Services Administration of George Washington University, says: "Many federal employees switch from low-option to high-option plans before expecting a baby—thus covering, for a few hundred dollars, expenses of $2,500 to $4,000." Others switch to HMOs, which include maternity benefits.

Similarly, a person who has had intestinal polyps knows that he will need a colonoscopy every two years, at a cost of approximately $800 each time. And people who have overexposed themselves to the sun for years can expect occasional skin-cancer excisions. "Where you have sure things like that," says Robert Hunter, "it's smart to pay for a top-dollar policy. You know your own health better than the companies do; you can beat them at the game."

People who work for small companies and the self-employed have to insure themselves. The most economical way to do so is through a professional or social organization that has a desirable group health plan or set of plans. Moreover, since many good plans and HMOs don't accept individuals, it's often the only way to become eligible for them.

These same criteria—cost, major medical coverage, comprehensiveness, and freedom of choice—can be used in evaluating association-provided plans. Some associations do have insurance advisers. Additional help also can be obtained from state insurance departments; many of them answer written or telephoned questions about plans offered by companies operating in their jurisdiction.

Protecting against catastrophe

Even a major medical policy provides only partial protection against the costs of some acute or long-term illnesses. A child stricken by leukemia and provided with months of intensive chemotherapy at a major hospital can run up a total bill of hundreds of thousands of dollars. A major medical policy might pay only $25,000 or $50,000 of that; the unpaid remainder would devastate many a family.

In the view of most experts, catastrophic protection—insurance against the possibility of enormous medical bills—is the most important consideration of all. While it is generally pitched to the elderly, whose fixed resources often cannot contend with their growing medical needs, it can be a godsend for people of all ages. "Ask yourself: Why should I have insurance at all? Economists answer: To protect yourself against unpredictable costly expenses—against catastrophe," says Warren Greenberg. "Unfortunately, most people underinsure for that and overinsure for smaller items."

Adds Robert Hunter: "It's economically smart to take a large deductible, meet the low-end expenses yourself, and invest the difference in protection against improbable but catastrophic contingencies."

Many Blue Cross and Blue Shield plans offer million-dollar coverage at a premium only moderately higher than their major medical plans. People with major medical coverage from other companies can buy "excess major medical" or catastrophic illness policies at relatively little expense. Coverage starting after a $25,000 deductible and paying up to $1,000,000 costs about $70 a year for a 35-year-old man. A 35-year-old woman would pay $118, the higher premium based on actuarial tables showing that women live longer than men. Rates are far higher for older people.

Unfortunately, few young people buy such cheap protection. "People don't buy catastrophic insurance when they perceive the horizon as far off; but it may not be," says Warren Greenberg.

The lowdown on HMOs

Whether to opt for traditional, fee-based insurance coverage or to join a health maintenance organization is probably the most confusing initial choice facing insurance buyers today. The advantages of prepaid HMO membership can be beguiling. A brochure for a typical health maintenance organization operated by Kaiser Permanente, one of the nation's oldest and largest HMO networks, notes "No Charge" next to most of its long list of services. Many HMOs even provide heart and liver transplants—worth about $150,000 and $350,000 respectively—now that these are considered standard rather than experimental procedures.

HMOs might have flourished long ago except for the opposition of the organized medical establishment, which induced most states to prohibit them by law. But in 1973, Congress, seeking ways to control rising medical costs, passed the HMO Act, legalizing HMOs everywhere and requiring firms with twenty-five or more employees to include an HMO in their employee health package if one was available in their area. As a result, the number of HMOs jumped from 39, serving about 3,500,000 subscribers, in 1972, to 595, with 21,000,000 members, in 1986. Some authorities predict that by the year 2000, HMOs will care for nearly 50 percent of the population.

But their critics—many patients and a majority of private practitioners—find much wrong with health maintenance organizations. The chief flaw is the patients' lack of freedom. Most HMOs require patients to use doctors on their official list. As Dr. Timothy Mattison, a Mt. Kisco, New York, dermatologist who is not contracted to an HMO, says: "The patient has to ask himself what choice is worth to him. Are you really willing to give up the right to go to the doctor you want to see? Or the hospital you want to be in?"

Private practitioners also claim that HMO economics, based on fixed charges, often encourages doctors to furnish minimal service. A joke told by anti-HMO doctors goes as follows:

Patient: "How long will I have to wait?"

Receptionist: "If you're fee-for-service, go right in. If you're Medicare, an hour. If you're an HMO patient, *I'm* the doctor."

Yet a Johns Hopkins University review of studies of the quality of HMO medical care showed that nineteen studies found it better than fee-for-service care, a handful found it comparable, and only one or two found it inferior. "HMOs make sense from a financial standpoint and also from a medical standpoint," says Dr. William Roper, the administrator of the Health Care Financing Administration (H.C.F.A.). "The HMO is responsible for the *whole* care of the patient at all levels. That makes for better medicine. The M.D.'s who are so sure HMOs will fail may be in for a rude awakening."

Still, HMOs aren't for everyone. As Seymour Kaplan, executive director of "alternative delivery systems" for the Blue Cross and Shield Association, says: "For people to whom choice of their doctor is very important, and who can afford the cost, conventional fee-for-service care or PPOs are the answer. HMOs appeal mostly to young and healthy people and their families; many older people with accumulating medical needs pay more for the freedom to cling to doctors they have had a long relationship with."

Anyone considering an HMO should visit its central facility; merely by walking in, one can see whether it's sleazy and overcrowded or attractive and comfortable. More important, check what lies behind appearances. "Look at the list of doctors," says Robert Hunter. "Note where they trained, how many are board certified. And see if the HMO has been around long enough" to have worked out its fee schedule and other start-up problems.

William Gold, president of the ANCHOR Organization for Health Maintenance in Chicago, suggests asking your state's insurance department about the quality of a given HMO. James F. Doherty, president of Group Health Association of America (G.H.A.A.), a national organization of HMOs, adds, "Be sure it's 'federally qualified'—that's a seal of approval by H.C.F.A." Membership in G.H.A.A. is another sign of high standards; so is membership in HMO-U.S.A., the organization of HMOs run by the Blues. (HMOs are a recent and growing part of the Blues' business.)

Medicare and beyond

Often, we hear friends or parents quip, "The only good thing about getting older is that once I'm 65, Medicare will pay all my medical bills." Surveys by the Gallup Organization and by Louis Harris have found that many people still share this illusion. The reality is quite different.

Currently Part A of Medicare, the hospitalization portion, requires a patient to pay the first $520 of his or her hospital bill. Medicare then pays the rest through the 60th day, but beyond that the patient pays $130 a day for the next month, then $260 a day to the 150th day, and the whole cost thereafter. And Medicare pays its share of the 91st to 150th days' costs only once in a lifetime. Medicare thus is more or less adequate for short to fairly long hospital stays, but grossly inadequate for prolonged ones or repeated spells of hospitalization.

Part B of Medicare, covering medical expenses, is concerned chiefly with doctors' bills. It is optional and costs $17.90 per person per month; 95 percent of Medicare-eligible people buy it. For that premium, Medicare pays 80 percent of what H.C.F.A. considers a reasonable fee for the service rendered in the doctors' geographical area. The patient pays the other 20 percent, plus the balance of the bill, if the doctor doesn't accept Medicare's frequently mingy rates—throughout the nation, 72 percent do not.

The result, as Robert M. Ball, former commissioner of the Social Security Administration, told the Senate Labor and Human Resources Committee last January, is that Medicare now meets only about 40 percent of the total health costs of the elderly. And since older people need three to four times as much health care as people under 65, their routine medical bills can strain their and their children's budgets, while their more serious illnesses can pauperize them.

Under the circumstances, a "medigap" policy is essential for people over 65. Medigap policies supplementing Medicare coverage come in all shapes and sizes; more than one hundred such policies are offered by insurance companies. Some are excellent, and others—because of multiple exclusions or extremely high deductibles—are worthless. In some states, regulations bar the bad buys; in New York, only thirty-four plans are acceptable. Most medigap insurance is sold through two reliable sources, the Blues and the American Association of Retired Persons (AARP).

If you or a working parent is approaching 65, check whether an employer-provided plan can be converted at retirement to an individual medigap policy; about one-third are convertible. The result is often better and cheaper coverage than an association medigap policy; the only way to be sure is to compare them carefully.

There are several things to steer clear of when purchasing a medigap policy. Coverage of all Medicare deductibles, for example, is a bad idea. An AARP insurance booklet states flatly: "Your goal should not be total coverage. Insurance ceases to make sense when the cost is disproportionately large in comparison with the risk."

Rehabilitation coverage is also generally not needed; Medicare covers it fairly well. And duplication of benefits is a waste of money. Scare advertising and high-pressure sales techniques cause some elderly people to throw away money on excess medigap insurance. Hubert H. Humphrey 3d, Attorney General of Minnesota, last year told a subcommittee of the House Select Committee on Aging of one 80-year-old woman who had been sold fourteen overlapping policies by agents from one insurance company.

A good medigap policy must include several essential elements. Comprehensiveness is crucial. Medigap policies cost anywhere from $150 to $1,500 a year per person, but the bargain models aren't comprehensive enough to protect the elderly. For those who can't afford a comprehensive policy, an HMO may be the answer. In HMOs that accept Medicare recipients—about one in four does—Medicare payments go to the HMO and the individual pays an additional medigap fee of $30 to $60 per month to the HMO for the same broad coverage other people get.

Catastrophic illness insurance on top of the medigap policy also is absolutely essential. Even good medigaps go only so far; most have a lifetime limit of about one year's hospital coverage and pay little or nothing toward doctors' fees above what Medicare deems reasonable. Such policies cover major illnesses but not catastrophic ones—a two-year hospitalization in a specialized facility for treatment of a stroke-induced coma, for example, which could cost a total of $1 million.

One solution, of course, is to sign up with an HMO that accepts Medicare recipients. For those who want to retain their freedom of medical choice, it makes sense to buy a separate catastrophic illness policy with a large ($25,000 or more) deductible and paying up to $1,000,000. They're relatively inexpensive and can cost only about $200 a year for persons over 65.

Nursing home care is the great economic threat to the elderly and their children. It can cost $20,000 to $25,000 per year, and can continue for years. No form of private catastrophic illness insurance covers custodial nursing home care; neither would President Reagan's proposed expansion of Medicare. Although Medicare and some private policies pay for nursing care during convalescence, most aged people in nursing homes are not convalescent but simple unable to take care of themselves. Medicaid will cover the entire amount, but only for the indigent elderly; half a million elderly people each year use up their life savings for nursing home care and then, practically penniless, go on Medicaid. An elderly person too proud to strip a decrepit spouse of assets and declare him or her indigent may use up family savings until he or she, too, is poor.

The good news is that special nursing home insurance is available, in widely differing forms, from some seventy companies. The bad news is that it's expensive—up to $1,500 a year or more per person for people in their seventies, even more for older people. Worse news: many policies pay only if the patient comes to the nursing home directly from a hospital, a restriction that makes these policies valueless to most purchasers. So far, only an estimated 170,000 subscribers hold nursing-home policies.

Choosing one's health insurance prudently, though a formidable task, is both possible and eminently worth the effort. But, as Ovid wrote: *"Nulla, nisi ardua, virtus"*—"Whatever is worthwhile is difficult."

20

Insurance for Long-Term Care

Charles Schaeffer

After Stanley Fetterman's mother suffered a disabling stroke at age 70, he decided to have her admitted to a nursing home, despite the thousands of dollars of annual out-of-pocket expense the decision involved. When his mother-in-law also passed age 70, the Fettermans grew increasingly concerned about the potential costs if she were to need similar care. Then Fetterman and his wife heard about insurance that helps pay nursing home bills. They bought a policy offered in the San Francisco area by the Fireman's Fund, now AMEX Life Assurance Company.

Ironically, his mother-in-law, who had previously been in good health, suffered an incapacitating stroke soon after the purchase. After trying to cope with caring for her at home, the Fettermans reluctantly activated the nursing home policy.

Since then the policy has paid about $1,000 a month, which is nearly half of some $2,200 in monthly nursing home bills. "I wish we had taken it out for more," says Fetterman. Even so, the protection has saved them nearly $26,000. They got an additional break because the policy provides that the $600 annual premium be waived three months after benefits start.

The biggest catastrophic health expense for which older Americans have no insurance is the long-term care required when age, illness, or disability renders them dependent. In 1986, nursing home costs alone averaged roughly $21,000 annually per person. At the most expensive centers the bill can go as high as $50,000.

As more Americans survive into old age, an estimated nine million of them will be candidates for long-term care by 1990. For the elderly, their children, and the country as a whole, the question is who will foot the bills.

Although a recent survey by the American Association of Retired Persons (AARP) revealed that a majority of its members polled believe Medicare or private insurance will pick up the tab, the facts are just the opposite.

Medicare covers no more than 100 days of nursing home skilled care, and private insurance typically follows the same pattern. In reality the average is more like 25 days, because out-of-pocket co-payments begin after 20 days, discouraging many Medicare beneficiaries and holders of "medigap" policies that don't pick up the co-payments from taking advantage of the full period. Compare this with the average stay in a nursing home of two and a half years.

Almost half of the cost of long-term care is borne by Medicaid, the medical assistance program financed jointly by the federal and state governments. But before a person can become eligible, assets, including life savings, must be pared down to a minimum. As many a horror story attests, that amounts to virtual impoverishment.

The fear of going broke in a nursing home and having to turn to public assistance haunts most independent elderly people. Until a couple of years ago, families like the Fettermans had little choice but to dig into personal assets. Now, about thirty insurance companies are offering policies designed to cover a large chunk of the costs of long-term care. Still others are in the early stages of deciding whether to proceed.

Coverage for long-term care is more like disability protection than conventional health insurance. Says Laurence F. Lane, an insurance specialist with the American Health Care Association, "It can offer seniors who have disposable income an opportunity to protect their assets."

Like any competing products, long-term policies have contingencies and options that fit the needs of one person but are inappropriate for another. Whether you want to consider such coverage for yourself or help an aging family member decide, it's essential to have the facts.

What the insurance does

For an annual premium of around $100 to as much as $2,500, you can cover a specified stay in a long-term-care facility and, in an increasing number of instances, be reimbursed for certain home health services. Nursing home coverage can be as little as two years or as long as a "lifetime," with a cap that can range from $12,000 to $200,000. Most insurers divide long-term care into four main categories: skilled, intermediate, custodial, and services rendered in the home. Entry to one level sometimes is contingent upon a period of confinement in another.

Coverage is essentially an indemnity type; that is, insurers pay a fixed sum (say $40 to $50 per day) rather than a percentage of the fees customary in the community, as with comprehensive insurance. An indemnity policy tends to become outdated almost as soon as you sign the agreement. If it has no index for inflation, the onus is on you to peer down the road and try to gauge the amount of protection you would need to make a dent in future bills.

Insurance for long-term care is also relatively expensive because policies are sold only on an individual basis, though trials with groups are under way. (See sidebar, "Going with a group.")

How the policies pay

Long-term-care policies don't provide blanket coverage for an extended nursing home stay simply because the family believes a frail elderly person would be better off in such surroundings. Before any level of care is covered, it must almost always be defined as medically necessary or be preceded by a medical event. Then, depending on the beneficiary's condition and the terms of the policy, care proceeds through applicable stages. Although limitations and reimbursement schedules vary from insurer to insurer and from state to state, it generally shapes up like this.

Skilled care   Skilled care is medically necessary care provided by licensed, skilled medical professionals—nurses and therapists, for example—working under supervision of a doctor. Restoring the patient to a condition approximating the state of health before the illness or accident is the goal.

Intermediate care   Intermediate care also requires supervision by a physician and skilled nursing care to keep the patient stabilized. The difference is that the care is needed intermittently, rather than continuously over a prescribed period.

Going with a group

Even though long-term-care insurance is not every health planner's way to solve the problem of caring for America's growing numbers of frail elderly, the idea is taking hold. Nearly 200,000 policies—most of them individual coverage—are in place, and some experts predict the number will double this year. Marketing long-term-care insurance through a group would make it cheaper, more available, and easier to cope with because it would be more standardized. That's why the idea is being explored by some large associations and even some corporations, which might offer the benefit as part of a pension package.

Last November the largest trial policy, developed by Prudential, was offered to members of the American Association of Retired Persons in eight states. The premiums are based on age, ranging from $15 monthly between ages 50 and 59 to $95 between ages 75 and 79. Benefits include payments of $40 per day for all levels of nursing home care with a lifetime maximum of $43,800, $25 per visit for a health professional's visit to the home, and $20 per visit for home-maker services. Beneficiaries will pay for the first 90 days, compared with 20 days in an earlier trial offering, but the new version eliminates a three-day hospitalization requirement before benefits begin.

An initial pilot effort last summer drew only 1,200 or so takers. The association believes the small response was due to the erroneous idea that Medicare picks up most bills for long-term care. A beefed-up education campaign to dispel that myth is part of the new trial run.

Another group plan, sponsored by the National Association of Retirement Services in Bloomington, Minnesota, puts no age limit on the benefits once the family pays the $10 membership fee to join the organization. B'nai B'rith, the Jewish membership organization, also offers members a plan with benefits up to $60 a day. It's underwritten by MONY Financial Services of New York.

Blue Cross plans to test group insurance for long-term care this spring in several places. Making private insurance more widely available by giving buyers IRA-like tax breaks to save for it is advocated in a recent report to the President of the Department of Health and Human Services. The outcome depends on how Congress deals with the administration's overall recommendations on insurance to cover medical catastrophes.

Custodial care   Even if they escape disabling illness and injury, many elderly people reach a stage when performing such simple tasks as bathing, dressing, and eating is unsettling. Having a younger person around to help is the ideal solution; but when this is impractical, supervised custodial care, which is the nursing home service in greatest demand, is an alternative. Benefits cover mainly room and board plus payments for assistance with daily living. Even if the aid is provided by a professional, it is classified as custodial care.

Home health care   Depending on the policy, benefits for home health care may range from homemaking and chore services to occupational therapy and laboratory services.

The restriction maze

Be wary of the sales agent who promotes any policy as a cure-all for nursing home financial headaches. Even the best policies have restrictions that define when care can begin and under what circumstances. Restrictions typically require a stay in a hospital or skilled nursing facility before you can claim other benefits. Even then, between discharge and entry into a nursing home there is usually a delay called a waiting, or elimination, period of up to 20 or even 100 days. The delay gives the doctor and patient an opportunity to think the decision over and also discourages automatic admission.

Like conventional health insurance, long-term-care policies carry exclusions for preexisting conditions, which usually won't be covered for six months or a year after a policy is in force.

Policies sometimes differ in the ways they reimburse for care. A so-called facilities policy pays for only those services provided in a skilled nursing facility, even if the care given is intermediate or custodial. A care policy will cover levels of care given in less intensive surroundings if it otherwise complies with standard definitions.

Answers to hard questions

The need for long-term care shoots up markedly with age, with about half of those over age 65 eventually in need of some kind of service. If the idea of covering the risk appeals to you, there's still the problem of deciding when to take out the protection. Premiums start out at relatively modest levels for those in their fifties and rise steeply with advancing years, making the insurance costly or even prohibitive.

David Walker, a deputy insurance commissioner in Washington State, says that buying at a younger age locks in the lower rate if the policy provides for a level premium and guarantees your insurability before a disqualifying condition or disease has had a chance to develop. He says he will buy a long-term policy at age 55, though other authorities believe that signing up in the mid-sixties is a good bet, if the beneficiary is in reasonably good health.

Comparing long-term-care insurance is difficult, because benefits overlap, and restrictions and limitations vary from company to company and even within the same policy. Still, the more closely a policy can be tailored to the beneficiary's needs, the more sense it will make in the long run. "Any plan that does not cover all levels of care including custodial care is of very limited value," according to LTC Inc., a consulting firm and innovator in the long-term-care insurance field. LTC helped prepare an insurance consumers' guide for Group Health Cooperative of Puget Sound in Washington, where the law will soon require minimum policy standards. There are other key points to pin down.

Where will care be delivered?   Language in the policy may require that care be provided in a skilled nursing facility or licensed nursing home. The proportion of such institutions varies from state to state, with more than 90 percent of California's facilities classified as skilled, for example, compared with only some 5 percent in Oklahoma. Ask local officials from agencies on health or aging for the makeup of various long-term-care facilities to help you evaluate competing policies.

Is there a health screen?   The insurer will want to know the state of the beneficiary's health even if that only involves filling out a questionnaire. Stretching the truth could later invalidate the policy. Whether a prospect is accepted depends on the flexibility of the insurer and, to a degree, how the agent sizes things up. "It is safe to assume that applicants with a recent record of illness or institutionalization will not be acceptable candidates for insurance, although this is not usually stated directly in the policies," warns a report from the government's National Center for Health Services Research.

When do benefits begin and end?   Most insurers require an elimination period between admission and the first payment by the company, with the beneficiary picking up the interim tab. The delay serves as a sort of deductible in days. The policy should be clear on this or the applicant should be told what levels of care are covered and for how long. Some policies offer custodial care for six months or not at all but cover skilled nursing for four years or more. Yet, according to an LTC guide, "Cases requiring skilled nursing care for as long as six months, let alone longer, are extremely rare." Some insurers now broaden nursing home policies to include home health care that reimburses for homemaker services as well as for skilled care. Prudential pays $25 a visit for up to 365 visits by a licensed home health aide, without the traditional three-day hospital stay, though the deductible is 90 days

Does the policy exclude any medical problems?   Nearly half of all nursing home patients are confined because of Alzheimer's disease or other organically related mental disorders, chiefly multiple infarct dementia, a form of senility. Pass up any policy that excludes "mental disorders" unless the seller satisfies you that organically based mental disease is covered. A report last year by Consumer Health Advocates Inc. and commissioned by the Massachusetts insurance division recommended that all policies incorporate a common set of minimum standards for preexisting conditions and waiting periods and that insurers be prevented from excluding anyone who has been diagnosed as having Alzheimer's disease or related disorders after the policy is in force.

Waiver of premiums once benefits start or three to six months later is an option to look for. Also look for language guaranteeing renewal of the policy; renewal at the company's option is more likely to protect the seller than you.

If your state has strict insurance rules and powers of enforcement, consider asking for help in shopping. A booklet highlighting the main points for comparing long-term-care insurance, along with worksheets to record your findings, is available from Group Health Cooperative of Puget Sound.[1] Another publication, *A Comprehensive Guide to Medicare and Health Insurance for Older People*, is available from LTC Inc.[2]

---

1. $3 from Group Health Cooperative of Puget Sound, Senior Programs, 1st Floor, 221 First Ave. W., Seattle, WA 98119.

2. $5 from LTC Inc., 10940 NE. 33rd Pl., Suite 205, Bellevue, WA 98004.

21

GETTING ORGANIZED: A RECORD-KEEPING SYSTEM THAT WORKS FOR YOU

Patricia Walsh

See if you know the answers to these questions: Where is the title to your car? What did the refrigerator cost? Is it still under warranty? Where is the warranty? What are the maturity dates on your certificates of deposit? What's the cash value of your life insurance policy?

Setting up and maintaining a basic record-keeping system will put the answers to these and other important questions at your fingertips. The time and effort it takes to organize a record-keeping system is a small price to pay for the rewards you will reap.

Your system can serve as a financial blueprint showing how your money is distributed among bank accounts, real estate, insurance policies, and other financial instruments. You'll know where your money is and how it's doing and be able to act quickly to take advantage of some opportunity, whether it's selling your second car or switching money between investments.

Having your records in order is the essential first step before you can prepare a net-worth statement, obtain sound advice from your financial planner or accountant, or have your lawyer draw up your will. A basic record-keeping system will enable you or another family member to act quickly in an emergency such as a serious illness or death, and it will prevent valuable resources from "falling through the cracks." Resources such as bank accounts, life insurance policies, and retirement benefits often go uncollected because they've been forgotten. Finally, a record-keeping system provides the basis for family members to set financial goals and work toward them as a team.

A basic record-keeping system

To be effective, a record-keeping system need not be elaborate. In fact, the simpler it is, the better. The three key components of a good, basic system are

- At-home files
- A safe deposit box
- A personal/financial planning logbook.

The first step in setting up a system is pulling all the pieces together—out of shoe boxes, desk drawers, manila folders, and closet shelves. Bite the bullet and start collecting, reviewing, and sorting your records. First decide what to keep and what to discard. Then determine where to keep the records and documents you wish to retain. It might take a few phone calls to your lawyer, banker, accountant, and others to fill in information gaps to complete your records.

Psych yourself up for this odious task any way you can. Remember, once it's done, it's done for good, because you will be religious about updating the information and keeping your system current.

Hold a record round-up. Assign each family member to track down specific information or documents. Or make it a weekend project for yourself. And reward yourself well once it's done—dinner and a movie, a new fishing rod, whatever it takes to get you in gear. Pay the price. It's an investment in your future.

At-home files

The records you decide to keep at home should be stored in a heat- and fire-resistant metal cabinet that can be locked. Put records and documents less than three years old in an active file. Everything else can go in an inactive file. Once a year it will be necessary to shift items between your active and inactive files and throw out those items that have become obsolete.

Here are some suggestions for what to keep at home:

- Appliance manuals and warranties in effect
- Credit-card records
- Education, medical, and employment records
- Federal and state tax returns with documentation (the IRS

has a three-year statute of limitations unless income is un-
derreported by 25 percent, fraud is suspected, or no return
was filed)
- Receipts for expensive items and items under warranty
- Paid bills (length of time depends on specific item)
- Unpaid bills
- Bank books and statements
- Canceled checks
- Insurance policies
- Home improvement records
- Loan statements and payment records
- Property tax receipts
- Passports
- Pension, profit-sharing, annuity, and personal retirement
  plan records
- Social Security cards
- Salary records to check against W-2 forms at end of the year
- Safe deposit box inventory, keys, appraisals of items in box
- Wills (you may keep the original of your will at home, but
  most people prefer to leave it with their attorney or execu-
  tor).

Safe deposit box

A safe deposit box is the place to store documents and valuables
that would be difficult, if not impossible, to replace.

Many states seal a safe deposit box upon the death of one of its
owners. For that reason, items such as the originals of wills, life
insurance policies, deeds to cemetery plots, and other information
needed to settle an estate should *not* be kept in a safe deposit box.
In addition, appraisals of and receipts for valuables kept in a safe
deposit box should be stored at home.

Before renting a safe deposit box, find out how much insurance the bank carries on box contents. Then find out if your homeowner's insurance covers the contents of your box. You may have
to obtain additional insurance.

Ask the bank personnel about restrictions on what can be kept
in the box and how access to the box can be obtained in case of
your disability or death.

Here are some suggestions for what to keep in a safe deposit
box:

- Adoption, birth, marriage, divorce, death, citizenship, and
  military discharge records

- Certificates of deposit, stock and bond certificates, trust agreements
- Contracts and promissory notes
- Titles to property (except cemetery plots)
- Court decrees
- Household inventory (including receipts, appraisals, and photographs of valuable items)
- Valuable jewelry, coins, stamps, mementos.

Personal/financial planning logbook

The key to making your record-keeping system work well either as a financial planning tool or in an emergency is your personal-financial planning logbook. Its purpose is to compile in one place

- Personal and family information
- Control forms listing the location of all important records and documents
- A summary of all important financial instruments.

You can buy a logbook at most bookstores or create your own, using a notebook. If your financial situation is complex and you have a personal computer, consider using one of the many computerized record-keeping/financial-planning programs on the market. Check their ratings in *Consumer Reports*, ask friends for recommendations, and then shop around for the best buy. For most of us, however, a logbook like those found in most bookstores will work quite well.

In selecting a logbook, consider which of the following items you want to record, then choose the book that comes closest to meeting your requirements. You'll probably want to record information for some or all of the categories listed below.

Personal and family information   For each member of the immediate family, it would be helpful to know

- Name, address, home and work telephone numbers
- Birthdate, Social Security number
- Marital status, place and date of marriage, date of divorce.

For yourself and your spouse, if married, you may also want to compile information on

- Educational history
- Military record

- Employment history
- Medical history, including allergies, medications, immunizations, and chronic or serious illnesses
- Specific instructions in case of incapacity or death
- Location of original of will; date will was executed; name, address, and telephone number of executor.

Control forms   Having everything neatly filed in your heat- and fire-resistant cabinet, your safe deposit box, office safe, or with your lawyer will not do much good unless you know what went where. Your logbook should include the following forms:

- Master form for recording the location of all documents
- Safe deposit box inventory listing contents of the box, location, names and telephone numbers of people with access to the box, and where you keep the keys to the box
- A professional advisers form listing the names, addresses, and telephone numbers of doctors, dentist, clergy, lawyers, accountant, investment broker, financial planner, trust officer, pension adviser, insurance agents, and other experts you contact regularly.

Financial summary   Most logbooks typically include forms for recording details for each of the following financial categories. Make sure the logbook you select goes into the amount of detail you wish to record for each category or allows space for you to add more information.

- Bank, savings and loan, and credit union accounts
- Trust agreements
- Investments (stocks, bonds, mutual funds, money-market funds)
- Real estate holdings
- Business interests
- Installment loans
- Home equity loan or account
- Credit cards and charge accounts
- Insurance policies and annuities
- Pensions, profit-sharing plans, and personal retirement plans, including information on survivors' benefits.

To remain useful, a record-keeping system must be kept up to date. Review it at least once a year or whenever a significant change in your circumstances—such as a job change, marriage, or divorce—warrants.

The financial summaries should be reviewed more frequently. A periodic review will jog your memory about things that need to be done: updating a will, changing a beneficiary, increasing liability coverage, or deciding what to do with a certificate of deposit that will mature shortly. As you review each category, make a "to do" list to prod you into action on these or other matters that require your attention.

22

DO SHOP AROUND
FOR THE RIGHT ADVICE

*Choosing the wrong personal planner
can be a costly mistake*

Richard Weatherington

The price on the gas pump reads 29.9¢ for regular, rib steak sells for 69¢ a pound and, if you drive a hard bargain, you can buy a new luxury car for only $3,300. Your passbook savings account earns 4 percent per year; about the only other "investment" choice you have, if you don't mind a little risk, is gold at $40 an ounce, a hot tip from Wall Street, or a long shot running at Santa Anita.

But that was the early sixties, before the Vietnam war and the Arab oil embargo. Then there was little need for financial planners, and there were few investment choices for those who *did* need them. Back then, true financial planners concentrated on the fiscal fat cat who could afford to smoke a Havana cigar or buy a Rolls Royce on a whim; the rest mainly used the title to help sell more insurance for their firms.

Now, however, there's a virtual supermarket of investments to whet even the modest financial palate. Options abound, and a fast-growing group of financial planners are eager to help the middle-class investor spend wisely—or, in some cases, to relieve that investor of money and provide little in return.

True, the right planner can help you steer your shopping cart efficiently through the mountains of quality and junk products being offered in today's financial marketplace. Before rushing headlong into the arms of one of these whiz kids, however, you should

Reprinted with permission of the author from *Modern Maturity* magazine, Special Financial Issue, 1988, 18, 20–22. Copyright 1988 by Richard Weatherington.

(1) determine if you really *need* a financial planner's services and (2) learn what traps to avoid when selecting one.

"The main thing a planner does is provide order and system for an individual's financial life. In the extreme case, that means making order out of chaos; in the best of all worlds, it means helping someone who's well organized become even *more* effective in his or her money management," according to Donald Pitti, a vice president for John Nuveen and Company of New York City and former chairman of the board of the International Association for Financial Planning.

Do you need help?

If you make more than $25,000 a year, financial planning may be beneficial; if your income is lower, there's usually little left after the bills and taxes to play with, much less to salt away; even so, "since financial planning is the coordination of a person's total finances, there's a need for some type of planning at *every* income level," says Becky Juhan Crawford, a certified public accountant and certified financial planner in Lakewood, Colorado. "Income of $25,000 or more is a starting point, but it shouldn't rule out someone below that level if positive results can be obtained from tax savings or proper investment planning."

The average person is, realistically speaking, ill equipped to deal effectively with the increasing number of ways to invest money and the divergent strategies available. Many are overwhelmed by such buzz words as high-tech stocks, T-bills, no-load mutual funds, and zero-coupon bonds, not to mention insurance, budgets, taxes, estates, and retirement programs—all of which a professional planner can and should coordinate. A private survey several years ago indicated that fewer than 17 percent of married couples earning over $50,000 a year felt secure about their personal financial decisions.

While you *may* be able to understand and handle these things yourself, you probably haven't done so. Too often, people procrastinate—then grumble about working so hard and keeping so little. A financial planner, however, can fit together all the pieces of your personal economic puzzle, provide a coordinated, written plan for you to adopt, then follow up in the years to come by adjusting the plan when changes occur and helping you implement it.

"Planning can help you become a better financial shopper and improve your money management," says Pitti. "It can help you better utilize what you already have and create more of what you haven't."

Any of the following "ifs" may signal a need to seek professional help:

- If you're ready to step off the sidelines and get serious about investing
- If you already pay too much in taxes (generally anything above a 28–33 percent effective bracket)
- If you can't seem to save money in spite of ever-increasing income
- If you're underinsured (and thus ripe for a loss)
- If you're starting to plan for a child's or grandchild's future education
- If a review of your Social Security benefits indicates they will be inadequate when you retire
- If you anticipate a major change—divorce, new business or job, relocation, income fluctuation, significant tax law revision—that will impact your savings or investments
- If you run a small business and your personal financial well-being is tied to its future
- If your financial affairs have grown beyond the capabilities of your present advisers—insurance agents, brokers, accountants, attorneys, etc.
- If your sleep is troubled because of increasing concern about your financial future
- If your investments languish year after year because you lack the time to do your own planning.

Locating a good planner

If the foregoing list convinces you that you need a financial planner, trying to find a good one could make you feel like you've just shot the Colorado rapids in a leaky rubber boat.

"When looking for a planner, proceed with caution," warns James H. Stevens Jr., a principal with Creative Planning Inc. of Kansas City, Missouri, a certified financial planner and a master of financial science. "You should ask the prospect what qualifications he or she has. Merely being a lawyer does *not* automatically qualify someone to do total financial planning."

The field of financial planning is hot right now, and, as usually is the case with any profession growing at a record rate, regulation lags behind. As a result there are hordes of vultures out there, posing as bona fide practitioners but ready to pick your bones. There are also countless recycled salesmen, agents, and dealers hoping to beef up their customer lists by adding another title to their business cards. Finding a good *anything* is 90 percent legwork, and financial planners are no different.

You can find financial planners through the Yellow Pages, of course—though going that route is a lot like selecting a family doctor by drawing straws. Or you can call or write one of the trade associations listed in the accompanying sidebar. Your best bet, however, is recommendations from friends you respect or from your attorney, banker, or accountant.

And you'll want to comparison-shop. If possible, talk to at least three different planners and compare their styles, programs, and fees. Take your spouse along if you're married so you can both express your needs and compare impressions.

You should feel comfortable with the planner since you'll likely end up telling him or her more about your personal affairs than you would your psychiatrist.

The planner should ask you a lot of questions about your financial situation; for example, What are the short- and long-range goals? How much risk are you willing to take? A good planner should also be prepared to

- Give you a comprehensive and written plan
- Recommend ways to improve your present situation
- Explain the basis for his or her recommendations
- Provide you with the pros and cons of each suggestion
- Identify financial problems.

Ask if the financial planner is willing to consult with your existing attorney, accountant, banker, broker, or insurance agent. If not, move on. An effective plan needs to be coordinated. As Crawford points out, "People have the view that financial planning is primarily associated with particular fields, such as insurance or investments. But true planning should involve *all* areas, including income, investments, retirement, and taxes. Planners should be willing to work with other professionals when necessary."

Ask about follow-up and monitoring of the plan. A planner should suggest follow-up reviews at least annually and after any major change in your situation or in the tax laws. Ask the planners you see to explain their areas of expertise, the types of clients they're seeking, and the techniques and procedures they use to reach their clients' goals. If the planner provides a newsletter for clients, ask for sample copies.

If you're comfortable with a planner at this point, find out about his or her professional background, credentials, and trade affiliations. There are a number of professional designations be-

---

Where to start

A good way to look for a financial planner is through a trade association. Write or call one or both of these for lists of planners in your area.

International Association for Financial Planning (IAFP), 2 Concourse Parkway, Suite 800, Atlanta, GA 30328; 404-395-1605. This 24,000-member organization will also include names of members who meet the tough experience, education, and examination requirements to qualify for IAFP's Registry of Financial Planning Practitioners. In addition, IAFP offers two free booklets: *A Consumer's Guide to Comprehensive Financial Planning*; and *Building a Capital Base*. The latter contains a general overview of financial planning and planners, the Association's code of ethics, a glossary of financial terms, and a three-page worksheet to compute your own cash-flow net worth. You can request the booklets by calling the Association's customer relations department toll-free at 800-241-2148.

Institute of Certified Financial Planners (ICFP), 10065 East Harvard Ave., Suite 320, Denver, CO 80231-5942; 303-751-7600. This 8,500-member organization works closely with the College for Financial Planning.

---

stowed on those who have completed some educational requirements and who have professional experience in accounting, law, insurance, investments, or similar fields. The three most common designations are Certified Financial Planner (CFP), Chartered Financial Consultant (ChFC), and Registry of Financial Planning Practitioners—which many consider the toughest to obtain.

While this alphabet soup behind the name may seem impressive, competency should still be measured by a track record. What do the planner's customers say about his or her service? How long has the planner been in business? How many clients continue each year? (If the prospect has been in the business or a related profession less than three years, or if his or her turnover exceeds 25 percent, look for the door.)

"A safety device few consumers understand is registration with the Securities and Exchange Commission," says Stevens. "By registering, a planner places his or her practice under the Commission's rules, which include total disclosure and liability to the client. The very detailed registration form is open for public inspection. Planners who are registered investment advisers are thus subject to tighter controls."

A planner's education should never stop. Does the planner attend seminars to keep up to date? Take continuation courses in new areas of planning? Avoid or refer some areas to another professional? A planner who claims to do everything is either suspect or a phenomenon. Find out what the planner did before becoming a financial adviser. In a practically unregulated trade, one could be a cook today, a financial planner tomorrow.

Be leery of planners who take little time to find out about you and your finances and instead spend most of their time touting specific plans to buy. Likewise, watch for planners who move you toward exotic tax shelters or urge you to reposition all of your present assets *immediately*. The IRS has all but declared war on most tax shelters, and financial planners should be very cautious about making changes with your assets all at once.

Paying the piper

Remembering that there's no free lunch, see how much such service will impact your bank account. Financial planners usually charge in one of three ways: flat or hourly fee only, commissions only, or a combination of the two. Hourly rates generally range from $50 to $150, flat fees from $500 to $5,000, depending on the complexity of your finances. Regardless of the fee, most true financial planners hope to earn you twice that amount in tax savings and return on your money the first year.

"There's a lot of controversy between commission-only and fee-only financial planners," says Crawford. "I believe fee-only planners can be more unbiased in their recommendations. Commission-only planners, I'm afraid, may be more likely to lean toward items that yield higher commissions."

Admittedly, a commission-based planner needs to sell his or her products—whether insurance, investments, or retirement plans—to provide the planning services. You should not, however, be pressured to buy a particular item. Be especially wary if the planner insists you buy all recommended items from him or her *personally*.

It would be wise to ask a commission-only planner what percentage of sales are of a particular investment vehicle; if that vehicle accounts for 85 percent of all products sold, you need to look at the setup very carefully. A planner who acts like a bumptious used-car salesman on a slow night may be nothing more than a product pusher.

Stevens points out that "planners need to disclose to their clients any conflict of interest that could possibly arise. There's a lot of product selling involved, and planners should reveal not only the fact that they'll make a commission on a sale, but how much. That way all the cards are on the table, and a planner won't violate the customer's trust or be committing fraud."

Besides the standard arrangements, there are computerized financial plans available for as little as $25. While this may be a beneficial first step for the uninitiated or undisciplined, you may get little more than a computer printout and a pat on the head.

Proceed with care

Now that you've spent the twenty-plus hours needed to adequately investigate the financial planning field, have enough reasons to seek help, and have found a planner you're comfortable with, don't suddenly kick back and send your brain out to lunch. There remain two important admonitions:

- *Never* delegate or abdicate your financial responsibility. The planner is not there to manage your money but to provide overall direction and make planning sensible. He or she should *not* make financial decisions for you.
- If you don't feel comfortable with a recommendation the planner makes, don't blindly follow it. Get a second opinion—as you would if your doctor recommended major surgery.

Be realistic

Don't go to a financial planner with unrealistic goals. He or she isn't Merlin incarnate. And don't expect the expert to dig through boxes looking for just the right data to produce the perfect plan for you. *You* have to gather that information.

By and large, these are some of the things your planner *won't* do: Balance your checkbook, set up an estate, choose your investments, guarantee a return on your money, plan your children's schooling or your retirement, set your future goals, try to read your mind, or hound you to carry out the plan he or she has designed for you. Planners are not nursemaids, Wall Street wizards, or crystal ball-gazers.

One final warning: The information a planner has about clients is not protected; it can be obtained through legal action. If you

What to start with

A financial planner can't create an economic plan for you out of thin air. He or she will need to know where you stand today in order to calculate where you should be in the future. Many planners will ask you to dig deep into your records and provide the following information:

1. Your present income from all sources and a history of past increases that may indicate future trends
2. Copies of all tax returns (federal, state, gift, corporate, etc.) for the past three to five years
3. Family data: marital status, dependents, and future family plans
4. Copies of any incorporation or partnership agreements that might impact your finances
5. Copies of any wills, divorce decrees, or trust agreements in effect
6. Insurance policies (including group) covering health, disability, life, property, and casualty
7. List of assets—including stocks, bonds, savings, educational trusts, and annuities
8. Data on any business activities indicating profits, loss, and history
9. Financial statements for your individual activities and business ventures
10. Data on your real estate holdings
11. Information on all employee benefits, IRAs, Keogh Plans and other retirement programs

have financial skeletons in your closet, therefore, consult your attorney before giving sensitive documents to your financial planner.

What tomorrow looks like

Though total financial planning as a profession is only about seventeen years old, it is estimated that 21 percent of all American households with combined incomes of over $67,000 per year are now using professional advisers. A growing number of companies are even offering financial planning to their executives as an employee benefit.

Never before has the financial supermarket offered such a smorgasbord to select from—and the variety is not about to shrink. Thus, picking and choosing the best products can be as difficult and time consuming as comparing a food chain's nutrition labels.

But the first bit of comparison-shopping that you must do involves looking for the right planner. Follow a good financial planner's advice as you would a consumer advocate's, and you should end up with a tasty meal. Fall prey to the fine print, however, and you could end up just another plucked duck.

23

KEEP YOUR ESTATE
SAFE FOR YOUR FAMILY

Walter W. David

Pity poor George Farmer. He always meant to draw up a will, but he never quite got around to it. He figured if anything happened to him, his wife would get everything anyway, so there was no rush.

But when George died from a stroke, his estate was thrown into disarray. Without a will, probate and administration of the estate siphoned off 25 percent of the estate's assets instead of the more usual 8 percent.

What was worse, the courts divided the estate among George's wife and four children according to a prescribed formula for that state. Because George's true wishes were not known, his wife didn't receive enough of the estate to support her income needs. For lack of a simple, relatively inexpensive document, George left behind confusion, an unnecessary financial drain on his estate, and potential hardship for his wife of many years.

For people of modest means, taxes and other estate costs will probably be minimal. However, the more substantial your assets, the more important it becomes to assess and minimize future liability. There are a number of ways to substantially reduce taxes and other estate costs—once you estimate what they will be.

The estate tax

The first step in estimating your estate taxes is to take an inventory of all the estate's taxable assets. This would include any life insur-

Reprinted with permission from *The 50 Plus Guide to Retirement Investing*, by Walter W. David. © Dow Jones-Irwin, 1987.

ance that is payable to your estate, business, or partnership interests; any patents or copyrights that you own; and the value of your retirement plans, whether they are IRA, pension, or Keogh plans. In addition, you must include all your personal assets such as automobiles, household goods, and jewelry.

Some assets that you will not need to include are insurance which is payable to other beneficiaries and in which you have no ownership and the value of future income that you may receive after your death. The worksheet (Figure 1) will help you.

Allowable deductions   The next step is to value each of the assets. The total of all these assets is called your gross estate. Fortunately, you do not have to pay tax on this entire amount; you're allowed deductions in five main categories:

1.   *Debts and liabilities.* These include the money owed on mortgages, bank loans, unpaid taxes, or similar debts.
2.   *Expenses for funeral and administration of estate.* These include attorney's fees, administrator's commissions, court

Stocks	$_____
Bonds	_____
Cash, including money markets	_____
Real estate owned and mortgages held	_____
Annuities	_____
Insurance you own	_____
Insurance payable to your estate	_____
Money owed you	_____
Partnerships	_____
Some retirement plan benefits	_____
Rights to taxable income	_____
Personal belongings, including cars, furniture, jewelry, etc.	_____
Total	$_____

Figure 1.   Value of taxable property for estate.

costs, and appraiser's fees. Also deductible are any losses in the value of the assets during the administration period, unless they are covered by insurance.

3. *Federal estate tax credit.* Under certain circumstances, any part of the property which has previously been taxed as part of another estate will not incur the full tax again.

4. *Contributions made to charity.* Any amounts left to charity are deducted from the gross estate.

5. *Marital deduction.* This is probably one of the most important deductions. Put simply, all assets that are given to a surviving spouse are exempt from estate tax.

Use the Federal Estate Tax Estimate worksheet (Figure 2) to help calculate the amount of your taxable estate. After you have that, you will receive one additional deduction—the unified tax credit.

The unified tax credit.   The federal government allows a specified amount to be deducted from each estate before a final tax figure is arrived at. After you calculate the taxable estate and determine the amount of tax owed on it from the tax table in Table 2, you are allowed to subtract the amount of the unified tax credit to get the amount of actual tax owed. In 1987 and thereafter, the unified tax credit is $192,800.

Sometimes it is easier to think of the unified tax credit as an

---

Gross estate		$ _____
Debts	_____	
Administrative expenses (approximately 8 percent)	_____	
Contributions to charity	_____	
Marital deduction		− _____
Taxable estate		= _____
Tax due before unified credit		= _____
Unified credit		− _____
Total tax due		$ _____

Figure 2. Federal estate tax estimate worksheet.

Table 1.   Federal gift and estate tax rates through 1987.

If taxable amount is		The tax is	Plus	Amount over
Over	But not over			
0	$10,000	0	18%	0
$10,000	20,000	$1,800	20	$10,000
20,000	40,000	3,800	22	20,000
40,000	60,000	8,200	24	40,000
60,000	80,000	13,000	26	60,000
80,000	100,000	18,200	28	80,000
100,000	150,000	23,800	30	100,000
150,000	250,000	38,800	32	150,000
250,000	500,000	70,800	34	250,000
500,000	750,000	155,800	37	500,000
750,000	1,000,000	248,300	39	750,000
1,000,000	1,250,000	345,800	41	1,000,000
1,250,000	1,500,000	448,300	43	1,250,000
1,500,000	2,000,000	555,800	45	1,500,000
2,000,000	2,500,000	780,800	49	2,000,000
2,500,000	3,000,000	1,025,800	53	2,500,000
3,000,000			55	3,000,000

exemption. Thinking of it that way, it means the first $600,000 of a taxable estate will not be subject to tax.

Another simple way of reducing your taxable estate is through the giving of gifts.

Gift giving

Gift giving should be considered a total part of your estate planning strategy. By giving away some of your holdings, instead of leaving them for an estate, you can not only reduce your taxes but also have the joy of seeing your loved ones benefit from your generosity.

However, there are four important things to consider before you decide to give a gift:

1. *Giving up control.* Once you have given something away, you have given up the right to it and all control over it. This sometimes can be very difficult to deal with psychologically, and the benefits of any tax reduction must be weighed against these considerations.
2. *Can you afford it?* Very large estates may find it easy to provide for some gift giving, but smaller estates must be very careful lest assets are depleted. Naturally, it is impossible to predict to the last penny what your future income needs

might be, but be as certain as possible that whatever you give away won't be needed in the future.

3. *Tax implications.* Because the government has already anticipated that you might use a gift as a method of escaping estate taxes, it levies a gift tax at approximately the same rate as estate taxes (more about this later). Be sure that you determine the tax implications. Will it benefit your estate? What effect will the gift have on the taxes of the person to whom you are giving it?

4. *Timing of the gift.* Achieving your personal objectives is an important part of any gift-giving program. The payoff may come not just from giving money to your loved ones but from giving it to them at a time when they need it most.

Non-cash gifts   When giving property other than cash, there are two important tax considerations:

1. *Don't give depreciated property.* It is normally not advisable to give property whose value has dropped below your original costs. You can't take a tax deduction for the lost value, and neither can the donees (the persons receiving the gift).

2. *Give appreciated property to charities only.* It is usually not a good idea to give away appreciated property unless it is given to a charity. If the donee should sell the property after receiving it, the donee will owe tax on the entire capital gain. If the same asset were left in your estate, any capital gains from your original purchase until your death would never be taxed.

    One exception to this rule might be a situation in which you have assets that you expect to appreciate significantly in the future. By giving away such an asset before it appreciates, you escape both gift and estate tax on the future appreciation.

    Another possible exception is when the donees have a much lower tax bracket than yours. If you give them your appreciated asset to sell, when they sell it they pay the capital gains at a lower rate.

Gift taxes

If estate taxes are designed to reduce the assets passed from one generation to another, gift taxes are designed to prevent you from avoiding the estate tax; they are figured at the same rate as the estate tax.

Gift taxes are paid by the giver on April 15 of the year following the gift. Taxes are paid on the fair market value of the property you've given away.

The unified credit   Each person making a gift may use the same unified credit that we discussed under estate taxes. But once you have used up your unified credit in gift giving, it is not available to be used against your future estate taxes. In 1987, a donor could give as much as $600,000 without incurring gift taxes. This means that a husband and wife together could give away $1,200,000 before incurring any gift taxes.

Four kinds of gifts help you avoid gift taxes completely:

1. *$10,000 annually.* You can give away as much money as you want without ever being taxed so long as you give no more than $10,000 to any one person in any one year. There is no limitation on the number of years this may be done. Each individual donor (the person doing the giving) is allowed $10,000 per year per donee. If a husband and wife decide to give gifts to their children, each child can receive $10,000 from his or her father and $10,000 from his or her mother, for a total of $20,000 per child. In the case of three children, for example, this allows parents to give away $60,000 tax free each year.
2. *Charitable organizations.* Gifts to bona fide charitable organizations are not subject to gift taxes.
3. *Tuition.* You may pay the tuition for your children or grandchildren or anyone else you would like without those payments being taxed as gifts. Only tuition is covered under this exemption. Books, room, board, and the like are not considered tax-free gifts. You must make the payments of the tuition directly to the educational institution, and not to the students involved.
4. *Medical costs.* Direct payments of the medical expenses of another are not subject to gift taxes so long as you make the payments directly to the provider of the medical services, not to the person receiving treatment.

The gift tax return   IRS forms 709 and 709A are used to report gifts on an annual basis. It is necessary to file the return if charitable gifts of over $10,000 are given, even if the charitable deduction would reduce the taxable gift to zero, and even if the unified credit completely offsets any taxes owed. It is not necessary to file if $10,000 or less is given to each donee, or if the gift is to a spouse qualifying for the unlimited marital deduction.

The will

Any money that you don't spend or give away will be distributed by the court after you're gone. To be sure that the money is distributed as you want, you should leave a legal will.

Many people feel that because they have their assets in joint tenancy with their spouses they don't need a will. As George Farmer proved, this simply is not true

Because your will is such an important document, you may want to utilize the services of an attorney who specializes in this area. Before sitting down with your attorney, however, you must decide how you want the division of your estate to be calculated: in percentages of the total value, or in terms of specific assets to be distributed to each beneficiary, or a combination of the two.

Another important decision is the choice of executor. Your executor is the one charged with the responsibility of taking care of all the administrative duties of your estate. In general, executors are entitled to compensation for these services and in most states must post a bond to ensure that they perform the duties adequately. If you are going to name a relative as executor, you can allow that person to serve without the necessary bond by stating that in your will.

Your will should be drafted, signed, and witnessed so as to meet all the requirements of state law. Once the will is drawn up, it may be changed from time to time. It is probable that you will want to periodically review your will to ensure that it still meets your personal objectives and is taking maximum advantage of any changes in federal or state tax laws.

If the changes in your will are major ones, you may want to draw up an entirely new document. If, however, the changes are minor, you may make the changes by simply amending the will with a codicil. Be sure, if you do make an amendment to your will, it does not contradict any of the other provisions of the will.

Because of the importance of this legal document, keep it safe and accessible. Many find it convenient to leave a copy of their will with their attorney. Be sure to tell a close friend or relative exactly where your will is kept so that it can be found in a timely manner. A delay in locating it could cause substantial inconvenience for your beneficiaries. It is also very practical to keep an unsigned copy of your will at home so that you can refer to it from time to time.

24

PASS IT ON

Where there's a will, there's a way to keep
Uncle Sam out of your family's inheritance

Julie Whitmore

It could happen to you. Kenneth McGee was 65 when he died un-expectedly in January of a heart attack. The sudden tragedy left his 58-year-old widow, Marilyn, broken-hearted—and broke.

Marilyn won't be able to receive Social Security until she is 62, although she will be entitled to survivorship benefits when she is 60. She has lost the motel business she and Kenneth had managed because it's too much work for just one person. And the mortgage on their new motor home, which Kenneth's monthly Social Security checks had been paying off, is much more than the $10,000 in life insurance Kenneth left her.

The result? Because Marilyn has no other means of support, she has been forced to move in with her stepdaughter, Judith and has become her dependent.

It's a ticklish situation that never should have happened, says Kenneth's daughter, Judith McGee, who heads a Spokane, Washington, financial planning firm called Associated Investment Advisers. McGee had always assumed her father had prepared his estate. Her father, on the other hand, had always assumed he had plenty of time for such things because longevity runs in the family. But a few simple preparations, like the purchase of credit life insurance, could have saved McGee's stepmother from financial disaster while she was experiencing the anguish of her husband's death.

Reprinted with permission of the author from *Mature Outlook*, September/October 1987, 44, 47–51, 53. Copyright 1987 by Julie Whitmore.

When you put off or avoid estate planning for any reason, you're making a big mistake. In fact, the planning you do now actually can make things easier for you and your family later.

Benefits of estate planning

How? According to Graydon Calder, a San Diego financial planner, preparing your estate now can pay off by

- Ensuring that you and your spouse will have enough money to live on in retirement. You can plan how to use your assets most efficiently while both of you are alive and minimize taxes for the survivor when the first spouse dies.
- Helping you avoid a court-supervised conservatorship (guardian) if you become incapacitated
- Passing your assets on to your heirs exactly as you wish
- Avoiding probate for your heirs, if you choose to
- Minimizing federal estate taxes and state inheritance taxes for your heirs.

Although estates under $600,000 are exempt from federal taxes, and spouses enjoy an unlimited exemption, state inheritance taxes can take a bite from even small estates.

Those are goals that everyone—no matter how large or small the size of his or her estate—can benefit from achieving. Even if you always have paid careful attention to financial planning and personal investments, your estate isn't necessarily in order.

Components of estate planning

Getting your estate in order is a two-step process: deciding on a plan, which might entail consulting with a financial planner, a lawyer, an accountant, and a life insurance salesperson; and following up on its implementation, which requires a lawyer. Although some financial planners are lawyers, make sure you check the planner's credentials thoroughly before you hire him or her. You need to be certain that your plans comply with the legal requirements of your state—and that takes special expertise.

As a general rule, estate planners recommend at least a valid will and one or both of these tools:

- A durable power of attorney
- A revocable or "living" trust.

The will   For smaller estates—those consisting of a home and a little nest egg, for example—a will might be enough, says Chicago attorney Judith McCue, a partner with Keck, Mahin & Cate who specializes in estate planning, probate, and trust administration.

If you don't have a will when you die, the state will distribute your assets according to its own laws, which might or might not correspond with your wishes. And the probate court, which handles all matters involving wills and estates, will appoint an administrator or executor, probably a family member or a lawyer.

For the will to be valid, it must be clear that you intended the document to be a will. Your signature usually is considered the most important evidence of that intent. Your lawyer can convert your ideas to standard language acceptable to your state courts.

The will must be witnessed by people who do not have anything to gain from it, such as neighbors or casual friends. Most states require two witnesses, but it's important to check with your lawyer for the specific number of witnesses required in your state.

Although some wills not drawn up by lawyers are accepted by the courts, don't count on that, notes Boston lawyer Steven Riemer. It's always best to work with a professional who knows the ins and outs of estate laws, which vary from state to state.

Lawyers generally charge by the hour, and legal fees vary across the country. But the simplest, most basic document will likely cost about $150 to prepare.

Your will can be as general or as specific as you wish, but it should include references to your financial assets, *and* to any prized personal possessions as well, such as the family silverware or a favorite stamp collection.

You should name an executor whom you trust and expect to outlive you. If you have children under age 25, you can set up a separate trust for them in the will or elsewhere to postpone distribution of their inheritances to them beyond age 18 (or 21, if provisions are made for distribution to a custodian under the Uniform Transfers to Minors Act). Otherwise, in most states, legal adulthood is assumed at 18—an age when most parents still would prefer some older and wiser supervision.

Although it's your property, one copy of the will should remain with your lawyer for safekeeping. The courts expect a will to be legible, and inserted corrections usually will not be considered valid. They may even serve to revoke the will. If you decide to make changes in your will later, you'll need to have your lawyer draw up a codicil (a supplement) or a completely new will.

Durable power of attorney After you've completed your will, ask your lawyer about drawing up a document designating someone to assume durable power of attorney for you. It will give authority to another person—not necessarily a lawyer—to act in the event of your disability or incompetence; for example, if you suffered a paralyzing stroke or were in a coma from an auto accident. Without the durable power of attorney clause, your physician or hospital would have to search for a family member and ask the court to approve that person's right to act on your behalf—and it might not necessarily be the family member of your choice.

The durable power of attorney clause is designed to be used if you are disabled or incompetent. It does not represent any loss of control for you: Instead, you are *extending* your control by choosing a person you trust to act when you no longer are able to, experts say. That person also may be named executor of the will.

Location of documents   After documents are drawn up, tell family members where they are. And the one place the documents *shouldn't* be is in a safe deposit box, because in many states those boxes are sealed on death. (Some lawyers, however, recommend keeping an extra copy there as an extra safeguard against loss.) A better place might be a fireproof box in your home; you should also leave a copy or the original with the lawyer. Along with estate documents should be any other vital records, such as birth, death, marriage, and divorce certificates.

You should review your estate documents at least every three years and especially after any major life changes. Mary B. knows firsthand how difficult it can be to locate a necessary record. When her husband, a retired lawyer, died at age 78, the federal government held up Mary's pension checks for two months until she submitted a valid death certificate for her husband's first wife, who had died years before their marriage in 1945. During thirty-five years of employment and subsequent retirement, her husband had never changed his beneficiary designation on his official federal benefit file.

But telling relatives where to find documents doesn't mean you have to tell them your plans in great detail, says Washington lawyer John Freeman Blake. Informing children of what you intend to leave them leads them to expect it and to act accordingly, he says. And that might make it more difficult to revise your plans later.

For example, a couple with three children initially might decide to split their estate equally among the three. But ten years after their original will is executed, one son is unmarried, while another is married with three children, including a severely handicapped daughter. The couple might find it psychologically more difficult to change their will to provide more support for the handicapped grandchild if all three children are expecting an equal share.

The living trust   A will and a durable power of attorney can cover the situations every family will encounter, but sometimes a different kind of protection is called for. That's where a "living" trust comes in. It involves maintenance fees, but it's increasingly recommended by estate planners for those with assets of $250,000 or more. The trust (a legal title to property held by one party for the benefit of another) avoids probate and allows arrangements to be completely private.

When Robert Tardiff's father-in-law died several years ago without a trust, his children were confident they had control of the situation. One son was a lawyer, another was an accountant. Nevertheless, "it took eighteen months to settle the estate," says Tardiff, president of Tardiff Financial Services in El Segundo, California. Tardiff's children had to sell the family home, and that required court-approved appraisals of the value of the house and of its final selling price. "Our biggest problem was getting court dates," adds Tardiff. In many states, if the family home had been part of a trust, it would have simply passed on to the successor trustee, who could have kept it or sold it as he pleased.

Financial planner William Kelly, in Little Rock, Arkansas, notes that many people prefer to keep private the extent of their assets and whom they go to. "Probate records are available to all kinds of salesmen [because they're public records]," he points out. Kelly has encountered a number of cases where a recently widowed woman invested her husband's estate proceeds unwisely under pressure from a smooth-talking huckster. By the time Kelly was consulted, the transaction costs for getting out of the investments were significant.

With a trust, a spouse can protect the surviving spouse from having to make investment decisions during the extremely stressful grief period, as long as the surviving spouse is not the successor trustee.

A trust agreement costs somewhat more to draw up than a simple will, and it involves filing additional federal and state tax returns, because the trust is considered a separate legal entity. Annual administrative costs generally run between $300 and $500 for a basic trust administered by a family member, lawyer, or trusted friend. (Most couples also designate one spouse as a trustee.)

Trusts managed by banks or other institutions are much more costly, with annual fees of about three-fourths of 1 percent of assets, plus investment transaction costs.

A typical trust includes a person's or a couple's real assets: farm, home, savings, life insurance, company profit-sharing proceeds, and even stock trading accounts.

The trust creators, called "grantors" in legal terminology, name themselves as beneficiaries of the trust. All the benefits (interest payments, investment returns, the right to live in their house) go to them as long as they live, and to the successor beneficiaries (the surviving spouse and then usually the children) after their deaths. From a practical point of view, there is no difference in how the grantors live or pay bills.

The grantors designate a successor trustee in case they become incapacitated and for when they die. This person takes no part in the decision making unless or until it becomes necessary.

Estate taxation   Most lawyers recommend a trust as part of a large estate so the ultimate beneficiaries can receive as much as possible of the inheritance built up by the couple during their lifetimes. That recommendation stems from the Economic Recovery Tax Act (ERTA) of 1981, still the major law affecting federal estate taxation. Under ERTA, a surviving husband or wife can inherit any amount from the other without paying any federal taxes, and each parent can pass along a total of $600,000 to his or her heirs, free of federal taxes.

But state taxes are another matter. They can be hefty, diminishing the estate that a couple has accumulated for their children. In Pennsylvania, for example, children are taxed at 6 percent of the amount they inherit; lateral heirs, including brothers and sisters, at 15 percent.

Both life insurance proceeds and assets in trust are excluded from the tax in Pennsylvania, according to financial planner Gary Brytcsuk in State College, Pennsylvania. Pennsylvania's law is fairly typical, and some states even are beginning to revise their inheritance taxes to reflect the higher federal limits. That's why it's important to consult a lawyer in your own state when you're planning your estate.

Transfer of titles   After you've decided to use a trust, don't make the common mistake of failing to put all your assets into it. John Freeman Blake calls this the "empty bowl" syndrome.

"A trust is an empty bowl which must be filled with 'soup' in order to provide nourishment," he says. But the bowl will stay empty if the trust is not designated as beneficiary on life insurance policies and if titles to real estate—including the family home—aren't transferred.

"I've had people spend $1,000 preparing a retirement financial plan and then balk at spending $200 to draw up the legal documents to implement it," says Brytcsuk. Like most certified financial planners, Brytcsuk and Tardiff include checklists at the end of their clients' plans and call them to be sure they have carried them out.

Because every insurance company and pension fund uses different language for trust designations, accomplishing transfers of title and beneficiary changes can be tricky. McCue recommends asking if a law firm can handle the chore with paralegal assistance, at a much lower hourly rate than a lawyer would charge.

Special situations

Some people will need more specialized advice from lawyers and accountants with expertise in a particular field:

- Stockholders of privately held companies or family businesses, for example, might want to consider a corporate buy-back agreement, in which the business agrees to purchase, the shares when the shareholder dies. Without a buy-back agreement, the spouse inheriting the stock probably won't be able to convert the holdings to cash if needed, because there will be no ready market in which to sell the stock. Be sure to check with your estate planner about potential tax problems if another close family member also owns part of the business.
- People with small interests in real estate, such as mineral rights from a grandparent's farm in Colorado or shares of the family farm in Kansas, should consider asking their attorney about a buy-sell agreement with other relatives or children upon death, to avoid the expense and trouble of out-of-state probate. Sometimes the probate costs more than the land itself is worth.
- A handicapped child living in a public institution may need to be provided for. If the child becomes a ward of the state when the parents die, the state will take over all of the child's assets and provide basic necessities. But special trusts can be created, with funding as low as $30,000 to

$50,000, to provide for "luxury" items like recreation, clothing, and birthday parties. This kind of planning is very important for people with smaller estates; consult a local handicapped advocacy group or your lawyer.

It's never too early—or too late—to plan an estate you can enjoy and pass on. Like a smoke detector in a home, an estate plan protects against what might happen in the worst case. In the best case, it's just another form of insurance for you and the people you care about.

CONCLUSION:
RETIREMENT PLANNING FOR LIFE FULFILLMENT

David S. Arnold

Retirement planning doesn't begin when you are looking at your Social Security earnings statement to see whether you'll start to draw at age 62 instead of age 65, or when you are shopping for insurance to supplement Medicare. By that time it is much too late. All your decisions, for better or worse, are locked in. As the chapters in this book have shown, retirement is a process that should begin when you are in your thirties.

The major reason is that the world has changed so much in the past generation. Job changes often involve moving to another city, sometimes across the country. We switch jobs much more often; and some of us, as we hit the middle years, change occupations, which may mean going back to school and a whole lot of other complications.

Education no longer stops with the diploma in hand. (It never did, but the penalties for not keeping up today are much more sudden and drastic.)

Family ties are stretched and thin. Relatives may be scattered all over the country. Couples in their middle years are called the "sandwich generation," financially responsible both for children in their teens and twenties and for elderly parents. Divorces and remarriages complicate family relationships still further.

And the financial world has been transformed. In the good old days, a worker had to think only about his (and it usually was "his") pension, the mortgage on his house, and his savings account. If he paid his bills on time, that was it. Today, the investment options are almost endless; Social Security is under constant scrutiny; inflation is built into all financial planning; international finance profoundly affects our money; and everyone has lots of advice about what you should do with your money, your house, and your car.

Sounds like a downer, doesn't it? But it won't be if you (1) think about what is most important in your personal life and (2) keep a few basic records.

On the first point, begin early, in your thirties if possible, to develop the habits of effective living. Your checklist is short but vital.

- Build and maintain your support system. Keep in touch with family and friends. Friendships are not guaranteed, but they can be cultivated.
- Stay fit. The basics for good health are well known and apply at any age, even for people in their seventies and eighties: get moderate exercise, eat a balanced diet, watch your weight, and don't smoke.
- Expand your interests. There's more to life than work, television, and visiting relatives. Seize the day!
- Learning has no age limit. Schooling in many forms will be a part of most jobs. But look beyond the job for educational opportunities—and they are everywhere—that will add zest to family relationships, leisure time, and travel.
- As you reach the middle years, start thinking about where you want to live. Remember, your best bet may well be to stay put.
- Make your home life a partners' program. Plan together.

Records are the legal lifelines for your income and assets. The number and complexity of records may seem overwhelming, but don't back off and say "Forget it!" Do keep the basic records that protect you and yours:

- Social Security earnings statements
- Your will
- Your family budget and annual net-worth statement
- Insurance policies: property, life, car, and health and hospital
- Pension contract and annuity documents
- Sales receipts and other records for furniture, appliances, and other personal property
- Income tax returns.

Do you sometimes answer a questionnaire by checking "All of

the above"? That's the way to look at these checklists. They don't take a lot of time, but they do need periodic attention. For most people, running through the lists once a year should be sufficient.

To conclude, think of this book as a guide for exploring how you want to live right now and in the years ahead and how much you can afford. When you get discouraged—and most of us do, especially about money—review your financial planning and savings objectives.

We live in one of the wealthiest nations in the world and in the best-housed nation in the world. We have the opportunities, unparalleled in history, to plan for fulfilling lives. And that's what retirement planning is all about.

SOURCES OF INFORMATION

Part One

General

Comfort Zones: A Practical Guide for Retirement Planning. Elwood N. Chapman. 1987. $14.95. Crisp Publications, Inc., 95 First Street, Los Altos, CA 94022 (415-949-4888). Highly readable book on taking charge of your life, utilizing your time, improving your health, developing human support systems, financial planning, and personal fulfillment.

Retiring Right. Laurence J. Kaplan. 1987. $12.95. Avery Publishing Group Inc., 350 Thorens Avenue, Garden City Park, NJ 11040 (516-741-2155). Work and play in retirement; understanding Social Security and pension benefits; savings and investments for retirement; life insurance; annuities; taxes; legal issues; housing; and Medicare, Medicaid, and other health insurance. Includes worksheets.

How To Plan Your Successful Retirement. 1988. $9.95 ($6.95 to AARP members) plus $1.75 shipping. AARP Books, Scott, Foresman & Co., 1865 Miner Street, Des Plaines, IL 60016. Health and fitness (exercise, nutrition, coping with stress, wise use of medications), changes in roles and relationships, meaningful use of time, work options in retirement, financial and estate planning, and legal issues facing pre-retirees. Includes checklists, tips, and worksheets.

Roles and relationships

Pathfinders. Gail Sheehy. 1985. $4.95. Bantam, 414 E. Golf Road, Des Plaines, IL 60016 (800-323-9872). A classic book that describes people who came through adult crises in a positive way. Addresses a variety of midlife concerns, including the importance of love and support systems.

The Three Boxes of Life: And How To Get Out of Them. Richard N. Bolles. 1981. $9.95. Ten Speed Press, P.O. Box 7123, Berkeley, CA 94707 (800-841-2665). Innovative ways to look at the time in our lives and how to combine work, leisure, and education in creative ways for greater life satisfaction.

Widow to Widow. Phyllis R. Silverman. 1986. $19.95. Springer Publication, 536 Broadway, New York, NY 10012 (212-431-4370).

Caregiving

Caring for Your Aging Parents. Robert R. Cadmus. 1984. $8.95. Prentice-Hall, 200 Old Tappan Road, Old Tappan, NJ 07675 (201-767-5054). Guidebook for children of aging parents. Provides advice on psychological changes and practical suggestions to make day-to-day living more pleasant for parent and child.

The following free publications are available from the American Association of Retired Persons (AARP). Send request to AARP Fulfillment, 1909 K Street, NW, Washington, DC 20049. Specify title and order number.

Miles Away and Still Caring (D12748): For caregivers who do not live near their elderly parent.

A Handbook About Care in the Home (D955).

The Right Place at the Right Time (D12381): Describes types of long-term-care services available.

Coping and Caring: Living with Alzheimer's Disease (D12441).

See also resource list, "To help your aging parent," in Chapter 4.

Health and fitness

The following two books are available from Random House, 400 Hahn Road, Westminster, MD 21157 (800-638-6460):

How a Man Ages—Growing Older: What To Expect and What You Can Do About It. Curtis Pesmen and the editors of *Esquire.* 1984. $7.95 plus $1.00 shipping. Provides recent medical findings and practical advice. Includes routines to help you stay healthy and fit.

How a Woman Ages—Growing Older: What To Expect and What You Can Do About It. Robin Marantz Heniz and the Editors of *Esquire.* 1985. $7.95 plus $1.00 shipping. Provides recent medical findings and practical advice. Includes routines for staying healthy and fit.

The following two books are available from AARP Books, Scott, Foresman & Co., 1865 Miner Street, Des Plains, IL 60016:

Medical and Health Guide for People Over Fifty. The Dartmouth Institute for Better Health. 1986. $14.95 ($10.95 to AARP members) plus $1.75 shipping. Explains how you can take charge of your health; includes self-care techniques.

Fitness for Life: Exercises for People Over Fifty. Theodore Berland. 1986. $12.95 ($9.45 to AARP members) plus $1.75 shipping.

How to design a fitness plan to achieve your objectives. Includes 14 exercises to assess your current fitness level.

Using Your Time

See the resources listed in Chapter 6: "Voluntary action resources," "Education resources," and "travel resources." See also the Sunday Travel Section of the *New York Times* for innovative travel and sightseeing ideas.

Work in retirement

Success Over Sixty. Albert Myers and Christopher Anderson. 1984. $15.95. Summit Books. Order from Simon & Schuster Order Dept., 200 Old Tappan Road, Old Tappan, NJ 07675 (212-698-7501). Discusses second careers and business and volunteer activities for people over 60. Suggestions for matching past experience to a new career, how to set up a new business, how to become a lifelong learner, and staying physically and mentally fit. Extensive resource section.

The Work Book: Getting the Job You Want. J. Michael Farr, Richard Gaither, and R. Michael Pickrell. 1983. $12.95. Order from Bennett & McKnight, Division of Glencoe, Front and Brown Streets, Riverside, NJ 08075 (800-257-5755). How to find the job you want. Networking, résumés, cover letters, gathering information, and interviewing.

The Age Discrimination in Employment Act Protects Your Rights. Here's How. Updated 1988. American Association of Retired Persons. Free from AARP Fulfillment, 1909 K Street, NW, Washington DC 20049. Specify the title and order number D12386.

Housing

Planning Your Retirement Housing. Michael Sumichrast, Ronald G. Shafer, and Marika Sumichrast. 1984. $8.95 (6.50 to AARP members) plus $1.75 shipping. From AARP Books, Scott, Foresman & Co., 1865 Miner Street, Des Plaines, IL 60016. How to evaluate types of housing, neighborhoods, and communities. Includes checklists for comparisons.

Places Rated Almanac: Your Guide to Finding the Best Places To Live in America. Richard Boyer and David Savageau. 1985. $14.95. Available in most bookstores or write to Rand McNally, P.O. Box 7600, Chicago, IL 60680 (800-323-4070). Rates over 300 American metropolitan areas on climate, housing, health care, safety, economics, recreation, and environmental pollution.

Organizations

American Association of Retired Persons, 1909 K Street, NW, Washington, DC 20049 (202-872-4700). This nonprofit membership/consumer advocacy organization offers many free and low-cost publications and programs on a wide range of topics, including health, Medicare, Social Security, supplementary health insurance, housing options, consumer fraud and protection, safety and crime prevention, retirement planning, caregiving, widowhood, and more. Write for a free publication list.

National Association of Home Care, 209 C Street, NE, Washington, DC 20002 (202-547-7424). National clearinghouse for information on home care agencies. Write for publication list.

Children of Aging Parents, 2761 Trenton Road, Levittown, PA 19056. Refers persons to local self-help groups.

Displaced Homemakers Network, Inc., 1010 Vermont Avenue, NW, Suite 817, Washington, DC 20005 (202-628-6767). Clearinghouse for information of value to displaced homemakers. Refers women to local programs in their communities.

International Franchise Association, 1350 New York Avenue, NW, Suite 900, Washington, DC 20005, (202-628-8000). Write for publication list.

Service Corps of Retired Executives (SCORE) assists people starting their own businesses. See resource listing in Chapter 6, "Voluntary action resources."

For information on programs and services geared toward local residents, contact your local Council on Aging. Check your local telephone directory for a listing

Part Two

General

Personal Financial Planning for Local Government Employees. Edited by Bruce K. Blaylock and Kenneth F. Kennedy. 1987.

$9.25. International City Management Association, 1120 G Street, NW, Washington, DC 20005 (202-626-4600). Topics include selecting a financial planner; the Tax Reform Act of 1986; life, disability, health, and other forms of insurance; investment basics; and financial planning for retirement.

Dow Jones-Irwin Guide to Retirement Planning. Ray Vickers. 1987. $19.95. Dow Jones-Irwin, 1818 Ridge Road, Homewood, IL 60430 (800-323-4560). Provides guidelines for lifetime money management leading to a financially secure retirement. Topics include investment strategies, tax shelters, options for collecting retirement benefits, potential insurance, and legal problems.

(Still!) The Only Investment Guide You'll Ever Need. Andrew Tobias. 1983. Paper, $3.95. (Hardcover edition has been updated to reflect 1986 Tax Reform Act.) Bantam, 414 E. Golf Road, Des Plaines, IL 60016 (800-323-9872). In easy to understand, entertaining language, explains the basics of money management and a common-sense approach to financial planning, the stock market, insurance, real estate, etc.

The following two publications are available free from the American Association of Retired Persons. Send request to AARP Fulfillment, 1909 K Street, NW, Washington, DC 20049.

Your Retirement Income Tax Guide. Revised annually. Provides help to people age 65 and older in filling out federal income tax returns.

Your Retirement State Tax Guide. Provides information by state on income tax, property taxes, sales tax, estate tax, and other taxes or tax credits.

We suggest that you routinely read one or more of the following financially oriented magazines, newsletters, and newspapers to keep up on financial topics. All are available at local libraries and magazine stands. *Business Week, MONEY, Changing Times, Consumer Reports, FORTUNE, The Wall Street Journal,* and *Forbes.*

Social Security

See resource list at the end of Chapter 13.

The Complete and Easy Guide to Social Security and Medicare. Faustin F. Jehle, Updated annually. $9.95. Fraser Publication Co., Madison, CT. Distributed by Williamson Publishing Co., Church Hill Road, P.O. Box 185, Charlotte, VT 05445 (802-425-2102). Explains determining your entitlement to retirement and survivors' benefits, filing a claim, computing your retirement benefits, and applying for disability benefits, Supplemental Security Income, and Medicare benefits. Includes sample forms and answers to frequently asked questions.

Getting the Most from Social Security, Medicare and Other Government Benefits. Leona Rubin and Gloria Klopman. $3.50. Signet, 120 Woodbine Street, Bergenfield, NJ 07621 (800-526-0275). How to figure your monthly benefit from Social Security, what Medicare will and will not cover, how to protect your benefits, how to prevent errors in your records and how to correct them, and more.

Pensions

The following publications are available from the Pension Rights Center, 918 Sixteenth Street, NW, Washington, DC 20006 (202-296-3776):

Protecting Your Pension Money. Barbara J. Coleman. 1987. $6.00. Explains rules pension managers must follow and what workers can do if they think the rules have been broken.

The Case of the Disappearing Pension. $3.50. Explains how some pension plans integrate their benefits with Social Security payments.

A Guide to Understanding Your Pension Plan. $3.00. What to look for when reviewing your pension plan document.

Your Pension Rights at Divorce. $2.20.

How to File a Claim for Your Benefit. U.S. Department of Labor, Pension and Welfare Administration, Room N5666, 200 Constitution Avenue, NW, Washington, DC 20210. Free. Outlines steps a worker may take to file a claim for benefits from a private employee benefit plan and what to do if the claim is denied.

Your Guaranteed Pension. Pension Benefit Guaranty Corporation, 2020 K Street, NW, Washington, DC 20006 (202-272-7440). Free.

Protect Yourself: A Woman's Guide to Pension Rights. American Association of Retired Persons. Describes how to request pension documents from the pension plan administrator and lists questions women should ask about pension benefits they expect to receive from their own or their husbands' pension plans. Free from AARP Fulfillment, 1909 K Street, NW, Washington, DC 20049. Specify the title and order number D12258.

Life Insurance

"Your Life as a Tax Shelter." Richard Eisenberg. *MONEY* magazine, March 1988, 153ff (available in most libraries). Describes kinds of cash-value insurance and compares them with respect to death benefit, premium, investment choices, rate of return on cash value, and access to cash value.

Home Equity

Home-Made Money: Consumer's Guide to Home Equity Conversion. Ken Scholen. 1987. American Association of Retired Persons. Describes the most popular forms of home equity conversion available to retirees. Free from AARP Fulfillment, 1909 K Street, NW, Washington, DC 20049. Specify the title and order number D12894

Organizations

American Association of Individual Investors, 612 N. Michigan Avenue, Chicago, IL 60611 (312-380-0170). Check the telephone directory or write for information on local chapters in your area.

No-Load Mutual Fund Association, 11 Penn Plaza, Suite 2204, New York, NY 10001. Write for free list of association services and for list of no-load mutual funds.

Investment Company Institute, 1600 M Street, NW, Washington, DC 20036 (202-293-7700).

Securities and Exchange Commission, Office of Consumer Affairs and Information Services, 450 Fifth Street, NW, Washington, DC 20549 (202-272-7440).

Pension Benefit Guaranty Corporation, 2020 K Street, NW, Suite 700, Washington, DC 20006 (202-254-4817).

Pension Rights Center, 918 Sixteenth Street, NW, Suite 704, Washington, DC 20006 (202-296-3776). This nonprofit group strives to educate the public about pension issues; protect the pension rights of workers, retirees, and their families; and promote pension reform. Provides help to individuals with pension problems. Write for a complete list of current low-cost publications.

U.S. Department of Labor, Welfare and Benefit Administration, 200 Constitution Avenue, NW, Room N5666, Washington, DC 20210 (202-523-8921). Offers a number of free publications on private pensions.

Home Equity Information Center, American Association of Retired Persons, 1909 K Street, NW, Washington, DC 20049. Upon written request, provides information on reverse equity mortgages and home equity conversion counseling programs available in each state.

See Sources of Information, Part Three, for life and health insurance and legal-service organizations.

Part Three

Life insurance

"Life Insurance: How To Protect Your Family." Three-part series in the June, July, and August 1986 issues of *Consumer Reports*. Available in most libraries. *Term Insurance* (June 1986, 371–400): Discusses what term insurance is, how to shop for it, and what it typically costs. Includes a worksheet for figuring how much life insurance a person/family needs. *Whole Life Insurance* (July 1986, 447–470): Explains how whole life works as an investment as well as protection, costs, and tax privileges. Also discusses what you should expect from a life insurance agent. *Universal Life Insurance* (August 1986, 515–529): Explains how universal life works, compares it with term and whole life, describes special features of universal life such as policy loans and timing of interest payments. Also discusses whether you should switch policies. Lists seven steps for buying life insurance.

Health insurance

A Guide to Choosing Medicare Supplemental Insurance. $4.95 postpaid. United Seniors Health Cooperative, 1334 G Street, NW, Washington, DC 20005 (202-393-6222).

Medicare, Medigap, Catastrophic Care and You. Randy Freudig. $17 postpaid. R.A. Freudig Associates, P.O. Box D, Warrington, PA 18976. A health insurance guide for people over 65. Contains thorough analysis of Medicare and medigap policies, tips on evaluating medigap policies, suggestions for selecting a company and an agent.

How To Use Private Health Insurance with Medicare. Updated 1988. Health Insurance Association of America, 1001 Pennsylvania Avenue, NW, Washington, DC 20004-2599 (202-628-1126). Discusses health care gaps left by Medicare and offers practical guidance on how to supplement Medicare with private health insurance. Single copy free.

Long-term care insurance

See also the sidebar "Going with a group," at the end of Chapter 20.

Understanding Long-Term Care Insurance. Max E. Lemberger. $4.95 plus $1 for shipping. National Association of Health Underwriters, 1000 Connecticut Avenue, NW, Suite 1111, Washington, DC 20036 (202-223-5533). In-depth discussion of long-term care contracts and coverage. Includes worksheet for comparing policies.

Record keeping

Check the financial sections of local bookstores for additional possibilities.

Your Personal Financial Fitness Program. Elizabeth S. Lewin, CFP. 1987. $9.95. Facts on File Publications, 460 Park Avenue South, New York, NY 10016 (800-322-8755). Contains comprehensive record-keeping section with examples and blank worksheets. Also discusses setting financial goals, figuring net worth, budgeting, using credit wisely, getting out of debt, social security benefits, evaluating your pension plan, determining your insurance needs, making a will, and keeping financially fit after retirement.

Your Vital Papers Logbook. 1988. $4.95 ($2.95 to AARP members) plus $1.75 shipping. AARP Books, Scott, Foresman & Co., 1865 Miner Street, Des Plaines, IL 60016. Explains how to organize your important papers. Provides forms for summarizing key personal and financial information to be at your fingertips in an emergency or when major decisions have to be made. Check the financial sections of local bookstores for other possibilities.

Professional advisers

See also the resources listed in Chapter 22, "Where to start."

How To Talk to and Select Lawyers, Financial Planners, Tax Preparers, and Real Estate Brokers. American Association of Retired Persons in cooperation with the Federal Trade Commission. 1986. Free from AARP Fulfillment, 1909 K Street, NW, Washington, DC 20049. Specify the title and order number D12380.

Estate planning

The following two books are available from AARP Books, Scott, Foresman & Co., 1865 Miner Street, Des Plaines, IL 60016.

The Essential Guide to Wills, Estates, Trusts and Death Taxes. Alex J. Soled. 1988. $12.95 ($9.45 to AARP members) plus $1.75 shipping. How to construct an effective will, reduce estate taxes, determine whether a trust is for you, and appoint a personal representative.

It's Your Choice: The Practical Guide to Planning a Funeral. Tom Nelson. $4.95 (3.00 for AARP members) plus $1.75 shipping. Guidebook for funeral arrangements. Discusses decisions that must be made, including legal and financial issues. Explains alternatives to the conventional funeral.

Organizations

American Council of Life Insurance (202-624-2000) and Health Insurance Association of America (202-628-1126), 1001 Pennsylvania Avenue, NW, Washington, DC 20004-2599. Free publications on life insurance, health insurance, and money management. Toll-free number for consumer questions about life and health insurance (800-423-8000).

International Association for Financial Planning (IAFP), 2 Concourse Parkway, Suite 800, Atlanta, GA 30328 (404-395-1605). Maintains Registry of Financial Planning Practitioners.

Institute of Certified Financial Planners (ICFP), 10065 East Harvard Avenue, Suite 320, Denver, CO 80231-5942 (303-751-7600). Maintains roster of Certified Financial Planners.

See Chapter 22 for additional information on locating financial planners.

Legal Counsel for the Elderly, 1909 K Street, NW, Washington, DC 20049 (202-872-4700). Works to improve legal services for older people. Offers publications on a variety of topics, including legal aspects of Social Security, Medicare, and Medicaid. Write for free publication list.

National Senior Citizen Law Center, 2025 M Street, NW, Washington, DC 20036, (202-887-5280). Focuses on legal issues surrounding Social Security, pension plans, Medicare, Medicaid, and nursing home rights.

**Lifelong Retirement Planning
for Local Government Employees**

Text type
Aster

Composition
Unicorn Graphics
Washington, D.C.

Printing and binding
Arcata Graphics

Cover design
Zebulon Rogerson